OXFORD GEOGRAPHICAL AND
ENVIRONMENTAL STUDIES

Editors: Gordon Clark, Andrew Goudie, and Ceri Peach

THE MODALITIES OF EUROPEAN UNION GOVERNANCE

The Modalities of European Union Governance

New Institutionalist Explanations of
Agri-Environment Policy

Alun Jones and Julian Clark

OXFORD
UNIVERSITY PRESS

OXFORD

UNIVERSITY PRESS

Great Clarendon Street, Oxford OX2 6DP

Oxford University Press is a department of the University of Oxford.
It furthers the University's objective of excellence in research, scholarship,
and education by publishing worldwide in

Oxford New York

Athens Auckland Bangkok Bogotá Buenos Aires Cape Town
Chennai Dar es Salaam Delhi Florence Hong Kong Istanbul Karachi
Kolkata Kuala Lumpur Madrid Melbourne Mexico City Mumbai Nairobi
Paris São Paulo Shanghai Singapore Taipei Tokyo Toronto Warsaw

and associated companies in Berlin Ibadan

Oxford is a registered trade mark of Oxford University Press
in the UK and in certain other countries

Published in the United States
by Oxford University Press Inc., New York

British Library Cataloguing in Publication Data
Data available

Library of Congress Cataloging in Publication Data
Jones, Alun.
The modalities of European Union governance:
new institutionalist explanations of agri-environmental policy /
Alun Jones and Julian Clark.
p. cm.—(Oxford geographical and environmental studies)
Includes bibliographical references and index.
1. Agriculture—Environmental aspects—Government policy—European
Union countries. 2. Agriculture and state—European Union countries.
3. Environmental policy—European Union countries.
I. Clark, Julian. II. Title. III. Series.
S589.76E85 J66 2001   338.1'84—dc21   2001016289
ISBN 0–19–924112–0

1 3 5 7 9 10 8 6 4 2

Typeset by Hope Services (Abingdon) Ltd.
Printed in Great Britain
on acid-free paper by
TJ International Ltd,
Padstow, Cornwall

We dedicate this book to our parents

EDITORS' PREFACE

Geography and environmental studies are two closely related and burgeoning fields of academic enquiry. Both have grown rapidly over the past two decades. At once catholic in its approach and yet strongly committed to a comprehensive understanding of the world, geography has focused upon the interaction between global and local phenomena. Environmental studies, on the other hand, have shared with the discipline of geography an engagement with different disciplines, addressing wide-ranging environmental issues in the scientific community and the policy community of great significance. Ranging from the analysis of climate change and physical processes to the cultural dislocations of post-modernism and human geography, these two fields of enquiry have been in the forefront of attempts to comprehend transformations taking place in the world, manifesting themselves in a variety of separate but interrelated spatial processes.

The new 'Oxford Geographical and Environmental Studies' series aims to reflect this diversity and engagement. It aims to publish the best and original research studies in the two related fields and in doing so, to demonstrate the significance of geographical and environmental perspectives for understanding the contemporary world. As a consequence, its scope will be international and will range widely in terms of its topics, approaches, and methodologies. Its authors will be welcomed from all corners of the globe. We hope the series will assist in redefining the frontiers of knowledge and build bridges within the fields of geography and environmental studies. We hope also that it will cement links with topics and approaches that have originated outside the strict confines of these disciplines. Resulting studies will contribute to frontiers of research and knowledge as well as representing individually the fruits of particular and diverse specialist expertise in the traditions of scholarly publication.

Gordon Clark
Andrew Goudie
Ceri Peach

ACKNOWLEDGEMENTS

This book is based upon research carried out between 1995 and 1999 as part of the European Union funded project *Regional Guidelines to Support Sustainable Land Use by EU Agri-Environment Programmes* (AIR–3–CT–94–1296). The project was financed under the EU's Agriculture Industry Research (AIR) Programme. A further tranche of research, carried out during the winter and spring of 1999–2000 in Brussels, London, and Paris, enabled us to corroborate and where necessary update our original findings, in what is a fluid and fast-moving arena of EU policy.

We wish to thank a number of individuals who have assisted us. First, Dominic Byatt, and latterly Ann Ashby, our editors at Oxford University Press, were unstinting in their support during the completion of the manuscript. Thanks are also due to our series editors, Professor Gordon Clark and Professor Andrew Goudie. We are grateful to Diana Harrop, Chief Scientific Editor at Pion Limited, London, for allowing us to draw upon some material that we have published in the international journals *Environment and Planning A* and *Environment and Planning C* on EU agri-environmental policy. In this context, we also express our gratitude to Professor Robert Bennett of the Department of Geography, University of Cambridge, who has been particularly supportive of our work.

Alun Jones would also like to thank Professor Colin Clarke and Professor Ceri Peach of the School of Geography and the Environment, Oxford University, for the kindness and hospitality they showed him during his Visiting Fellowship at St Catherine's College in 1999.

Over the last five years, we have collated a tremendous amount of published data and archival materials, and many interview transcripts. Over 100 interviews were conducted with senior politicians, EU policy practitioners, administrators, and representatives from farming and environmental groups in Belgium, France, Germany, the Netherlands, Spain, and the UK. While for reasons of confidentiality it is not possible to thank all interviewees individually, we express our profound debt of gratitude to each of them. Their thoughtful and insightful comments on EU policy-making have been instrumental in the writing of this book.

Lastly, we reserve our greatest thanks to our partners, Jackie and Lucy, for their untiring support and encouragement.

A.J.
J.C.

London
July 2000

CONTENTS

LIST OF FIGURES

ABBREVIATIONS

ADASEA	*Association Départementale pour l'Aménagement des Structures des Exploitations Agricoles*
ALURE	Alternative Land Use and Rural Economy
ASAJA	*Asociación Agraria-Jóvenes Agricultores*
ASG	Agricultural Structures Group
BGMCS	Broads Grazing Marsh Conservation Scheme
CAMA	*Consejería de Agricultura y Medio Ambiente*
CAP	Common Agricultural Policy
CC	Countryside Commission
CHG	*Confederación Hidrográfica del Guadiana*
CDOA	*Comité Départemental d'Orientation de l'Agriculture*
CEC	Commission of the European Communities
CLA	Country Landowners' Association
CMO	Common Market Organization
CNASEA	*Centre National pour l'Aménagement des Structures des Exploitations Agricoles*
CoEC	Council of the European Communities
COGECA	*Comité Générale de la Coopération Agricole de la Communauté Européene*
COPA	*Comité des Organisations Professionnelles Agricoles*
COREPER	Committee of Permanent Representatives
CPL	*Centrale Paysanne Luxembourgoise*
COP	*Comité de Pilotage de l'Opération*
CPRE	Council for the Protection of Rural England
CRDP	Common Rural Development Policy
CRAE	*Comité Regional Agriculture-Environnemental*
DBV	*Deutscher Bauernverband*
DG	Directorate-General
DG Agri	Agriculture and Rural Development Directorate-General of the European Commission
DG Env	Environment Directorate-General of the European Commission
DDAF	*Direction Départementale de l'Agriculture et de la Forêt*
DETR	Department of Transport, Environment, and the Regions
DIREN	*Direction Régionale de l'Environnement*
DoE	Department of the Environment
DRAF	*Direction Régionale de l'Agriculture et de la Forêt*
EAGGF	European Agricultural Guidance and Guarantee Fund
ECOSOC	Economic and Social Committee of the European Community

EP	European Parliament
EPP	European People's Party
ESA	Environmentally Sensitive Area
EU	European Union
FEOGA	*Fonds Européen d'Orientation et de Garantie Agricole*
FNSEA	*Fédération Nationale des Syndicats d'Exploitants Agricoles*
GATT	General Agreement on Tariffs and Trade
GUE	*Le Groupe Confédéral de la Gauche Unitaire Européenne*
HoC	House of Commons
IA	Irrigators' Association
ICONA	*Instituto Nacional para la Conservación de la Naturaleza*
IFA	Irish Farmers' Association
LFA	Less Favoured Area
LTO-Nederland	*Land-en-Tuinbouw Organisatie-Nederland*
LUPA	*L'Union des Petits Agriculteurs*
MAF	*Ministère de l'Agriculture et de la Forêt*
MAFF	Ministry of Agriculture, Fisheries, and Food
MAPA	*Ministerio de Agricultura, Pesca y Alimentación*
MEKA	*Marktentlastungs-und-Kulturlandschaftsausgleich*
MEP	Member of the European Parliament
MLG	Multi-Level Governance
MoI	Ministry of Information
MOPTMA	*Ministerio de Obras Públicas, Transportes y Medio Ambiente*
NCC	Nature Conservancy Council
NFU	National Farmers' Union
NGO	Non-Governmental Organization
NSA	Nitrate Sensitive Area
PCR	*Programa Compensación de las Rentas Agrarias*
PES	Party of European Socialists
QMV	Qualified Majority Voting
RDA	Regional Development Agency
RDR	Rural Development Regulation
RSPB	Royal Society for the Protection of Birds
SCA	Special Committee on Agriculture
SEO	*Sociedad Española de Ornitologia*
SERAD	Scottish Executive's Rural Affairs Department
SSSI	Site of Special Scientific Interest
STAR	*Comité des Structures Agricoles*
UKREP	United Kingdom Permanent Representation/Representative
WOAD	Welsh Office Agriculture Department
WP	Working Party
WTO	World Trade Organization

1

The Modalities of European Union Governance

Against a backcloth of changing political geometries of European integration, there has been a burgeoning academic interest in the nature and functioning of the European Union (EU) polity. It has been in the field of political science that the greatest theoretical developments on the nature and dynamics of EU integration processes have taken place. Hix (1998: 54) notes for example: 'Never before in the study of the EU has there been such explicit . . . debate on so many levels of analysis.' In sharp relief to political geography, political science is now awash with ontological, methodological, and epistemological debates over the nature of European integration and governance (Marks *et al.* 1996; Risse-Kappen 1996; Armstrong and Bulmer 1998; Moravcsik 1998; Puchala 1999; Rosamond 2000). These debates have not, unfortunately, transcended the disciplinary boundaries between political geography and political science (see e.g. Taylor and Flint 2000). Our aim in this book, therefore, is to present to (though not exclusively) the political geography community a theoretically informed interpretation of EU political processes using the empirical canvas of the initiation, development, and implementation of agri-environment policy, in the context of the EU's reforming Common Agricultural Policy (CAP). We deploy both policy network analysis and new institutionalism from political science to explore the mechanisms and procedures of EU governance in this policy area, approaches that have recently attracted considerable interest among geographers working in other substantive contexts (Martin 2000). These approaches highlight issues of scale and territorial identity, agenda formation and deliberative process, scalar flows of knowledge and ideas, and embedded institutional norms and values—all of which, unquestionably, are profoundly relevant to geographical enquiry.

The revival in European integration from the mid-1980s onwards was centred upon geographical enlargement and increased political competence for the EU, and triggered considerable discussion of the governance of the 'New Europe' (Pinder 1995; Sandholtz and Stone Sweet 1998). In recent years, theoretical debate within political science on the EU polity has focused upon two particular lines of thought: state-centrism and multi-level governance (MLG) (Moravcsik 1993; Marks 1996; Pollack 1996; Rosamond 2000). State-centrism asserts the centrality of nation states to the nature, speed, and scale of EU integration, and in turn accords primacy to the state in the EU polity. The context for state action is that of 'intergovernmentalism', with states coming together in the EU polity to cooperate for certain specified purposes (Nugent 1999). From this perspective, national governments are the main channels of communication between the EU member states, thereby controlling the overall direction and pace of EU decision-making. State-centrism suggests that the primary source of EU integration lies in the interests of the states themselves, a function too of the relative power each brings to the negotiating table. The corollary of according primacy to the state is that supranational and subnational actors within the EU integration process do not have significant independent powers in their own right, but function essentially as agents and facilitators of the collective will of the national governments.

Criticisms of the intergovernmentalist approach have centred upon so-called 'history-making' decisions in EU integration, the dialectic tension between nation-state sovereignty and integration efforts, and the analytical neglect of the 'low politics' and day-to-day processes by which EU policies are initiated, formulated, and implemented. Consequently, concern over integration has now ceded ground to attention on governance. The 'regulatory thicket' of EU governance (Rosamond 2000: 106) and the evolving complex scalar processes of institutional interaction in the EU are deemed thus to require a more politically sensitive approach that acknowledges that EU governance incorporates a dispersal of authority among a variety of actors, not just nation states. As Richardson (1996*a*: 3–4) explains: 'The EU is . . . a complex and unique policy-making system . . . the extreme openness of decision-making to lobbyists, and the considerable weight of national [and subnational] politico-administrative elites within the process, create an unpredictable and multi-level policy making environment.' This 'governance turn' in EU studies (Majone 1996*b*; Marks *et al.* 1996) has sparked a number of new conceptualizations of the political processes of the EU, which recognize the *sui generis* nature of the EU polity. The multi-levelness of the EU has prompted the development of a notion (or 'compelling metaphor' (Rosamond 2000: 110)) of MLG, which emphasizes the 'fluidity, the permanence of uncertainty and *multiple modalities* of authority [in the EU]' (Rosamond 2000: 111; emphasis added) (see also Hooghe and Keating 1994). These 'modalities' are the strategies and methods of procedure in EU policy making that are selected by policy elites and institutions to advance their own interests and influence. Hence, they condition the operation of the constituent governance regimes of the EU polity, be they national, subnational, or supranational. Critical to MLG, these modalities also furnish the linkage between the different scales of governance operation. They can be interrelated, independent, formalized, less formalized, though what they have in common is a perceived legitimacy to specific EU policy communities. They are licit practices and methods of policy procedure that enable the furtherance of political goals, ambitions, and strategies with the MLG system, and can be defined at individual actor, institutional, and indeed territorial levels in the EU polity.

Exponents of MLG highlight a number of its important attributes (based on Marks *et al.* 1996). Principally, they argue that the process of governing in the EU is no longer conducted exclusively by the state. However, MLG exponents do *not* reject the view that state executives and state arenas remain the most important pieces of the European jigsaw, but, rather, elaborate the position that the state no longer *monopolizes* European level policy making. In addition, they maintain that not only does the state no longer provide the sole interface between supranational and subnational arenas, but supranational agencies, such as the European Commission, are themselves political actors interested in enhancing their power in the EU polity. MLG exponents therefore contend that the locus of decision has shifted away from the national administrations of member states to be replaced by a complex structure of EU policy-making involving also supranational and subnational agents (Richardson 1996*a*). They argue that supranational actors, including the European Parliament, European Commission, and the EU's Court of Justice, exercise independent influence in EU policy-making that cannot be 'derived from their role as agents of state executives' (Marks *et al.* 1996: 346). Furthermore, they maintain that European integration is a polity-creating process in which authority and policy-making influence are shared across multiple levels of government—subnational, national, and supranational. As such, state sovereignty is diluted in the EU by collective decision-making across various political scales, and by the roles and activities of bodies such as the European Parliament, European Commission, and the European Court of Justice.

The collective decision-making by states at the EU level is regarded as involving a loss of national sovereignty that stems not only from particular voting arrangements in the EU's Council of Ministers (notably qualified majority voting (QMV)), but also, specifically, from the ability of supranational institutions to extend their influence in the EU polity. In the case of the European Commission, this is achieved as a result of 'its position as an interlocutor with national governments, sub-national authorities and numerous interest groups which gives it a unique informational base' (Marks *et al* 1996: 355). Importantly, MLG exponents emphasize not only the role played by supranational actors, but also that of interest groups in shaping the agendas and influencing the legislative outcomes of EU policy business. Significantly, too, MLG recognizes both the competition and the interdependence between these various actors in the EU polity. The relationship between state and non-state actors in the EU polity is polycentric, non-hierarchical, and mutually dependent, which stands in stark contrast to the traditional 'command and control' modalities of policy-making (Jessop 1995*a,b*).

MLG also stresses the complexity of the political processes associated with the initiation, formulation, adoption, and implementation of EU policies. Intrinsic to this complexity is that, within the EU polity, decision-making arenas are interleaved rather than nested, enabling subnational-level actors to operate at a variety of political scales. The implementation of EU policies in member states thus brings a spectrum of subnational actors such as regional and local authorities, as well as specific interest groups into the MLG system. Hence, subnational participation in EU policy implementation creates a bargained, negotiated form of policy-making that has a direct bearing upon implementation outcomes. In particular, subnational actors are able to engage in policy activities that are not wholly controllable by national governments. Of overriding importance, then, is that within EU MLG there are complex webs of interrelation and interaction between actors involved in policy-making, with these relational networks linking together policy-makers at different politico-geographical scales.

There has not been any attempt to unravel the modalities underpinning the different characteristics of MLG in the EU *across* these various politico-geographic scales. While acknowledging the complexity of the EU polity, scholars have attempted to develop the notion of MLG by recourse to two important theoretical literatures—policy network analysis and new institutionalism. These literatures, drawn mainly from the comparative politics and policy studies subdisciplines of political science, focus attention on what have been termed 'middle range theories' of the EU, and furnish a very useful means for critically analysing the functioning of the EU polity (Mazey and Richardson 1993*b*; Bulmer 1994; Hix 1994; Peterson 1995*a*; Armstrong and Bulmer 1998; Nugent 1999). The central argument for the deployment of these approaches is well summed up by Richardson (1996*a*: 5):

the stuff of European integration is as much about detailed, often technical, Euro-legislation as it is about high politics issues such as monetary union or the creation of a European superstate . . . the European policy game continues to be played at the detailed policy level . . . Low politics this may be, but it is probably the nine-tenths of the EU's policy iceberg that is below the water line [and] . . . some means has to be found of analysing it and conceptualising it.

In this book, we suggest that what is required is a closer examination of the strategies and tactics of engagement in EU policy-making selected by scalar policy elites and institutions. Actors within the EU polity deploy strategies of engagement to advance their interests and influence, which are shaped by the bounded constraints imposed by the particular institutional settings of the EU polity. This focus upon interests, agendas, network operation, and actor influence, configured by the specific settings of the EU, constitutes the modalities of EU governance. In turn, as we show in subsequent chapters, these modalities are powerfully illuminated by the policy networks and new institutionalist literatures.

1.1. Policy Network Analysis and Multi-Level Governance

Policy network analysis has been championed as a valuable approach to understanding multi-level governance in the EU, particularly for sectoral analyses (Peterson 1995*a*). In essence, policy networks and policy communities provide arenas for the mediation of the interests of governments, supranational institutions, and interest groups, and as such can be used to characterize the dispersal of power across the multi-levelled EU polity. As Peterson (1995*b*: 391) explains: 'The term network implies that clusters of actors representing multiple organizations interact with one another and share information and resources. Mediation implies that the networks usually are settings for the playing of positive sum games: they facilitate reconciliation, settlement or compromise between different interests which have a stake in outcomes in a particular policy sector.'

However, when applied to the EU context, the policy networks approach has not been without criticism (Kassim 1994). The grounds for this criticism are that the fluidity of EU governance eludes 'capture' by the networks model, and that the model is not sufficiently sensitive to the complexities of EU institutions. Furthermore, it is argued, there are real difficulties in demarcating the boundaries of stable policy networks at the EU level. The counter-arguments have been focused upon the degree to which informal bargaining impacts upon EU governance, the ways in which policy networks emerge with the purpose of establishing 'order' in the EU system of MLG, and that, although it might be difficult to delimit policy networks, this is not to deny their existence, nor their importance. The central element in the network approach to EU MLG is that the 'policy arenas' are not equally accessible to all interested or affected parties, and that the participants in the network may devise a variety of strategies to deter and prevent intrusion by others. Sainteny (1995), for example, has outlined four such strategies: excluding from the political arena the 'theme' used by the 'intruder' to enter or to try and enter it; harnessing the 'theme' (that is, manipulating it to the policy community's own advantage); excluding from the arena the 'intruder' who has entered it or is trying to do so; and, fourthly, harnessing the 'intruder' once this player has penetrated the arena. In this sense ideas, knowledge, and interests are critical components of the functioning of policy networks, and, in our view, offer a useful analytical vehicle for exploring the MLG system.

The policy networks approach to MLG is pitched at a relatively 'low' level of EU politics, enabling explanations to be advanced for what are often described as 'policy-shaping' decisions in EU governance (Peterson 1995*b*). These are decisions taken at a relatively early stage of the EU policy process, when options and proposals are in the process of political formulation. However, this actor-based approach is less well able to explain the decisions that 'set' policy after policy options have been formulated. It is in an effort to fill this conceptual vacuum that exponents of MLG have turned to new institutionalist approaches, in which the focus is upon norms and values of institutional actors, embedded socio-cultural processes, and the inertias of institutional structure, routines, and procedures (Jones and Clark 1998). The use of alternative complementary literatures is accepted by MLG exponents, for, as Richardson (1996a: 5) makes clear: 'Different models of analysis may be useful at different levels within the EU and at different stages of the policy process. For example, if we were to conceptualize the EU policy process into . . . agenda setting, policy formulation, policy decision, and policy implementation . . . we need a fairly eclectic use of concepts and models.'

1.2. New Institutionalist Perspectives and Multi-Level Governance

The institutionalist literature is characterized by a tremendous diversity of approaches, and does not constitute a single, uniform perspective that can support MLG. In essence its message is clear: institutions matter to political outcomes (March and Olsen 1984). New institutionalism defines institutions in a broader sense than the 'older' school, where emphasis was tightly focused upon the formal powers and structures of decision-making. New institutionalism, by contrast, incorporates informal and formal procedures, practices, actor relationships, customs, norms, and traditions. This breadth of coverage is reflected in the number of strands of new institutionalist thinking (Peters 1999). Four mainstream institutionalist perspectives are generally recognized: normative, rational choice, historical, and sociological institutionalism. Some political scientists cite empirical and international variants, though their 'direct connections to institutionalism may become . . . remote' (Peters 1999: 20).

Normative institutionalism places considerable emphasis upon the norms of institutions as a means of understanding how they function, and how they shape individual actor behaviour (March and Olsen 1984). The most important feature of this variant of institutionalism is that institutions have a 'logic of appropriateness'—that is, actors will make conscious choices, but those choices will remain within the parameters established by the dominant institutional values (Peters 1999). Political institutions are thus collections of interrelated rules and routines that define appropriate actions in terms of relations between actor roles and situations. Enforcement and sanctioning of this appropriateness is built into the structure of the institution, and is sustained through processes of socialization between actors (March and Olsen 1984).

By contrast, rational-choice institutionalism defines institutions as formal legalistic entities and sets of rules that impose obligations upon individual actors in their pursuit of maximum self-interest (Weingast 1996; Rosamond 2000). These systems of rules and procedures not only constrain political actors: they also impact significantly upon their behaviour. Rational-choice institutionalists therefore analyse how actors and institutions interact in order for these actors to maximize their preferences, and embrace notions of how actors learn more accommodative norms, and routines, and how they become respectful of institutional values, in order to further their political goals (North 1990). Implicit is that actors can gain some benefit from membership of an institution, and are thus prepared to sacrifice 'some latitude of action in order to receive those benefits' (Peters 1999: 47). Such benefits include an increased predictability in the political process as actors realize that their competitors are also restricted by the same institutional rules and procedures.

The third variant of new institutionalism is historical institutionalism, where the focus is upon the 'distributions of power that are produced by institutional arrangements, the ways in which these arrangements result in path dependence . . . and the relationships between institutions and other factors that shape political activities and outcomes . . .' (Nugent 1999: 516). Important in this perspective is that the policy choices made when an institution is formed, or when a policy is initiated, will have a continuing and largely determinate influence over the future development of the policy (Hall 1986). Institutions thus serve as 'carriers of history', with the ideas behind early policy choices continuing to serve as parameters in which actors respond to new politico-economic challenges (Majone 1996*a*).

A fourth variant is sociological institutionalism, which stresses the key role played by values and symbols in defining an institution and in steering the behaviour of its actors. This institutionalism draws heavily on its sociological roots, though there are strong similarities with the normative institutionalism outlined above. There is, though, one principal difference between these two strands of new institutionalism. In the sociological model, the focus shifts to the perceptions that actors hold of particular situations and the particular 'cognitive frames' that they bring to such situations in order to make decisions about them. In the normative model, on the other hand, the focus lies with the appropriateness of actor behaviour.

The application of these institutionalisms to the study of EU political processes has been attempted by several scholars (see Pollack 1996). Given the different emphases within these institutionalisms, it is not surprising that their application to the study of the EU has focused upon a variety of features of the political processes surrounding integration, be it the 'path dependencies' fashioned by early choices in the creation of the EU and the development of its decision-making structure (Pierson 1996; Armstrong and Bulmer 1998); constraints upon actors in inter-state bargaining (Aspinwall and Schneider 1998; Heritier 1999), or the values upheld by actors in supranational institutions, like the European Commission (Hooghe 1999). Overall, there is no single institutionalist explanation of the EU (Hix 1998), and MLG exponents accept that a variety of approaches is required to undertake a 'pathology of the collective governance of the EU, [in which] a core concern is with mapping the institutions, decision-making procedures, [and] rules and norms embedded in these across policy areas' (Bulmer 1994: 355).

1.3. Synthesizing Policy Networks and New Institutionalist Perspectives

Governance explanations of the processes surrounding EU policy development can be enhanced by the deployment of new institutionalist/policy network approaches. In particular, using this 'toolkit' (Peterson 1995*a*) in the context of specific EU sectoral areas should enable light to be shed on the intricacies of multi-scalar policy-making. Aspects of this include: discourses surrounding the choice of policy options by particular elites, and how ideas, beliefs, and knowledges become embedded in the EU policy process (see Risse-Kappen 1996; Jachtenfuchs 1997); and the prevailing narratives within supranational institutions, such as the European Commission, that mould these particular discourses into policy initiatives (Cram 1996; Laffan 1997). Rosamond (2000: 120), for example, acknowledges that the 'capacity to shape and deploy ideas is a powerful strategic tool [for EU institutions]'. Also, the synthesis of new institutionalist and policy network approaches could enable the examination of deliberative processes by which consensus is reached around policy initiatives, both between and within EU institutional arenas, and, not least, an analysis of the role played by interest groups in multi-scalar policy-making. At other scales of EU MLG, these approaches are useful devices for exploring the implementation of particular policies—for example, the institutional arrangements and locally embedded values that shape policy outcomes.

Synthesizing policy networks and new institutionalist approaches also offers a valuable means of examining the mechanisms and procedures used by actors and institutions in their quest to further their strategic agendas within the EU MLG system. In this book, we contend that these 'modalities' constitute the substance of EU policy-making, and are, in fact, the everyday procedures used by actors to process EU business referred to by Richardson (1996*b*). Although policy modalities are tremendously varied, we suggest that they can be characterized in four principal ways:

- as *mechanisms of coordination* within the EU polity, operating at macro-, meso-, or micro-scales, for example: multi-level policy networks in particular policy areas (see Chapters 6 and 9); multiple points of access or nodes in the MLG system; and by facilitating agenda interlocking between EU institutions (see Chapter 4) that brings influence to bear upon both policy-shaping and policy-setting decisions (see Chapters 4 and 5);
- as *strategies that enable power resources between actors to be redistributed*, thereby creating new 'pockets' of policy discretion in EU MLG, for

example: counter-lobbying strategies; use of 'nationality networks'; and the brokerage of bilateral agreements within the Council of Ministers (see Chapters 4, 5, and 7);

- as *procedures that optimize the use of knowledge, skills, and expertise*, hence facilitating the deliberative process of EU decision-making, for example: the European Commission's astute use of national experts in fashioning policy proposals (see Chapter 3);
- as *attributes of policy areas that prioritize the selection of certain policy instruments over others* (see Chapter 2); such attributes can, for example, rule out the use of a regulatory as opposed to a discretionary approach to the operational aspects of certain policies.

Importantly, these modalities can be policy based, institution based, or indeed actor based. They can be complementary or conflicting, though crucially they are all legitimate forms of political procedure and process within specific policy sectors in the EU polity. All are geared around the deliberative, negotiated, consensual form of policy-making evolving within the EU, and provide a linkage between structure and agency. Focusing upon modalities, therefore, takes us to the centre of the new institutionalist/policy network dynamic.

1.4. Environmentalization of the EU's Common Agricultural Policy

We have selected agri-environmental policy as the empirical context to examine the modalities of EU governance using the analytical toolkit set out above. There are several reasons for this empirical selection. First, EU agricultural policy is characterized by deeply entrenched interests, reflected not only in the domination of EU budgetary expenditure by agricultural issues and the high profile traditionally accorded agricultural policy in the EU integration process, but also by the success of these interests in thwarting major policy reforms. Key actors within the agricultural policy community in EU governance include Agriculture Departments in the member states; highly vocal farm lobby groups under the umbrella organization *Comité des Organisations Professionnelles Agricoles* (*COPA*); a powerful Directorate-General (DG) of the European Commission (DG Agri) (the Agriculture and Rural Development Directorate-General of the European Commission, formerly Directorate-General VI (DGVI)) responsible for the strategic management of the Common Agricultural Policy (CAP); and an influential Working Committee in the European Parliament, dominated by Members of the European Parliament (MEPs) with vested agricultural interests. Historically, they have represented a formidable barrier to efforts to reform the CAP.

Secondly, however, from the mid-late 1980s, pressures for CAP reform intensified as its productivist basis was increasingly called into question, particularly with budgetary expenditure remaining high (hence constraining EU efforts to broaden the basis of EU integration into other sectors) and an international community manifestly hostile to the worsening trade implications of the operation of the CAP's market regimes (Swinbank 1993, 1999). In addition, the agricultural policy community was confronted by growing demands for it to be more respectful of its environmental obligations, as evidence mounted on the CAP's negative impacts upon the farmed landscape of western Europe. These forces for the 'environmentalization' of the CAP (a multifaceted process, examined in Chapter 2) were thus pitted against the trenchant interests of agricultural productivism. The key question for members of the agricultural policy community was how to respond tactically to these pressures, without damaging their strategic interests in the EU polity. In this respect the community sought legitimate mechanisms to maintain its privileged position in the EU polity, whilst at the same time being able to demonstrate publicly some support for the agriculture–environment relation. This dynamic is the primary focus for the modalities of EU governance in agricultural policy set out in the book.

The environmentalization of the CAP is an ongoing process. A recent high point came in 1992, with the ratification of EC Regulation 2078/92, which was agreed upon as an 'Accompanying Measure' to the CAP reform package by EU farm ministers in June of that year (CEC 1992). Farmers were to be encouraged through grant aid to adopt environmentally sound production methods or implement measures to safeguard the environment and preserve the countryside. In keeping with the principle of 'subsidiarity', the Regulation enabled member states to implement locally appropriate agri-environmental programmes, tailor-made to their own specific agricultural and environmental circumstances. Subject to approval by the European Commission, the EU would reimburse member states up to 50 per cent of the costs (up to 75 per cent in the EU's poorest regions) of these 'zonal programmes'. In the first two years after the launch of the agri-environmental Regulation the implementation of some of the programmes was slow, and not all the funds allocated to it were taken up. A number of reasons have been cited for this, not least the adjustments that were required in management practices by participating farmers, and the need for local institutions to put in place operating procedures for the policy. However, by the beginning of 1997, most of the 130 agri-environmental schemes approved by the European Commission were up and running. By late 1998, the Commission was in a position to report on its evaluation of the implementation of Regulation 2078/92 (CEC 1998*b*). Over 1.6 million EU farmers were in receipt of grant aid for agri-environmental schemes, embracing over 26 million hectares of land. DGAgri's comparison across the member states of the number of beneficiaries and the number of holdings involved showed tremendous variation. For example, in 1998 78 per cent of Austrian farmers were participating in agri-environmental schemes, while less than 7 per cent of farmers were involved in Greece, Spain, Belgium, and the Netherlands (CEC 1998*b*). The most recent tranche of CAP reforms has witnessed EC 2078/92 subsumed as the flagship measure of the Rural Development Regulation (see Chapter 2).

1.5. Methodological Approach

We have endeavoured to achieve a strong empirical focus for this book. We have been fortunate in being granted access to restricted documentation on the formulation and negotiation of EC Regulation 2078/92 held by EU institutions, and have been able to corroborate this material through interviews with over 100 actors in the EU MLG system. These individuals have covered the full spectrum of opinion, from those actively engaged in the environmentalization of the CAP, to steadfast supporters of productivist agriculture. Interviewees included the draftsman of the Regulation; senior officials in the DG Agri; the Environment Directorate (DG Env); and Secretariat General of the Commission; Members of the European Parliament (EP), including its former President; Chairs of the EP's Agriculture and Environment Working Committees and Rapporteurs; some forty current and former members of the EP's Agriculture and Environment Committees, from different political groupings and EU Member States; Council negotiators; EP Secretariat staff in Luxembourg; senior negotiators in *COPA*; officials from national agriculture ministries in France, Germany, Spain, Netherlands, and the UK; and regional and local agricultural officials in Languedoc (France), Castilla la Mancha (Spain), Baden-Wurttemberg (Germany), Beemster and Vaterland provinces in the Netherlands, and Flanders in Belgium. These semi-structured interviews were conducted across the EU between November 1995 and January 2000. In total, they represent one of the largest analyses of a specific policy sector undertaken in EU governance.

Using new institutionalist/policy network approaches in the context of MLG, in the following chapters we examine the modalities deployed in the initiation, formulation, negotiation, and implementation of the agri-environmental Regulation. We chart the development of the new agri-environmental policy domain over an extended period from the early–mid-1980s to the beginning of the new millennium. The book therefore represents a comprehensive longitudinal policy analysis, setting it apart from more restricted interpretations of specific elements of sectoral policies.

1.6. Plan of the Book

The book's principal objective is to develop the 'compelling metaphor' of MLG into a more analytically rigorous framework, by scrutinizing the modalities of EU governance as they apply to agri-environmental policy. We do so by drawing on elements of new institutionalism and policy network approaches. In Chapter 2 we focus on the 'environmentalization' of the CAP, and demonstrate the fundamentally discursive nature of this multifaceted process. As such environmentalization has been, and continues to be, shaped by the diverse less formal institutions of the EU—the particular norms associated with the CAP, the different preferences of actors associated with this policy, and the socio-cultural beliefs arising in the EU–15. Crucially though, the chapter shows a communality in these less formal institutions that has created a 'discursive motif' at the supranational level, shaping the trajectory of EU agri-environmental policy, by favouring particular policy options over others. The modalities demonstrated here are profoundly cultural in origin, steeped in the interests and predilections of member states, while being tempered and reconfigured at the supranational level into distinctive 'European' patterns. The discursive motif we highlight obviously has substantial consequences for organizational and structural learning among EU policy elites. In turn, this chapter provides compelling evidence of the existence of policy communities in the EU, and of a shared knowledge and expertise base that provides compatibility and coherence both for the EU agricultural policy community and, indirectly, for the emerging EU polity.

Chapters 3 and 4 build on this analysis, by demonstrating that the formal EU institutions of the European Commission and the EP had their own agendas regarding 'environmentalization' of the CAP. In support of the MLG perspective on supranational institutions, we demonstrate how these two key EU institutions have used a variety of policy modalities not only to further their objectives with regard to the 'environmentalization' of the CAP *per se*, but also to advance their strategic situation in the EU polity more generally. These modalities have included the mobilization of political and nationality networks, the use of agenda interlocking, and the plundering of policy expertise by the DG Agri from all quarters of EU MLG. Both institutions have sought to play a key role in how and on what terms 'environmentalization' of the CAP should proceed, and consequently what issues this multifaceted process should encompass.

In particular, Chapter 3 shows the DG Agri of the European Commission as the 'spider in web' of EU agricultural policy, an organization that has utilized comprehensively the resources offered by the EU multi-level polity to promote its influence and extend its own strategic agenda through agri-environmental policy. Notably, inter-institutional coordination in the MLG system has been a most effective modality for the DG Agri in pursuing these goals. This has meant nurturing close relations with particular member states at the supranational level, demonstrating responsiveness to the expressed opinions of the EP positions, and careful sensitivity to the needs of other member states in the Committees of the Council of Ministers. The Commission clearly emerges as a strategically sophisticated actor, with the political sagacity and institutional shrewdness to expand its own role in EU governance.

Chapter 4 examines the EP's role within the environmentalization of the CAP. We show that the EP, despite its growing powers in many sectoral areas within EU governance, has only limited formal powers in the field of agricultural policy. Nevertheless, actors within this institution have deployed a variety of modalities to shape the development of agri-environmental policy. We focus in particular upon agenda interlocking as a modality of governance, a hitherto little studied procedure that enabled the EP to work across the formally prescribed contours of power in the EU polity.

In Chapter 5 we explore inter-institutional modalities at the supranational scale, with specific reference to the multinational lobby group *COPA* and its efforts to counter the forces of environmentalization. We highlight how, somewhat contrary to expectations, supranational lobbying spaces in EU MLG are not necessarily more open, receptive, and 'accessible' to lobbyists than national political arenas, and contain as many pitfalls as opportunities. This is particularly the case for 'umbrella' groups such as *COPA*, which seek to represent accurately the territorial identities of a multiplicity of local and regional interests. We highlight crucial missed opportunities and failures in *COPA*'s lobbying on EC 2078/92, and demonstrate how these shortcomings enabled the DG Agri to use counter-lobbying modalities against this organization.

The analysis in Chapter 6 moves to the political interface between national and supranational scales of governance. Using the case of the UK's position on the environmentalization of the CAP, we reveal not only the synergies of interests and policy influence between the UK's Ministry of Agriculture, Fisheries, and Food (MAFF) and the European Commission, but also the obstructions between these two institutions situated at different political scales. For the UK, the supranational arena offered an important opportunity for advancing national goals and objectives in the field of agri-environmental policy. Deeply ingrained beliefs in British society relating to 'trusteeship' by farming of the natural environment were deployed by policy elites in the MAFF in the development of the UK negotiating position in the EU's Council of Ministers.

However, as Chapter 7 shows, the EU's Council of Ministers is characterized by its own historically embedded rules and accepted codes of procedure and behaviour, and member states, in their search for maximum benefits from political engagement in supranational decision-making, are forced to work within such bounded constraints. In this chapter we investigate the modalities by which national delegations attempt to secure maximum benefits from their participation in Council decision-making. We consider effective briefing, forceful interventions in debates, interstate deals, occupancy of the Council Presidency, and synchronizing the member state position with that of the European Commission.

Chapters 8 and 9 expose how the actions within EU political activity spaces have been translated into territorial policy outcomes. Using examples from France and Spain of the implementation of the agri-environmental

Regulation, we show how territorial identities are being refashioned and redefined by local and regional elites to influence the political actions within EU activity spaces, particularly those at national and supranational levels. Our analysis in these two chapters clearly demonstrates the heterarchical, rather than the hierarchical, nature of policy-making within the multi-scaled polity of the EU. Crucially, bargaining, negotiation, and compromise among locally based actors over EC 2078/92, mediated through particular sets of power relations, have characterized agri-environmental policy-making in both states, just as it had done during policy-shaping and policy-setting at the supranational level. Chapter 10 presents our conclusions from this study of the modalities of EU governance.

2

The Environmentalization of EU Public Policies: The Case of the Common Agricultural Policy

Since its introduction in 1962, the European Union's Common Agricultural Policy has remained remarkably unchanged, both in a policy-design and in a practical sense (see e.g. Harris and Swinbank 1997). At the start of a new millennium, not only are the policy's goals and aims the same as those drafted by its creators almost four decades ago. Many of its operational mechanisms have also survived largely unscathed, in the face of tremendous political and socio-economic upheavals in European and global economies. Such reforms of the policy as were reluctantly agreed by the EU's Agriculture Council during the 1970s and the early 1980s were incremental and reactive in nature, carried out in response to steadily mounting evidence of the CAP's negative economic, social, and environmental effects. (Pretty (1998) provides a comprehensive summary of these critiques.) However, these piecemeal reforms provided a foundation for potentially more far-reaching reorganizations of the CAP, undertaken in the mid to late 1990s.

On 23 March 1999 the Agriculture Council agreed modifications in the policy's architecture as part of the so-called Agenda 2000 programme (Buckwell 1997; CEC 1998a; HoC Agriculture Select Committee 1998). Against the backdrop of a continuing reduction in CAP price support, first introduced under the 'MacSharry' reforms[1] of 1992, agriculture ministers ratified the creation of a 'second [policy] pillar' for the CAP, the 'Rural Development Regulation' (RDR) (CEC 1999a; HoC Agriculture Select Committee 1999), which potentially places rural development objectives at the heart of the EU agricultural policy. This Regulation represented the most innovative element of the 1999 reforms, seeking to counterbalance the CAP's exclusive forty-year focus on agricultural markets and farm income support. Ministers also agreed that environmental stipulations should be built into the policy, although the precise nature of these environmental standards were left at the discretion of

---

[1] Named after the then European Commissioner responsible for Agriculture, Ray MacSharry.

member state administrations. While, therefore, some have observed rightly that the opportunity for fundamental agricultural reform has been missed yet again (Swinbank 1999), at the least the agricultural component of Agenda 2000 shows that EU policy elites are attaching greater importance to the production of 'environmental goods'[2] by European farmers.

The centrepiece of the 1999 reforms, the RDR, is an omnibus measure, comprising fifty-six Articles. It draws together in a single legislative framework a range of new and existing EU instruments on rural development and agricultural restructuring. Among the pre-existing instruments are nine EU Regulations, affecting upland livestock farming, processing and marketing facilities for agricultural produce, incentives for afforestation and forestry management, early retirement, the establishment of young farmers, and agri-environmental policies. However, it is only the last of these measures, a Regulation introduced in 1992 to encourage 'agricultural production methods compatible with the requirements of the protection of the environment and the maintenance of the countryside' (CEC 1992), that member states must implement. The RDR draws upon the core budget line of the CAP, the Guarantee Fund, to finance these disparate instruments—a major departure for this policy's socio-structural, as opposed to its market dimension.

As its only obligatory measure, it has been argued that agri-environmental policy constitutes the singlemost important element of the RDR.[3] Another innovation, which again points to the significance vested in this Regulation, and to the agri-environment policy it sponsors, is that member states can syphon off funds from the budgetary heart of the CAP—its 'Common Market Organizations'—to subsidize the expansion of their own 'rural development programmes' instituted under the RDR. Clearly, rural development, and, in particular, its compulsory agri-environmental element, has at last come of age in European agricultural policy. This situation prompts a number of questions: why has this change in the CAP come about, specifically why has a policy consensus emerged in the EU polity around what has been described in other contexts as the 'environmentalization'[4] (Buttel 1993: 12) of policy? Secondly, how has the growing global importance attached to qualitative issues—especially the conservation of the natural environment—been mediated by the diffuse multi-tiered structure of the EU polity?

We argue in this chapter that the answer to both questions is bound up with the institutionalized form of forty years of agricultural decision-making within

---

[2] In this context, the production and management by farmers of agricultural landscapes on behalf of the public for explicit environmental purposes, including environmental protection.

[3] The importance attached by the European Commission to agri-environmental policy is evident in the preamble to the RDR (CEC 1999*a*: 82): 'in the coming years, a prominent role should be given to agri-environmental instruments to support the sustainable development of rural areas and to respond to society's increasing demand for environmental services.'

[4] Defined by Buttel (1993: 12) as 'the trend towards environmental considerations being increasingly brought to bear in political and economic decisions, in educational and scientific research . . . [and] in geopolitics . . .'.

the EU—in short, with the fundamental tenets of the CAP itself. We contend that globalizing forces for 'environmentalization', arising in response to changing socio-economic contexts, have been reinterpreted by EU member states, and by EU institutions, through the medium of these policy tenets to be supportive of their own strategic goals and organizational agendas. Hence, the environmentalization of European agricultural policy is linked fundamentally to the modalities of governance operating within the EU agricultural sector. We substantiate this claim in the chapter by using the combination of theoretical approaches set out in Chapter 1—namely, new institutionalism and policy networks.

2.1. Environmentalization and the Modalities of EU Agricultural Policy-Making

The origins of environmentalization of EU public policies, such as the CAP, are to be found both within the multi-level polity, and in the global politico-economic context that conditions and defines this evolving political metastructure (cf. Rosamond 1999; Laffan *et al.* 2000). Environmentalism has been mediated by the institutional forms comprising the EU polity, and has been subject to manipulation and reinterpretation by them—in particular, by EU policy cartels. As discussed in Chapter 1, the EU agricultural policy community is especially durable and cohesive, and, we argue, has been particularly adroit in shaping environmentalization to suit its membership's goals and objectives. While, therefore, environmentalization has galvanized attitudinal and institutional change in the EU agricultural policy community, it has also been redefined by the prescribed modalities of operation within this sector.

This two-way dynamic can be seen to operate at different geographical scales, although we contend it is the cumulative effect of its multi-levelled operation that constitutes 'environmentalization'. At a micro-level, there has been real flux in the beliefs and values of subnational, national, and supranational policy and administrative elites towards the environment, arising from the changing dynamics of agricultural markets; new production technologies; growing awareness of environmental problems in agriculture; and the universalization and widespread acceptance of neo-liberal orthodoxes (see Spaargaren and Mol 1992; Hajer 1995; Buttel 1997, 1998; Leroy and van Tattenhove, forthcoming). Subsequent chapters examine aspects of this complex process in more detail. At the meso-level, regional and state modalities of agricultural policy-making, largely hierarchical and centralized in their operation, have struggled to cope with the activities of environmental interest groups and other social movements promoting environmentalization of sectoral decision-making (see Chapter 6; van Tattenhove and Liefferink 1992). Among the first regions where this became apparent was northern Europe, in particular Scandinavia (Vail *et al.* 1994). Environmentalization of the CAP at this meso-level has been assisted by the emergence of new policy procedures and processes, especially the development of what we term 'multi-level agri-environmental policy networks' (see Chapters 8 and 9). Significantly, the emergence of these networks has been actively encouraged by particular Directorates of the European Commission (see Chapters 8 and 9; see also Rhodes 1997).

Creeping environmentalization of European agricultural policy has also taken place at the macro-level, through global obligations on the EU in the environmental policy field. These include the UN's ground-breaking Stockholm conference of 1972 and that at Rio twenty years later, which prompted the incremental elaboration of the EU's own environmental agenda throughout the 1970s and 1980s, culminating in the environmental Articles of the Single European Act (1987), and the Treaty of Economic Union (1992). Increasingly, environmental accountability in EU public policies is also being ramped up through transnational institutions, such as the global trade forum, the General Agreement on Tariffs and Trade (GATT), and its successor, the World Trade Organization (WTO) (Lenschow 1998).

The dispersed decision-making and decision-taking competencies of EU agriculture, and the 'multiple points of access' (Grande 1996; see also below, Chapter 5) in this emerging polity, have resulted in the adoption of proactive and reactive stances towards environmentalization. Consequently, the underlying common policy structures of the CAP, which link together the different scales of the multi-level polity, have assumed a particular importance. The CAP binds together the day-to-day activities of the myriad sectoral policy constituencies, key actors, and organizations that comprise EU agriculture, and regulates the operation of the relevant formal institutions across the EU–15. It follows that a critical element in determining the way in which the 'environmentalization' of the CAP has unfolded is the policy's underlying tenets and assumptions. Forty years of policy deliberation and decision-taking have created a discursive frame of reference within which the activities of policy elites have been routinized and, to an extent, circumscribed. Over this period, the CAP's modalities have been defined, including, for example, the terms of engagement between the DG Agri and the Agriculture Council (these include the 'legitimate' operating procedures of both institutions, and the less formalized but equally important practices used to advance their ambitions through this EU public policy (see Chapters 3 and 7)).

As we show in this chapter, this shaping of policy options is clearly evident with respect to agriculture's interrelationship with the natural environment. The perceptual frame of the CAP as it relates to the environment has enabled the European Commission and the EU Agriculture Council to render environmentalization tractable to their different constituencies, by defining the range, scope, and aims of collective agri-environmental policy choice. This has provided the means for these prominent EU institutions to manage strategic opportunities in this policy domain (see also Chapters 3 and 7). In effect, the discursive frame of reference established by the policy has become the dominant conception of environmentalization as it applies to the EU, although, of course, this has not precluded the development of alternative discursive interpretations, as we show in later chapters (see chapters 5, 6, 8, and 9). The tremendous influence exercised by this hegemonic conception largely explains why territorial actors within the EU polity were persuaded to 'turn to Europe' in pursuit of agri-environmental legislation, rather than to regulate in this field solely at the national/state level.

In order to understand the environmentalization of the CAP more fully, a methodology is needed that specifies the interplay between the ideologies of agricultural interests in EU member states, and emergent environmental discourses, while at the same time being fully conversant with wider changes in the global political economy. Such an approach concurs with Hall's assertion (1993: 278) that a key component of policy-making is 'the deliberate attempt to adjust the goals or techniques of policy in response to past experience and new information'. Hall's approach has very strong complementarities with historical institutionalism, by providing a medium for linking structure (formal and informal institutional constructs, which constitute the substance of the EU multi-level polity) with agency (the activities and actions of EU policy elites at different politico-geographic scales) (see also Hall 1986). Such an approach is particularly important in EU sectors, where considerable discretion is given to elites over the development of policies, often as a result of their specialized or highly technical nature.

In the context of the EU CAP, these conditions are echoed in the joint administration of the policy by the European Commission's DG Agri and territorial agriculture departments and ministries (see Chapter 1). While we contend that other actors within the EU exert considerable influence on supranational policy-making (particularly subnational actors during its 'post-decisional' stages (Puchala 1975); see especially Chapters 6, 8, and 9), the DG Agri and delegates to the Agriculture Council are privileged, especially in the initial stages of policy formulation (see Chapters 3 and 7). In this chapter, therefore, we draw upon a theory that unravels the interrelationship between policy concepts and beliefs, and the impact these historical institutionalized forms have upon the trajectories of policy-making, Majone's model of public policy change (1989, 1991, 1992*a*, 1996*a*). Our reason for using this model reflects our view that political scientists and geographers have been overly preoccupied with theorizing the role of interests, at the expense of ideas, in their analyses of national and supranational policy-making. In this respect, agricultural policy studies lag behind work in other fields of academic enquiry—for example, environmental policy (Weale 1993) and land-use planning (Healey and Shaw 1995).

2.2. Ideas, Beliefs, and Deliberative Policy-Making

In a series of thought-provoking articles, Giandomenico Majone (1989, 1991, 1992*a*, 1996) has outlined a theory linking the mobilization by policy elites of socio-cultural beliefs to the evolution of public policies. Majone argues that elites are continually provided with concepts that furnish the basis for novel policy initiatives. These concepts are advanced by a tightly defined community of actors who may be motivated by different and sometimes conflicting opinions, but who nonetheless share an active interest in a specific policy area. Particular concepts are selected by policy elites to provide solutions to issues perceived as 'problems', with these issues being prioritized in response to flux in the political-economic forces impinging on the 'policy space' (Majone 1992*a*). An existing fund of concepts, 'the result of . . . intellectual efforts and practical experiences [of actors] over preceding years' (Majone 1991: 2), plays an important role in offering potential solutions to these problems. In their transformation into novel policy initiatives, these concepts are tailored to suit the politico-administrative environment in which they will operate, which at the same time provokes a subtle alteration in their substance. Thus, 'policy development is always accompanied by a parallel process of conceptual development' (Majone 1992*a*: 14).

Over time, the accumulation of policy decisions becomes codified as a policy's *core principles*. These principles provide an overarching conceptual frame of reference for elites, and dictate an underlying logic for the policy's future development. It follows that, if effective solutions to policy problems are to be found, policy communities need to be 'open and competitive' (Majone 1989: 163) to allow genuinely innovative ideas to emerge. According to Majone, without the regular emergence of novel ideas and concepts, policy-making stagnates and policies become moribund. For example, where new ideas are not forthcoming because of policy community 'closure', the constant cycling of deliberative processes that constitutes policy praxis ceases, and the flux in policy community values that is dependent upon this praxis is stifled. In this situation, core principles come to dominate policy development, and fundamental policy reform becomes increasingly difficult to achieve. Policy elites tend to seek solutions to problems on the basis of the core principles, which may have contributed to the perceived difficulties.

Novel policy initiatives, and the often highly politicized arguments supporting their adoption, are seldom inducted into this *policy core*. Instead, they provide a protective discursive belt around the basic assumptions of the policy. Chiefly this *periphery* provides the mechanisms 'that are intended to give effect to the core principles' (Majone 1989: 151), but it also blunts criticism or deflects it away from the core, reducing the need for time-consuming and often costly reappraisal of basic policy dogma. Peripheral mechanisms can thus be amended or dropped completely without affecting the integrity of core principles, providing a policy with the flexibility and responsiveness to adapt to political-economic change. Reliance on public monies also means virtually all policies need to be legitimized to society at large. As the periphery more accurately reflects recent political-economic developments, this 'external' legitimation is often conferred by the peripheral mechanisms rather than the core.

By contrast, the policy core 'changes more gradually and continuously' (Majone 1989: 150) through interaction with those novel concepts accepted as being highly compatible with policy goals and objectives. Where policy communities are 'closed' (i.e. have restricted membership), the core provides a set of criteria for accepting or rejecting ideas, ensuring consistency in selection, and guaranteeing continuity of policy objectives that are especially important in upholding the interests of influential policy elites. In effect, they define the fundamental modalities of policy-making. In doing so, core principles provide 'internal' legitimation for new initiatives to policy community actors, by ensuring that these new initiatives are reinterpreted in such a way as to be compatible with existing policy.

Applying Majone's model to the evolution of the CAP suggests that the designation by EU elites of an agri-environmental policy was made as a response to the potent threat posed to agriculture by environmentalization. Moreover, this designation was made in the certain knowledge that the agri-environmental 'problem' could be reinterpreted through the prescribed methods and procedures of the CAP to support its core doctrines. At the same time, the new initiative would provide external legitimacy for EU agriculture, which, by the mid-1980s, was in acute crisis, through buttressing its existing policy entitlements in the face of public demands for a new environmental dimension to be introduced. Following our earlier argument, to assess how environmentalization was mediated by the CAP's modalities, we need first to identify the policy's core principles.

2.3. The Modalities of the CAP and the Accretion of its Core and Periphery

Elucidating core doctrines of public policies is not easy. Difficulty arises because these doctrines are the result of countless earlier decisions, preventing their precise specification. Moreover, their importance in underpinning current policy alignments makes their disclosure a politically sensitive issue. For these and other reasons, policy elites may have difficulty in articulating them (Majone 1989). But Majone notes (1989: 157): 'The inability or reluctance [of policy-makers] to spell out basic norms and commitments is no proof that their policies lack a more or less well defined core.'

Core principles can instead be inferred by scrutinizing long-term modalities of decision-taking in particular sectors, as they provide continuity in the judgements made by policy elites. Majone (1989) divides these modalities into *positive* and *negative decision strategies.* Positive decision strategies refer to affirmative choices made to specify the operating procedures of a policy. Some instruments will emerge as 'preferred', as they are highly compatible with the policy's underlying principles. In effect, the core principles are a historical-institutional form, circumscribing policy options, shaping the reactions of elites to perceived 'problems', and defining policy 'opportunities'.

Majone cites two negative decision strategies. First, there are *rejected alternatives,* instances where viable new decision pathways are considered by policy elites but turned down because they conflict with the imperatives of the policy core; and, secondly, there are *non-decisions,* affecting routine administrative choices, where a consistent trend emerges in excluding certain policy options from consideration. Applying these categories to the CAP enables a judgement to be made regarding its core principles, and, by default, allows identification of the policy's peripheral mechanisms.

Majone's theoretical approach yields some surprising results. For example, the five objectives of the CAP instituted under Article 39 of the Treaty of Rome (1957), often cited as its guiding concepts, are peripheral to the core.[5] Even though they provide the CAP with its enabling instruments, including the price policies and 'Common Market Organizations' that regulate its daily functioning, these objectives do not guide the policy's strategic development, a quality characterizing core principles. Similarly, the policy core is often conflated with an ethos glossed as 'agricultural productivism' (Clunies-Ross and Cox 1994). In fact, productivism is another peripheral mechanism fulfilling the basic goals of the CAP, exemplified by a definition of the productivist era as 'dominated by a concern [among policy-makers] to increase [agricultural] productivity *as a step towards* farmer prosperity' (Whitby and Lowe 1994: 1; emphasis added).

However, the rationales of Article 39 of the CAP, and the productivist approach it inculcated in EU agriculture, are very closely interrelated. Both aim to increase farm incomes by creating guaranteed markets, introducing commodity price support, and providing incentives to maximize commodity production. Productivism also exhorts the EU's farmers to optimize their production practices, so as to exact the highest possible crop yields from agricultural land. Furthermore, it connotes a wider communal responsibility on the part of the farmer to provide food and raw materials for rural societies and economies. The overall aim of these peripheral mechanisms is therefore not just to raise farm incomes generally. They also seek to boost farmer incomes on the grounds of the socio-economic benefits that agriculture can provide. By inference, one of the core principles of the CAP is to *guarantee the continued occupancy of land by a viable agricultural workforce with the aim of ensuring long-term rural stability.* As the preferred instruments of the policy, produc-

---

[5] These objectives are: increasing agricultural productivity; ensuring a fair standard of living for the agricultural community; stabilizing agricultural markets; assuring availability of food supplies; and ensuring food is supplied to consumers at reasonable prices.

tivism and the objectives laid down in Article 39 are quintessential to achieving this doctrinal ambition.

This core principle recurs either directly or in a more oblique form in the great majority of EU agricultural documentation. Perhaps its most clear-cut expression is found in the 1991 report *The Development and Future of the CAP* (CEC 1991*a*), in which the Commission outlined to member states its proposals for the reform of the CAP. In drafting this reform package, the DG Agri took care to stress that: 'Sufficient numbers of farmers must be kept on the land. There is no other way to preserve the natural environment, traditional landscapes and a model of agriculture favoured by society generally' (CEC 1991*a*: 9–10).

Examination of the *negative decision strategies* adopted by EU policy elites demonstrates that there is at least one other core principle flanking this doctrine. A clear example of a rejected alternative was the serious reverse suffered by the DG Agri in its presentation to member states of the so-called Mansholt Memorandum (CEC 1968). This document proposed the amalgamation of existing 'inefficient' EU agricultural holdings, to create units dubbed 'modern farms' (Louwes 1985), which would be the cornerstone of an ambitious plan for reform of agricultural structures across the Union. Nonetheless this undertaking presupposed national agriculture ministries would assist in the recasting of the socio-cultural conceptions of the farm specific to each member state, by encouraging domestic policy constituencies to aspire to this new 'ideal type' of holding. But the notion of the 'modern farm' directly challenged another bedrock principle of domestic agriculture, based on *the centrality of small-scale farming (chiefly in southern member states) and family farming (predominantly in northern member states) to the (re)structuring of rural space*; a conceptual opposition that resulted in the Memorandum's rejection.

These two core principles also find their expression through the modality of *non-decisions*, chiefly reluctance on the part of the EU Agriculture Council and the DG Agri to introduce regulatory, as opposed to incentive-driven, policy instruments into the CAP. One argument in the protective belt of the CAP, for example, that arises from the small-scale/family-farm principle is that a general derogation is warranted for these holdings from pollution legislation imposed on other industries, because of the disproportionately negative impact on small-farm incomes (Baldock 1992). This rationale seems to have contributed to the long-standing presumption that, wherever legislation is applied in EU agricultural policy, it should be voluntary or subject to 'self-regulation' by the industry, rather than rigorously enforced by external agencies.

Majone's theory reveals that socio-cultural traditions in member states, and national experience of domestic agricultural policies, were directly implicated in the emergence of the core principles of the CAP. These principles were first aired at the EU level during the conference of Stresa (1958). Tracy (1994) identifies two ideas that were advanced by participating member states at this conference as a basis for the development of the CAP. The first was that the policy should encourage the creation of larger more efficient holdings as a route to higher farm incomes, prefiguring the argument advanced later by Mansholt. Invoking economies of scale in this way implied that EU agriculture was an economic sector to be treated like any other. But at the same time delegates stressed the centrality of small-scale and family farms to European rural life, and the occupancy of agricultural land as a means of ensuring territorial stability—national convictions that already underpinned the farm policies of the EU's six member states (EU–6).

These national convictions convinced EU policy elites of the need to view agriculture as in some way atypical, implicitly ruling out the first approach. Across the intervening years the core principles of the CAP, flagged at Stresa, stand out. In effect, the policy's core was codified in 1958, and has remained virtually unchanged ever since, providing a historical-institutional structure for policy development, and ensuring the CAP's evolution as a mechanism for farm survival.[6] This process was hastened by the accession to the EU of southern member states with large agricultural workforces, leading to the widespread impression that the CAP was 'ideally designed to conserve an impoverished peasantry in southern Europe' (Allington and O'Shaughnessy 1987: 1).

Although the policy core emerged from the cultural rootstock of domestic 'agrarian ideologies' (Baldock and Lowe 1996: 13), it has also been underwritten by national interests within the emergent EU polity, and a seeming reluctance on the part of the European Commission to challenge these interests. As the trade journal *Agra Europe* scathingly observed of the piecemeal reforms of the late 1970s and mid-1980s:

Because of the unwillingness of the Council to agree relevant solutions to the CAP's problems and . . . the unwillingness of the Commission to make the correct policy proposals, the [Union's] problems in the agricultural sphere have become more intense. The reason for this is quite clear: Member States will go on providing money to maintain the CAP in its present form . . . since maintenance of the status quo maximizes their advantage . . . (*Agra Europe* 1985: 1, 15)

Not surprisingly, there are benefits for national and supranational actors from perpetuation of the CAP's core doctrines. They have provided DG Agri with a design around which to fashion policy proposals that are highly likely to achieve consensus among national delegations in the Agriculture Council, thus raising the Directorate's reputation as a decision-maker among other Union institutions (see Chapters 3 and 7).[7] Another important explanation of

---

[6] As Wallace (1999: 23) observes: 'In a relatively small EC, in which relatively tight-knit policy communities could be built, there were special opportunities for these [communities] to be bound together by shared ideas as well as by a shared concern with a particular policy sector, and for these to take root as an important influence on policy outcomes.'

[7] Cf. Laffan *et al.* (2000: 78–9): '[The Commission's] Directorates-General carry the institutional memory of past policy proposals, choices and responses of member States [which places DGs] in a position to propose packages that [will] find favour with a sufficient number of Member States.'

their longevity is the cumulative decisions taken on the basis of these core criteria in member states. Such decisions represent a tremendous amount of sunken capital in terms of assets, infrastructure, and land investment. So the perpetuation of core principles does not arise simply from the work of policy elites in supranational and national decision-making forums; their persistence can be attributed largely to trenchant defence by powerful interest coalitions in all EU states (Keeler 1996).

Hall (1993), in outlining an historical-institutional approach complementary to Majone's, clarifies the determinacy of the policy core on the evolution of the CAP between the 1970s and the late 1980s. Hall characterizes the gravity of policy change in terms of three levels, or 'orders'. Minor fluctuation in global agricultural markets, or in international political economic conditions, has required no more than tinkering with existing policy 'settings', which in the case of the CAP has meant altering levels of price support—a ritual undertaken annually by farm Ministers during the agricultural price review. Hall describes this as 'first-order [policy] change'.

More challenging politico-economic problems have required 'second-order change'—that is the introduction of new policy instruments or mechanisms that, however, do not 'radically alter . . . the hierarchy of goals behind policy' (Hall 1993: 282). Hence, as overproduction provoked near bankruptcy of the CAP during the 1980s, to use Majone's terminology, a troop of new peripheral mechanisms was recruited into the protective belt around the policy core, including milk quotas, coresponsibility levies, budgetary stabilizers, extensification, and set-aside policies. 'Third-order change' takes place only when a fundamental reappraisal of the principles guiding policy and defining its instruments is needed to address irreconcilable difficulties.

The CAP story of the 1980s–1990s was of policy elites within the EU's multi-level polity striving to keep change within Hall's first two 'orders'. In fact, since its inception, reforms of the CAP have always been of this first-order and second-order nature, prompted by political-economic upheaval affecting the Union's agricultural policy, such as the profound budgetary crisis of 1984, and the first substantive discussions on agricultural trade during the Uruguay Round of the GATT (1986–93). Incremental reforms of the policy have followed, with their substance dependent largely on the fleeting preoccupations and predispositions of national and supranational actors.

Drawing together Majone's and Hall's institutionalist insights suggests that the introduction of EU agri-environment policy represented a 'second-order change' in response to new institutional and public mandates to intervene on environmental grounds in agricultural policy—in short, the environmentalization of the CAP. This introduction has permitted a radical alteration in the legitimizing arguments used by agricultural interests to justify their traditional policy entitlements. We contend that that the emergence of EU agri-environmentalism must be seen against this backdrop of the continuing need for bestowing political legitimacy on the CAP.

The germ of the idea for this initiative can be traced back to the decisions taken at Stresa. Implicitly, agreement was reached at this conference on a rationale for intervention in the CAP, based on agriculture's production of 'public goods', which policy elites believed could not be secured through other gainful activities (Hagedorn 1985). These public goods included raw materials and foodstuffs produced in guaranteed quantities, and more intangible socio-cultural artefacts that are powerfully represented by the core principles, such as maintenance of the 'social tissue' (CEC 1985*a*: 12) of the EU's rural areas and management and conservation of the natural environment.

As EU food surpluses escalated during the mid–late 1980s, so the require-ment grew for a socio-cultural justification for agriculture's continued subsi-dization. By the late 1980s the legitimacy conferred by the production of foodstuffs had worn thin, as a polemical piece from the UK's Adam Smith Institute made plain: 'CAP supporters claim that food prices have risen less than the rate of inflation—an extraordinary defence, given the high growth of production. They assert that if we bought food on world markets "this would reduce supply and raise prices". Why? The economic case for liberal trade is impregnable: the strongest arguments against it are all really political' (Allington and O'Shaughnessy 1987: 1–3).[8]

With concern for the 'environment', overwhelmingly cultural in its interpre-tation, already embedded in the policy core of the CAP, it was easy for the CAP's legitimizing arguments to be adjusted by national and supranational policy elites in the 1980s and 1990s to suit the increasing 'political salience' (Mazey and Richardson 1993*a*) of environmentalization. At the same time, this socio-cultural notion of 'environment' played a crucial role in legitimizing the EU's new agri-environmental policy domain to territorial constituencies in member states. Arguably the environmentalization of the CAP owed as much to the incremental elaboration of this innate concept as to growing public interest in environmental issues, especially given the hermeticism of the EU agricultural policy community. It is this concept of 'environment', emanating from the policy core, that has configured, and continues to configure, EU agri-environmental policy.

2.4. Environmentalization of the CAP: The Evolution of EU Agri-Environmental Policy

The interrelationship between the modalities of agricultural policy-making under the CAP, and the way in which environmentalization of this policy has unfolded, finds strong echoes in the interpretation and treatment of agri-

---

[8] This reflected the emergence of neo-liberal discourses in OECD economies, advocating effi-ciency and effectiveness rather than satisfying clientelistic objectives as the overall goal of policy-making.

environmental relations by EU policy elites. Asked to reflect on the evolution of EU agri-environmentalism, specifically on the difficulties of incorporating explicit environmental objectives within the CAP, a senior Commission official commented: 'The first big problem was the learning process, not only across the professional agricultural world but also in large parts of the agricultural administration. At the very beginning many people simply didn't believe that agriculture had [negative] environmental side effects. And so there had really to be a change in mentalities and a learning process had to be introduced' (DG Agri source, Dec. 1995).

The focus of this 'learning process' was the socio-cultural conception of environment held by policy elites and embodied in the core principles of the CAP, principles that originated in the agrarian ideologies of the EU–6. The core of the CAP has provided policy-makers with a discursive motif of human–environmental relations, which has been supplemented and redefined by later accessions to the EU, each state refashioning the motif with its own specific environmental traditions. This situation has obliged the DG Agri and Agriculture Council delegations to adhere to this motif in fashioning EU agri-environmental policy (Chapters 3 and 7). In effect, supranational and national policy actors have had to operate within a circumscribed 'decision corridor' defined by the CAP's core principles, which has provided delineation of agri-environmental policy.

In essence, this discursive motif portrays the interrelationship between EU agriculture and the natural environment in a culturally hegemonic way. European agricultural landscapes are depicted as palimpsests of centuries of sedentary farming activity, with each locality having its own unique examples representing the hard-won communal efforts of earlier generations. This condition of agricultural landscapes as irreplaceable cultural assets endorses the CAP's core imperative for continued occupancy of farmland at all costs.

The veneration of agriculture's civilizing influence owes much to the heavily populated and urbanized character of northern Europe, from whence the motif emerged, creating an image of potent symbolic power among policy elites in these states especially. But, crucially, Mediterranean agricultural policies also exhibit features compatible with the CAP's core doctrines, such as prevention of land abandonment, encouragement of small-scale farms, and an emphasis on the territorial independence of the farmer, preoccupations enshrined, for example, in the agrarian reforms in Greece (Louloudis *et al.* 1989) and southern Italy (Gay and Wagret 1986).

Hence southern accessions to the EU in the early to mid-1980s brought amendment and elaboration of discursive traditions relating to the environment, but did not require their fundamental reformulation; southern and northern conceptions of rurality were essentially more compatible than conflicting. Any need on the part of policy elites in Greece, Spain, and Portugal to recast these principles was probably dampened also by the essentially distributive nature of EU agri-environmental policy, which, alongside other elements of EU structural policy, contributed to alleviating the perceived bias in the CAP towards north European agricultural production.

This discursive motif has found concrete expression by shaping the modalities of the EU agricultural policy community, which, as Majone notes, is the forum in which new concepts emerge, and existing policy precedents are reinterpreted. In the case of the EU agri-environmental policy, this was manifested in the increasing specification of the latent environmental responsibility of the EU farmer to be consistent with the two core principles—a continuous process that has given substance to this new EU policy domain. This specification has gradually redefined elite perceptions of the natural environment, from being viewed as a constraint on farming activities, to recognizing its compatibility with existing agricultural preoccupations, and, latterly, to perceiving agri-environmental relations as a key element in the struggle of the industry to legitimize its historic policy entitlements.

The Less Favoured Areas (LFA) Directive, EC Directive 75/268 (CEC 1975*a*), played a vital part in this specification. EC 75/268 was introduced to compensate farmers working in areas deemed to be disadvantaged on the basis of certain criteria, compared with the Union average. In the original proposal for the Directive, drafted in 1973, farmers' environmental duties in these areas were determined largely by the discursive socio-cultural conception of the environment at the CAP's heart: 'small areas affected by special handicaps in which farming must be continued in order to protect the countryside and to preserve the tourist potential of the area. The total extent of such areas may not in any Member State exceed 2.5 per cent of the area of the State concerned' (CEC 1973: 10).

In this form, environmental obligations on the farmer were non-existent, reinforcing a widespread perception among EU policy-makers in the 1970s and early 1980s that agricultural instruments targeted at the environment were 'marginal measures for marginal areas' (DG Agri source, Dec. 1995).

However, shortly after the Directive had been ratified by the Agriculture Council, and as part of its response to the Community's Second Environmental Action Plan, the DG Agri proposed the LFA measure be used to embrace environmental management in farming:

where the countryside needs to be maintained from an ecological point of view . . . This aim can be achieved . . . by means of direct subsidies to encourage farmers to farm in a given area . . . Under [this] heading comes the Directive on hill farming and farming in certain other less favoured areas . . . At the same time, agriculture can also have certain unfavourable effects on the natural environment. In particular efforts should be made to mitigate the dangerous consequences of certain modern production techniques, for example cultivation methods which impoverish the soil . . .   (CEC 1975*b*: 27)

This statement would not have been out of place in the agri-environmental policy debates of the mid-1980s. But in its contentious portrayal of some environmental problems arising directly from intensive agricultural practice, the

DG Agri offered a far more politically challenging formulation of the agriculture–environment interaction than hitherto, which proved too controversial for agriculture ministries in member states—traditional bastions of the CAP's core principles. Among these institutions and their domestic policy constituencies, this statement reinforced the perception that environmental concerns in agriculture were constraints upon farming practice, perhaps explaining the elapse of a decade before the introduction of the Union's first *bona fide* agri-environmental measure, Article 19 of EC Regulation 797/85 (CEC 1985*b*).

For this reason—and although the DG Agri's comments did not constitute a formal proposal of any sort—it might easily have become, in Majone's terminology, another 'rejected alternative'. However, during the mid-1970s the initial impetus was given for the environmentalization of EU agricultural policy, as problems arising from intensive agricultural practice became commonplace in northern member states (Conrad 1991). In turn this prompted change in the 'political salience' of environmental issues within member states, which Majone notes catalyzes alteration of the modalities of policy-making used by elites. This was the case first in the Netherlands, where, in response to widespread agricultural 'improvements', provincial administrations chose to interpret the LFA 'specific handicaps' category to include areas of farmed semi-natural habitat.

By the mid-1980s pressure was also building on the UK's MAFF to incorporate environmental considerations more fully into agricultural policy (see Chapter 6), provoking wider discussion within the EU multi-level polity, and leading to elaboration of the precedent set by the Dutch. This resulted in the introduction of a voluntary mechanism, Article 19 of EC Regulation 797/85, whereby states were permitted to implement 'special national schemes in environmentally sensitive areas' (CEC 1985*b*: 10). Farmers' environmental responsibilities under the Article were set out only in general terms. But an annex to the Regulation recast the LFA precedent cited above to read: 'small areas affected by specific handicaps and in which farming must be continued, if *necessary subject to certain conditions,* in order to *ensure the conservation of the environment, to maintain* the countryside and to preserve the tourist potential of the area . . . The total extent of such areas may not in any Member State exceed *4 per cent* of the area of the State concerned' (CEC 1985*b*: 14; emphasis added).

This marked the onset of an evolving deliberative policy process within the EU polity, focused on the agricultural environment, through which farmers were transformed from the passive environmental guardians depicted by the CAP's policy core to active environmental stewards, following specific management guidelines over much larger swathes of the European agricultural landscape than formerly (eligible area of land in member states rising from 2.5 per cent to 4 per cent of the utilized agricultural area of member states).

In effect, environmentalization discourses, as they applied to EU agriculture, were being redefined by administrators within the DG Agri to be largely supportive of the core principles of the CAP, rather than infringing them, as implied in the latter part of the Directorate's response to the Second Environmental Action Plan. This redefinition was an acknowledgment that, in order to fashion a Union-wide initiative, the Commission had to work within particular modalities of policy-making defined by the traditional expectations of agricultural constituencies in member states. Henceforth, the notion of the environment espoused by the DG Agri was one that accorded with the CAP's core doctrines.

The progressive specification of EU agri-environmental policy received greater impetus with the ratification of the Single European Act (1987), which required the Commission to take environmental considerations into account in all new EU policy measures. The DG Agri examined the policy options that could realistically be employed at the supranational level in the document *Environment and the CAP* (CEC 1987*a*).

An important conclusion was that the Agriculture Council's powers, established under the Treaty of Rome, could be employed to remunerate farmers for the production of 'environmental goods'. This permitted cofinancing by the EU of Article 19—that is, the use of EU monies alongside national expenditures—which was introduced with immediate effect. But the Council concluded that EU funds could be used in this way only if agri-environmental policies were included within the ambit of *common measures,* 'the main purpose of which has a direct link with improvement of [agricultural] structures, the rationalization of farming practices or the ensuring of a fair standard of living for the agricultural population' (CEC 1987*a*: 6). Environmental objectives were not mentioned as a goal of these 'common measures', instead being proposed as a means of *contributing to all three objectives.* We contend that this formulation represented a fundamental flaw in their policy design. While 'common measure' status ensured EU cofinancing of agri-environmental policy, by approving this formulation the environmental basis of the policy *sensu stricto* was fatally compromised, as single policy instruments with multiple objectives are inefficient mechanisms for achieving specific policy goals (Tinbergen 1966).

Using Majone's conceptualization, the introduction of EU cofinancing of agri-environmental policies by designating them as 'common measures' permitted a new peripheral mechanism to be introduced to the protective belt of the CAP, deployed crucially to reinterpret agriculture–environment problems so as to reinforce, rather than undermine, core policy doctrines. This designation has had profound long-term effects for this emerging policy domain. In effect, 'common measure' status has prevented agri-environmental policy from developing either a coherent focus, or a set of explicit environmental (as opposed to income support, or socio-structural) goals. Moreover, it has codified policy incrementalism, while ensuring this initiative is tied firmly to the doctrines of the CAP.

Certainly, the first agri-environmental policy measures were promoted as having environmental benefits on quite dubious grounds. For example, in its report *Environment and Agriculture* (CEC 1988) the DG Agri discussed the recently introduced 'extensification' initiative, and its function within the CAP.[9] This term described a suite of measures with the aim of curbing the excessive use of agricultural inputs, including fertilizers and pesticides, in order to reduce commodity production. But the DG Agri also asserted that 'extensification schemes offer great possibilities for the protection of agricultural ecosystems' (CEC 1988: 11), an altogether more complex managerial task, quite beyond the scope offered by measures with simple quantitative goals.

One reason for this designation of agri-environmental instruments as 'common measures' by the Agriculture Council was to facilitate legitimation of the new initiative to sceptical agricultural constituencies. Not only did this bring environmental concerns closer to the main preoccupations of territorial agriculture ministries and departments, pre-eminent among them overproduction. It also untapped EU cofinancing, raising the profile of the new policy among member states, and enabling the DG Agri to claim: 'The schemes [introduced under EC Regulation 797/85] were designed to help solve the income difficulties certain farmers might face and at the same time avoid the production of surpluses. This was the thinking behind action to . . . encourage development of "extensive" agriculture . . . and to . . . induce farmers to give greater attention to environmental problems' (CEC 1987c: 25).

'Common measure' status also allowed agri-environmental policies to be adapted to suit the agrarian ideologies of different member states. For example, a press release describing Article 19 to a French audience stated '[the Article] is necessary to bring about extensification of production' (CEC 1986), omitting its environmental function altogether, chiefly because of its unpalatability to powerful agricultural unions in that country (see Chapters 5 and 9).

We argue that these evolutionary controls upon the EU's agri-environmental policy—the discursive motif provided by the CAP's core doctrines, the political mores and cultural traditions of member states crowding out ecological and scientific considerations, and the designation of agri-environmental initiatives as 'common measures'—enabled environmentalization of the CAP to be recast in a form supportive of established policy elite interests. Perhaps most importantly, they guaranteed an incentive-led, rather than a regulatory, approach to the new policy domain, which was absolutely critical in securing a favourable reception among sectoral groups within the EU multi-level polity. This was confirmed by a senior official in the DG Agri:

I think [a regulatory approach] was far away from what was considered in the mid-1980s. Certainly there was no discussion about having a regulatory approach on something like Article 19. From the very beginning, the idea was to give incentives for environmentally friendly behaviour and production techniques. Personally I would

---

[9] The EU's first extensification programme was introduced under EC Regulation 1760/87 (CEC 1987b).

have doubted if member states would have been prepared to accept it on a regulatory basis from the Commission. To do it through incentives was the only way to get this type of measure acceptable.   (DG Agri source, Dec. 1995)

As Majone's classifications of non-decisions and rejected alternatives imply, the lack of any regulatory element in the canon of agri-environmental policy is mute testimony to the power of the policy's core principles. Commission documentation is peppered with phrases pushing a discretionary policy line— for example, urging member states 'to do their best to ensure that the [envi- ronmental] objectives can be reached through the active and voluntary participation of farmers' (CEC 1988: 14).

A significant example of a 'rejected (regulatory) alternative' was a Dutch proposal made in October 1991 to the Agriculture Council's Agricultural Structures Group, which, if accepted, would have radically altered the config- uration of the agri-environmental Regulation (EC 2078/92) (CEC 1992). The Dutch argued for environmental obligations to be clearly specified in the main corpus of the CAP, urging other national delegations that an EU code of good agricultural practice be adopted across European farmland, with punitive levies on farmers failing to observe its requirements (CoEC 1991*a*). The pro- posal was voted down. As both Majone and Hall suggest, novel ideas are never enlisted into the heart of policies, especially, as in this case, where they infringe core doctrines.

One profound consequence of shelving a regulatory approach to EU agri- environmental policy has been a reduction in the range of policy instruments available to tackle the tremendous variety of issues in member states. This sit- uation partly explains the conflation in this policy of the twin aims of encour- aging the production of environmental goods, and the control of 'negative externalities': both are treated through incentive payments under the agri- environmental component of the RDR. But Majone's discourse approach seeks a deeper explanation, rooted in the changing modalities of deliberation within the EU's agricultural policy community. In this context, one feature that emerged from the national implementation of the voluntary Article 19 measure was its concentration in northern, rather than southern, member states. In making this an EU-wide initiative, the problem that faced the DG Agri is captured by Majone (1989: 153): 'members of the coalition built around the [policy] core may not be seriously concerned with particular peripheral programmes'.

This is overcome by legitimizing new initiatives to policy clienteles, first by asserting the continuity of their objectives with the principles supporting the existing policy architecture; secondly, by ensuring that the stated objectives are consistently applied. So in attempting to diffuse and universalize agri-environ- mentalism throughout the EU polity, a paramount aim of the DG Agri was to ensure all member states' agri-environmental concerns were adequately repre- sented, and that the level of environmental responsibility imposed on national farming communities was broadly similar.

This process of consolidating and refining the environmental responsibilities of the EU farmer characterized EU policy debate of the early 1990s, and was made explicit in policy terms with the broadening of the remit of Article 19 in July 1990 to include 'maintenance of traditional agricultural features and practices beneficial to the environment', an alteration reflecting predominately southern preoccupations (CEC 1990*a*). In contrast, the interests of northern states, particularly France and the Netherlands, seem to have been better represented in the codification of the rationale for farmer compensation given in 'The Development and Future of the CAP': 'A system of aids will be provided to encourage farmers to use production methods with low risks of pollution and damage to the environment . . . participating farmers would undertake to respect constraints on their farming methods and would be paid compensation in return for associated losses' (CEC 1991*a*: 33). This consolidation of farmers' environmental responsibilities across the Union enabled the European Commission to bring forward proposals for a more elaborate policy approach, encompassing all member states.

2.5. EC Regulation 2078/92: Central or Peripheral to the CAP?

The deliberative process of redefining agri-environmental responsibilities was not sufficient in itself to bring forward the Union-wide policy represented by the agri-environmental Regulation, EC 2078/92. But the fact that policy instruments within this new domain had the status of 'common measures' ensured that agri-environmentalism became embroiled in the larger plans for far-reaching reform of the CAP taking shape in the late 1980s, an inevitable consequence of the inclusion of agriculture as a single agenda item in the GATT. It was through this global institution that the EU's major trading partners, notably the USA, began steadily to increase pressure on the EU for CAP reform, demanding substantial reduction in price support for the first time in the policy's history (Swinbank 1993).

Administrators within the DG Agri recognized that 'deep' CAP reform of the sort required under GATT would not be agreed within the EU polity without recourse to ameliorative 'common measures', the aim of which would be both to facilitate the reform objectives, and to address the inevitable grievances of domestic producer groups. This was the role foreseen for an expanded Union-wide agri-environmental Regulation. As a senior source in the Directorate commented:

Regulation 2078 was created to flank reform of the CAP—it emerged from a clear need to implement and at the same time facilitate the reform. This was negotiated at the same time as the GATT agreement, and our first idea was, well, we had to conceive some aids to accommodate the reform which were acceptable under the GATT framework, and at that moment the need for these agri-environment measures became quite clear. (DG Agri source, Nov. 1995)

But the Regulation had more than a facilitative purpose. EC 2078/92 also represented a high point of deliberation within the EU polity over the agriculture–environment relationship, with the aim of making this relationship fully compatible with the CAP's core principles. The status of the Regulation as an established part of the design of the CAP was corroborated by its direct linkage to the financial heart of the policy, the 'Guarantee' section of the agricultural budget.

Whereas EC 2078/92's deviation from the CAP's core principles was only slight, the reciprocal concessions made by environmental interests in bringing about this Regulation were substantial. For instance, during its development an implicit bargain had been struck between agricultural and conservation interests, which placed monetary values on the production by farmers of 'environmental goods'—the production of landscape, environmental protection, and the like. But, according to van der Weijden (Club de Bruxelles 1995: 82), EC 2078/92 represented the codification of this bargain as a 'stewardship principle', a concept now so generalized within the EU as to be 'a . . . principle to be added to the other four principles of EU environmental policy'.

Since 1992, this codification has had a number of consequences for the EU agricultural policy community. Not least, it appears to have endorsed the continued exemption of the sector from the EU 'polluter-pays' principle, applied in other industries. It also represented a major step in justifying agriculture's claim as the pre-eminent land use for securing environmental protection in Europe's post-production landscapes, hence providing farming interests with a viable platform for legitimizing continuation of their highly subsidized and protected status.

The fusion of Majone's and Hall's historical institutional approaches provides powerful insights into the modalities of policy-making under the CAP, and how these modalities have mediated 'environmentalization'. In particular, 'common measure' status has enabled agri-environmental policy to be cast quite legitimately as an aid for the EU's economically disadvantaged producers—the small-scale and family farmers championed by the policy core—and as a complementary measure for controlling commodity production. And, by its induction into the periphery of the CAP, Regulation 2078/92 diffused environmental critiques of the negative impacts of agricultural practice in the wider countryside by playing on the belief that, given limited financial resources, the targeting of marginal farmed land of high biodiversity provides member states with the greatest environmental dividend.

But the theoretical approach deployed here, based upon the centrality of core principles to deliberative policy-making, demonstrates that for environmentalization to proceed at all it had to be articulated in farming's argot. Ratification of the agri-environmental Regulation also secured environmentalization an important foot-hold within the CAP. Majone suggests that, just as peripheral mechanisms can be discarded, their inclusion in the protective belt of a policy can also be a precursor to future elaboration—a process inevitably bringing these initiatives closer to the policy core. This seems to be confirmed by the introduction of the RDR in 1999.

2.6. Conclusions

We have sought in this chapter to provide an overview of the environmental-ization of the emergent EU polity, specifically as it relates to the modalities of agricultural policy-making under the CAP, in order to inform and contextual-ize our subsequent arguments. We have also demonstrated how a consensus emerged in the EU agricultural policy community around environmentaliza-tion, and how this complex suite of processes has been mediated by the EU's diffuse multi-tiered structure. Our analysis demonstrates that environmental-ization within the EU has proceeded in an incremental fashion, and, far from being an 'exogenous' process, has received considerable impetus from the myr-iad actors and decision-making arenas within the EU. At different times and in different forums, national administrations and supranational actors (espe-cially the DG Agri and the Agriculture Council) have sought to utilize the potentially destabilizing discourses of environmentalization, in order to develop an agri-environmental policy domain that actively enhanced their own strategic purposes and organizational agendas. We examine how this has proceeded in subsequent chapters.

Ironically for a relatively new EU policy domain, we have shown that agri-environmentalism has a pronounced 'evolutionary' quality, as supranational and national policy elites have adhered to shared agrarian beliefs implicit in the CAP in their configuring of agri-environmental policy proposals. Indeed, the importance of the CAP's policy doctrines cannot be overestimated in terms of their providing cohesion by binding and interrelating the daily activities of agricultural policy communities situated at different politico-geographical scales. EU agri-environmentalism emerges as indissolubly linked to the pol-icy's core principles, which in turn have been shaped by the diverse cultural concepts of rurality inherent in northern and southern member states.

Certain of these socio-cultural traditions in member states are transnational in character, and on this basis we have identified a discursive motif relating to agriculture and the role of farmers within the landscape. Derived from the core principles of the CAP, this motif has created particular modalities for the evo-lution of EU agri-environmental policy. It has determined those issues per-ceived as critical by supranational and national policy elites, leading to certain mechanisms being favoured over others for implementation of this policy, and has ensured the pre-eminence of socio-cultural norms over more objective sci-entific criteria as the *modus operandi* of policy in the longer term. Its hegemonic status within the EU polity explains why the 'solutions' to the agri-environmental 'problems' of the EU–15 are broadly similar, and have been sought at the European, rather than the domestic level. This perceptual framing of the policy has enabled the European Commission and the EU Agriculture Council to render environmentalization tractable to established policy constituencies, by defining the range, scope, and aims of collective agri-environmental policy choice, and to manage effectively strategic opportunities in this emergent policy domain (see Chapters 3 and 7).

We have also specified how the underlying socio-cultural doctrines of the CAP have impacted upon the agri-environmental policy. In 1985, instead of the Agriculture Council designating a new suite of policy instruments targeted at the management of agriculture–environment interactions, the notion of the 'common measure' was introduced to address three disparate policy goals: the socio-structural, socio-economic, and environmental problems that were then all beginning to pose serious difficulties in northern and southern member states. We contend that this 'common measure' mechanism is fundamental to understanding how this EU policy has developed since the mid-1980s. It established a policy precedent for the multiple objectives of EC Regulation 2078/92, and indeed, for the RDR. In turn, this is certain to have a major impact on any objective appraisal of the outcome of agri-environmental programmes implemented in member states under the RDR. As Tinbergen (1966) intimates, single policy instruments with multiple objectives are prone to inefficiency and reduced effectiveness.

This historical institutional analysis also provides insights into the subsequent development of EU agri-environmentalism. While there is a very strong commonality of beliefs within the EU polity relating to agriculture and the environment, greater recognition of the preoccupations of southern member states—in particular the role of agriculture in sustaining rural economies—is apparent in the ratification of the RDR, as is the strategic agenda of the European Commission in seeking to expand the scope of the CAP's rural policy dimension. It is highly appropriate that the RDR has been characterized as the CAP's 'second pillar', as this Regulation is fully consonant with the policy's core principles of maintaining rural stability and the farmer's role as a key actor in the (re)structuring of rural space.[10] Given the prevalence of these doctrines among supranational and national policy elites, and the importance of both actor sets in implementing these policy programmes in the future, it seems likely that cultural rather than ecological goals will continue to be promoted as the basis of 'successful' EU agri-environmental policy.

We have presented here an overview of the 'environmentalization' of the CAP, from its origins in the mid-1970s to its maturation in the 1990s. In the following chapters, we seek to tease out the modalities deployed by different

---

[10] For example, Lowe and Ward (1998: 31) note that: 'The conception of rural development implicit in the [RDR is] a distinctly land-based notion that intimately associates "rural" policy with "agricultural" policy.'

actors and institutions in this multifaceted process. We focus in particular on the use of informal and formal policy-making procedures relating to the formulation and implementation of the agri-environmental Regulation, an important precursor to the RDR. We start in Chapter 3 by analysing how the DG Agri of the European Commission established a commanding role as a 'policy entrepreneur' in this new policy domain, by exploiting the range and breadth of its contacts within the EU multi-level polity.

3

The Role of the European Commission in the Environmentalization of the CAP: Political Entrepreneurship and Institutional Agendas

In this chapter we examine the role of the European Commission in the formulation and negotiation of the agri-environmental Regulation. We begin by examining the various conceptualizations of the European Commission in EU governance, and highlight the recent burst of literature that depicts the Commission as a 'policy entrepreneur'. In particular, we focus upon the modalities by which the Commission gains an important margin of autonomy and capacity to influence outcomes in the EU policy process, portrayals that lend support to the 'compelling metaphor' of multi-level governance. The Commission's role and position in EU governance endow it with particular modalities as a policy entrepreneur, not least its power of policy initiative, its function as a marketplace for policy solutions, and its central position in seeking compromises between varying national interests and standpoints. In this chapter we illustrate how the agri-environmental Regulation offered tremendous scope for political opportunism by the European Commission. In particular, we demonstrate the strategic importance and perceived political value to the Commission's DG Agri of the environmentalization of the CAP. We argue that environmentalization provided the DG Agri with the opportunity to protect the agricultural policy community and the Directorate's central position within it, the potential to divest itself of certain financial and administrative responsibilities for agricultural policy, and the chance to commandeer a new policy domain in the face of competitive pressures from other DGs within the Commission.

3.1. Conceptualizing the Role of the European Commission in EU Multi-Level Governance

Despite the legal entitlements of the European Commission to act as initiator, executor, and guardian of EU policy (Jones 1994*a*), there were until relatively recently surprisingly few detailed analyses of the precise modalities by which the Commission fulfills these roles. For example, Peterson (1999: 46) argues that 'For years, one of the great mysteries of scholarship on European integration was the dearth of literature on the European Commission . . . as recently as the early 1990s, the Commission had received only limited serious coverage.' However, at the turn of the millennium, as Peterson (1999: 46) maintains, 'the new problem for EU scholars is trying to stay on top of an enormously expanded literature [on the European Commission]'. Since the mid-1990s a succession of important papers on the European Commission's role, power, and effectiveness in EU governance has appeared (see Cini 1996; Christiansen 1996; Mendrinou 1996; Metcalfe 1996; Cram 1997; Laffan 1997; Jones and Clark 1998; Schmidt 1998; Smyrl 1998; Wendon, 1998). Collectively, these papers represent an impressive body of empirical evidence that increasingly demonstrates 'the Commission's autonomous influence on policy outcomes in a variety of sectors' (Wendon 1998: 339). This point is also made by Cram (1996: 199) in the following terms: 'the Commission has learnt to respond to opportunities for action as they present themselves, and even to facilitate the emergence of these opportunities'—an implicit reference to the modalities of engagement deployed by the Commission in the EU MLG system. Furthermore, the 'maturing' Commission (Christiansen 1996) has been represented as 'a strategically sophisticated bureaucracy with the ability to expand its own role' (Wendon 1998: 340), particularly during periods of strong Commission leadership and favourable political-economic climates for strategic activity on its part (Peterson 1999). Some writers have suggested that the MLG system may also enable the Commission to expand its powers incrementally (Schmidt 1998), since its role in the EU polity brings it into contact with a multitude of state and non-state actors, often allowing scope for policy discretion.

Below we set out the principal interpretations of the Commission's role in EU MLG. They are not mutually exclusive, but, rather, reveal the multidimensionality of the Commission's activities in the EU polity.

3.1.1. The Commission as Honest Broker and as a Marketplace for Ideas

In this conceptualization of the European Commission's activities, the Commission fulfils its role by bringing together relevant national and sectoral interests and their different ideas, based around which it must develop a policy proposal that secures the agreement of a majority of member states. The Commission is indeed permeated by national interests, and acts as an important forum for competition between them (Peterson 1999). As such, the Commission acts as a facilitator of intergovernmental discussions taking up the role of 'honest broker' in areas of disagreement between national delegations (Obradovic 1995; see also below, Chapter 7). Implicit in this role is that this institution does not seek to widen its own competences. Instead, the Commission's activities are viewed largely as a passive fulfilment of the three roles (those of initiator, executor, and guardian of European legislation) assigned to it under the Treaty of Rome. Hence, in its capacity as the initiator of EU policies, the Commission's principal aim is to orchestrate good relations with client groups whose input and support are crucial to the functioning of the policy process, by providing a degree of predictability and stability within different sectoral policy communities (see Chapter 5). In intersectoral policy areas, such as agriculture and the environment, constituent DGs are perceived as working seamlessly together to bring this aim to fruition. Furthermore, in this 'passive' conceptualization, the Commission acts as a 'marketplace' (Mazey and Richardson 1994) for ideas, by convening various working groups, normally comprising experts and officials from national ministries to exchange scientific information, define potential management and technical problems and difficulties, and establish some initial agreement between the member states over the spirit and direction of policy proposals.

3.1.2. The Commission as an Internally Differentiated Actor

In contrast to the above description of the Commission as a unitary policy actor with the different DGs working in concert and having equal access to resources of influence, expertise, and finance, other authors have drawn attention to the fissiparous nature of this Union institution, the lack of a unitary mindset (Hooghe 1999), and the tremendous variation in ways of working that exist among its twenty-four constituent DGs. For example, although the formal mechanisms for the emergence of a proposal through the Commission have been well documented (see Spence 1994), it must be recognized that the relative influence that particular DGs may exert on a proposal circulated through the College of Commissioners differs both in nature and in effect. Proposals that emerge from the European Commission are the product of a complex series of interactions and sometimes of fierce infighting between the various DGs (Ross 1993). Consequently, as Christiansen (1996) suggests, the Commission is a segmented organization, which makes policy coordination highly problematic across a range of policy networks; thus, establishing a Commission line, as opposed to the policy preferences of individual DGs, is tortuous.

Furthermore, in this conceptualization policy proposals drafted by the Commission have not only to address the interests of member states, but also to serve the Commission's medium-term and long-term strategic agendas. Such agendas underpin the Commission's task of promoting closer European integration and securing its own position within this process. This reading of the Commission's objectives is supported by the work of Sasse *et al.* (1977), who suggested that the merits of a Commission proposal have to be assessed on the basis of three criteria: its intrinsic quality in terms of its potential for achieving desired results in a given policy field; its relevance to the priorities and long-term objectives of the Union; and the likelihood of the Commission securing political consensus on the basis of the proposal in the Council of Ministers. These conditions require the Commission to refine continually its strategy for integration, and to have at its disposal an appropriate planning policy to take all contingencies into account (Sasse *et al.* 1977). The Commission must have mapped out its likely responses to change in the political environment in which it operates—an environment that, at particular times, may give the Commission greater flexibility, influence, or authority in initiating proposals and securing their agreement by member states.

The means by which the Commission consults with member states and other interested parties varies with the particular policy sector. As we have already noted, the agricultural policy area is often characterized as being a very tightly knit policy community, with the DG Agri at its core. Indeed, the DG Agri could be regarded as occupying the 'control tower' overseeing management and security of the EU agricultural policy space. Hence, Sasse *et al.* (1977: 155) note that the DG Agri is 'within its own particular orbit . . . the prototype of a powerful organization'. Within the policy network, the DG Agri has regular contact with working groups in the Council of Ministers (see Chapter 7), with the Agriculture Committee in the European Parliament (see Chapter 4), and indeed with the specific policy constituency of interests vocalized by the farm lobby *COPA* (see Chapter 5). The logical corollary of this is that, depending on their power base, individual DGs may have varying scope for what Majone (1995) describes as 'policy entrepreneurship'.

3.1.3. The Commission as a Policy Entrepreneur

The entrepreneurial role of the European Commission in EU multi-level governance is demonstrated by it being one of the most important of the Council's agenda setters (Peters 1994; Majone 1995). However, the Commission's initiatives do not emerge *sui generis*, but are most frequently the result of factors exogenous to the Commission (Westlake 1995: 64). The debate surrounding CAP reform is a good example of this point, with growing budgetary costs, market imbalances, and intense international pressures for EU market access driving demands for the overhaul of the policy (see Chapter 2). The Commission's effectiveness in exercising its power of initiative often depends, as Coombes (1970: 335) states, 'on the general political circumstances of the time, on the disposition of the major political parties and groups (or of the national governments in an international context) and on the degree to which electorates and key political activists are positive or neutral with regard to the aims the bureaucracy is intended to serve'. It is the Commission that is expected to harness the ideas and provide the drive and creative imagination to further the process of European integration. As Peterson (1999: 47) observes: '[the Commission] is expected to be the "conscience of the Community" and identify new and promising avenues for European integration.' The Commission is thus not just a reactive institution 'living constantly with the pressure of urgent deadlines and the necessity of responding rapidly to unforeseen events' (Ross 1995: 75); rather it is proactive, with its own short-term and long-term strategic agendas. This view is supported by Nguyen-Dan *et al.* (1993: 94), who claim that 'The European Commission . . . is more than an agency passively registering and executing orders issued by the Member States by the Council . . . The Commission has shown its ability to act as an autonomous actor with a tendency to enlarge its areas of competence, to mobilize new action resources (including legitimacy) and to enter new policy fields.' This entrepreneurial conceptualization of the European Commission has received increasing endorsement by a number of writers (Cram 1996; M.P. Smith 1996; Jones and Clark 1998). The Commission, acting as 'purposeful opportunist', has employed a variety of modalities aimed at expanding the scope of Union competence, and the extent of its own scope for action. Supporting this view, M.P. Smith (1996: 567) contends that 'the Commission not only attempts to capitalize on permissive conditions, but undertakes to create opportunities for itself . . . the Commission is highly flexible in how it pursues these opportunities to expand its competence and influence'. Most recently, Wendon (1998: 340) has portrayed the Commission as a sophisticated bureaucracy, with adept strategists able to marshall 'inocuous-looking instruments to achieve surprising results'. The Commission performs a dual function of having to provide both stability and dynamism within EU multi-level governance. It must generate not only legislative proposals but, in a broader sense, ideas to resolve what are often complex political problems. At the same time, it must ensure that it retains the trust and confidence of other actors in the multi-level governance system (Christiansen 1996).

Despite these assertions about the Commission's opportunism and entrepreneurship within EU governance, the modalities by which it achieves its goals are less well understood. Using the environmentalization of the CAP as our substantive context, we set out below the modalities surrounding three key aspects of Commission activities. First, the process by which ideas for Commission policy initiatives evolve and develop; secondly, the mechanisms by which the Commission engineers consensus around these initiatives; and, thirdly, how these ideas are shaped to fit the strategic agendas of the European Commission.

3.2. The Origins and Development of European Commission Legislative Proposals in EU Multi-Level Governance

The identification of the origins of ideas behind EU policy is by no means a straightforward task, nor is accounting for the way in which these ideas are transformed into policy proposals at the supranational level. One single approach is unlikely to be able to explain fully the range or the relative importance of factors that influence the policy-evolution process in multi-level governance. For example, Clark *et al.* (1997) have argued that ideas for EU agricultural policy come about incrementally, with their acceptance by the policy community (including member states and the DG Agri) being largely determined on the basis to which they support the 'core principles' of existing policy and beliefs of policy-makers (see also Chapter 2). Majone (1989) has contended that policy-makers are confronted by a range of policy 'problems' that they seek to resolve with recourse to a pool of ideas that uphold the existing core principles of established policy.

Focusing upon the role of national administrations, Heritier (1996) suggests that the majority of Commission proposals originate as a result of a particular member state making what are described as the 'first moves' to secure the EU political agenda. However, others have contended that it is also possible for the European Commission to act as 'first mover', particularly when the political environment is conducive for Commission entrpreneurialism. For example, Ross (1995) has investigated the role of Jacques Delors's *cabinet* in the process of European integration, at a time when there was 'a favourable array of three contextual variables' (Peterson 1999: 51) for Commission activity: receptivity by EU member governments to EU-level solutions, changes in the political geography of Europe, and a generally favourable economic situation in the EU. A central element in Delors's entrepreneurial agenda was the reform of the CAP. According to Ross (1995: 110) the agri-environmental issue was embroiled by the Commission in the CAP reform debate in early 1990:

Delors had sounded the alert and set out initial lines of thought. Jean-Luc Demarty, Delors' agricultural expert [in Delors's *cabinet*], had then begun working with key people [in the DG Agri] including Guy Legras, the Director General, Michel Jacquot, Demarty's predecessor in the *cabinet*, Jerome Vignon, and Pascal Lamy. The first full brainstorming had begun in September 1990, prodded further over the summer by budgetary problems, with serious conceptualization starting in September.

This process of entrepreneurialism by the Commission is confirmed by Hooghe (1999: 363), who notes: 'If you put together a few people [within the Commission] who are *visionnaire*: a commissioner, a head of unit or a director . . . you can get things done.' Ross's view (1995) is that the origins of the agri-environmental initiative lie within the small *équipe* of administrators gathered around Delors, in the highest echelon of the Commission. Indeed, the notion of the Delors *cabinet* spearheading CAP reform, and this initiative within it, is supported by Delors's speech to the *Assises du Monde Rural* in Brussels in November 1990. This marked the first public indication of the thinking of the Delors *équipe* over the reform of the CAP. In March 1991, Delors elaborated this position in a speech to French farmers in Bordeaux, and was able to declare soon after that 'CAP reform was prepared . . . but now it has to marinade for a while' (quoted in Ross 1995: 108).

Delors's key role in the emergence of the agri-environmental Regulation as suggested by Ross is, however, contradicted by national representatives at the cutting edge of the 1992 CAP reform negotiations. As one negotiator put it:

I'm not sure that Delors's *cabinet* had a tremendous role in this. Delors's cabinet was rather more focused on the CAP market regime element of the reform, I don't think they were pushing very strongly for anything on the environmental side. There was a political interest in [the Regulation], as you might imagine, but it was left to officials in DG Agri, Mr X in particular, to work up a text that would go through . . . he was the most important single Commission official and fortunately he had this earlier shot in his back pocket [that is, COM (90) 366], which had been widely rubbished, which he was able to amend to make it more acceptable.   (UKREP source, Oct. 1996)

The 'marinade period' referred to by Delors culminated in the publication of a 'Reflections Paper' by the Commission in February 1991, under the title 'The Development and Future of the CAP' (CEC 1991*a*). In this paper, the three key measures complementary to the quite radical changes proposed in the market organizations, which were designed to 'offer special opportunities for rural development (CEC 1991*a*: 32)', were outlined. To be known as the 'Accompanying Measures', they included a specific environmental action programme for agriculture. The Commission emphasized that the farmers' role in the protection of the rural environment and the management of the landscape should be recognized more fully and remunerated accordingly. More specifically, farmers would receive payments for using production methods with low risks of pollution and damage to the environment. For arable production, this would mean a significant reduction in the use of potentially polluting inputs (fertilizers, pesticides, and herbicides), and, in livestock farming, a reduction of stocking densities. However, participation in the schemes was to be on a voluntary basis, with participants being paid compensation within set limits for loss of income. In addition, the Commission would cofinance schemes to promote environmentally beneficial management of farmed land. The Commission also proposed to introduce a system of aids to ensure the environmental upkeep of abandoned agricultural land—a proposal clearly directed at the Mediterranean states. Each member state would be obliged to introduce schemes under this Regulation and to define the programmes, the areas affected, the levels of payment, and the conditions for participation. Submissions by member states for funding of schemes under this Regulation would be scrutinized by the Commission.

Between February and November 1991, the Commission undertook an extended dialogue with member states and, in addition, conducted discussions with producer and interest groups (see Chapter 5). These consultations culminated in November 1991 with the publication of a repackaged, reworked, and considerably revised draft for the agri-environmental Regulation, published as COM (91) 415. Nonetheless, there appears to be no consensus on the part of Commission officials over the pre-eminent source of ideas for this Regulation, as the following comments from members of the DG Agri and the DG Env, respectively, demonstrate:

It's really a Commission initiative, but there is no, let me say, no unit of brainstormings [in the Commission]. We finance research, we are in touch with universities, with NGOs [non-governmental organizations], with interest groups and the ideas are there, and when you have to conceive a proposal to discuss with all the member states, well, the ideas should be taken from somewhere.   (DG Agri source, Dec. 1996)

I think it attracted a big attention in 1991 when the Commission was preparing the CAP reform . . . during the summer the Director General and another Director, a powerful Director, they went back to their own country and there discovered uncultivated land and problems on the hills, and they came back and said 'OK, why not try and find money to help farmers to bring about upkeep of the landscape?'. The second point was that they were looking for, let's say, something attractive for the general public, because when drafting the new CAP reform they were expecting a lot of resistance from farming communities, so they wanted to have at least one or two things which would be appealing, creating interest, so at that time they started to take it [ie. agriculture and the environment] more seriously.   (DG Env source, Jan. 1997)

This detail supports the point made by Peterson (1999: 58) that 'Commissioners themselves, as well as officials in the services, all carry "national baggage". . .', and that made by Hooghe (1999: 366), who states that the Commission is a 'particularly porously bounded institution into which officials can . . . import their own interests and ideas and advocate them'.

Irrespective of the source of ideas for its proposals, the Commission is dependent upon member states for their elaboration and refinement, based upon their experience of relevant domestic policies. In the case of the agri-environmental proposal, the Commission derived this expertise from a limited number of national quarters. As the UK negotiator explained: 'We found this Commission proposal more important than any other delegation and we did a lot of work in getting it shaped to meet our needs, and we think improved . . . I think it is fair to say that a number of delegations were highly sceptical, some were completely indifferent, others were quite interested, but we were the most enthusiastic of all' (MAFF source, Apr. 1996). The Commission's consultations with MAFF led to the UK being able to exercise some leverage in what Heritier (1996) refers to as the definition, 'framing', and solving stages of policy (see Chapter 6). As the UK negotiator explained:

The Commission listened to us a good deal because we had practical experience with agri-environmental schemes . . . we took it tremendously seriously and the Commission on the whole does respond if people are taking them seriously in a constructive way . . . they are willing to take points on board. After all, people sitting in DG Agri don't have tremendous experience in this area, so they need to plunder expertise from all quarters. (MAFF source, Apr. 1996)

According to the German Commission official responsible for formulating the agri-environmental proposal, the German experience in this policy area was instrumental in shaping Commission thinking:

I was invited to participate in a working group in Stuttgart to see whether MEKA [*Marktentlastungs-und-Kulturlandschaftsausgleich*, an agri-environmental scheme in Baden-Wurttemberg (see Jones and Clark 1997)] could be extended. Personally I gained a lot from these discussions. These influences were increased through contacts with countries both interested in, and engaged with, this policy, though particularly Germany. They were central to our position and attitudes. (DG Agri source, Dec. 1996)

For the UK, the Commission's proposal served a useful political objective, as it was not possible to introduce additional agri-environmental measures in the UK without recourse to primary legislation. The MAFF was keen to extend the scope of this policy, but, as a senior MAFF official explained:

We wanted to do things for the environment without necessarily moulding it into the Environmentally Sensitive Areas [ESA] framework . . . but we didn't have the primary powers and we had no prospect of getting parliamentary time for a new Act. So another way of doing things is if it becomes a Community obligation; you then use the European Communities Act to introduce measures under your Community obligations by Statutory Instrument, which is of course rather easier to do, if the government wishes to do it . . . so we had an interest in getting a decent Council regulation through. (MAFF source, Feb. 1997)

There are several pertinent issues concerning MLG and modalities that emerge from this discussion. First, it shows that the Commission *does* play an autonomous role in policy initiation as evidenced by the Delors *équipe* and individual Director Generals in the DG Agri taking the lead on agri-environmental measures. Secondly, it reveals that an important mechanism in policy initiation by the DG Agri is the plundering of expertise on agri-environmental policy from particular national and regional scales in the MLG system. And, thirdly, it demonstrates the ways in which the DG Agri identified enthusiasm for agri-environmental measures as advanced by certain member states, which could be harnessed to further Commission objectives in this policy domain. The accommodation of these particular national and territorial interests by the Commission at an early point in the development of the agri-environmental proposal was a critically important mechanism for depoliticizing the issues and, importantly, reducing the likelihood of more public (and therefore potentially more harmful) disputes over the policy at later stages of the policy process.

3.3. Modalities of Consensus Engineering in EU Multi-Level Governance

Engineering consensus over a Commission policy proposal can be examined in terms of securing *internal* and *external consensus.* Even before a proposal has been presented to national delegations, internal consensus within the Commission must be reached over the aims and objectives of the proposed legislation. Inevitably, where a proposal affects cross-sectoral issues, such as agri-environmental relations, this process of achieving internal consensus may be deeply problematic. This is because such policy initiatives inevitably challenge the competences of the relevant DGs, as Peterson (1999: 53) notes: 'rivalries between different sectoral policy networks within the Commission are fierce.'

In the case of the agri-environmental proposal, securing internal consensus within the Commission depended crucially upon a reconciliation between the rival interests of new environmental constituencies with those of the long-established EU agricultural policy community. Hence within the Commission, the DG Agri appears to have been at pains to prevent the Environment Directorate from having too significant an input into the emerging 'agri-environmental' Regulation. This is summed up well by a national official involved in the negotiations on COM (91) 415:

[The Environment Directorate] was irrelevant. They were not exactly a forceful presence in the Commission; DG Agri, of course, has always been a tremendously influential DG, they know how to operate the system, how to get things done, and have the budget. The Environment Directorate were really messing about in the margins, making a lot of not entirely helpful comments much of the time. They weren't a major force . . . although no doubt under Collegiate rules DG Agri were obliged to keep them on-side. (UKREP source, Oct. 1996)

For the DG Agri official in charge of agri-environmental policy at that time, the problem was summed up in the following way 'It was a question of personalities . . . it was a fraught relationship between the two DGs' (DG Agri source, Dec. 1996).These comments also confirm Mazey and Richardson's observation (1994) that there are often jurisdictional disputes between different parts of a supposedly unified bureaucracy and problems of horizontal coordination across related policy sectors.

In accommodating environmental interests within the Regulation, the mechanism by which the DG Agri was able to keep the Environment Directorate on board was by offering it a policy input of a token nature, as a senior official from the Environment Directorate confirmed:

DG Agri was a powerful DG in charge of the CAP reform, so when we reached the level of the cabinet discussions between the different heads of cabinet [within the Commission], DG Agri and Delors's cabinet wanted to give something to the Environment Directorate but a minor part . . . so they gave us the possibility to create a new *prime* [subsidy] for endangered breeds of livestock . . . nobody in DG Agri had any confidence in agri-environmental measures.   (DG Env source, Dec. 1996)

For many members of the agricultural policy community there was a less than sympathetic reception to this particular inclusion in the proposal. As one Council delegate explained: 'The Environment Directorate can have the endangered breeds thing on their tombstone. They've managed to waste a lot of public money. It was a rather extraneous bit "tacked on" . . . in essence, their contribution didn't surprise me" (MAFF source, Oct. 1996).

The DG Agri's uncompromising approach as 'spider in web' of agricultural policy is explained largely by the concern that the Environment Directorate's intrusion into the emergent agri-environmental 'policy space' (Majone 1989) would complicate the DG Agri's brokerage function in engineering consensus. Without it, interest groups may have found it difficult to discern just who the broker was on the proposal. As Mazey and Richardson (1994: 174) argue: 'while the "lead" DG can be identified easily this still leaves the problem of how to interface with the relevant DGs and leaves interests to cope with the general lack of coordination within the Commission . . . interest groups themselves may be brokers between different parts of the Commission.'

The competitive element between the two DGs and their poor working relations over agri-environmental policy and, moreover, the DG Agri's efforts to curtail the environmentalization of the CAP are confirmed by a senior *COPA* official, who claimed: 'We would have liked it if the DG Agri were more active in this field, because the Environment Directorate was trying to do everything and this was a slight problem for us [as part of the agricultural policy community] . . . I know from the Environment Directorate that we gave more input to their work on agri-environmental policy than the DG Agri' (*COPA* source, May 1998). In consensus-building in MLG, the Commission must convince the policy community of its firm commitment to the proposal it is launching. This becomes something of a problem if competing Commission Directorates are allowed too much involvement in the formulation of policy. For example, the Environment Directorate publicly questioned not only the DG Agri's interest in the environmental aspects of agricultural policy, but also its ability to implement and evaluate it. As one Environment Directorate source complained: 'DG Agri think that the *travail noble,* the most important part of their job, is market organizations; there's a very strong culture in DG Agri that the good jobs, the promotion jobs, are jobs dealing with market organization' (DG Env source, Dec. 1996).

With regard to the achievement of *external consensus*—that is, consensus between member states and the Commission over a policy proposal—the DGs have a variety of modalities at their disposal. Coombes (1970: 332) suggests that the power of the Commission is partly 'technical; the engineering of consensus involved in an economic concertee results not so much from an underlying social and political unity as from a skilled putting together of varying demands in a way which pays off to every important sector'. This skill involves careful timing, an ability to discern a common interest among the member states (or a large number of them), and to promote that interest effectively by whatever means. Dialogue and consultation are vital mechanisms in this process. Indeed, the Commission comes to depend upon this consultative procedure as much as the various national, territorial, and sectoral interests themselves. In essence it is mutually reinforcing, ensuring that the policy community remains tightly bound (Adshead 1996), and, in addition, provides a device for the Commission to legitimize its entrepreneurial activities. This is explained by Christiansen (1996: 80): '[in addition to member states] a wide range of non-governmental groups and interests . . . [are] regularly drawn into the ambit of the Commission [and they] would then emerge favourable to the development of a European policy which they had helped to design'.

Within multi-level governance, mutual sensitivity and responsiveness between actors are key components, creating predictability and stability in the system (see Chapter 7). To echo Peterson's view (1995*a*: 82): 'a range of actors in any policy sector will have an interest in ensuring that the policy-making process reflects a minimum degree of predictability and stability.' For the European Commission, this means keeping national delegations well informed about its own intentions regarding particular proposals, being receptive to national worries and concerns, and ensuring that proposals are adopted by the member states with the minimum amount of change and disruption to the Commission agenda. An important modality in this process is the 'bilateral'—that is, an agreed meeting between the Commission and a member state's negotiator(s) instigated by either party. Once the Commission has tabled a proposal, although this becomes part of the province of the Council, it is still possible for member states to request bilaterals with the Commission. Such meetings and their regularity will depend upon a number of factors, in particular how much concern there is about the legislative text in a member state, and the strength of the negotiator's relationship with the Commission personnel responsible for the text. In terms of the agri-environmental Regulation, there was shared, tacit ways of thinking and reacting between the DG Agri and certain member states, as one negotiator explained: 'the bilateral meetings [on the agri-environmental Regulation] were sought by us, and agreed to by Mr X [senior Commission official], and as such they were demand-led; it wouldn't necessarily be as easy to do that with all Commission officials. Mr X was actually very interested in the text, and open to suggestions on how to improve it' (MAFF source, Oct. 1996).

A variety of modalities are open to the European Commission to secure agreement among member states over a policy proposal. First, depending on how confident it is in its proposal, the Commission can adopt a 'take it or leave it' stance, putting pressure on member states to go along with the proposal, although, as a Council negotiator suggested, 'this very rarely works, since the chances are the Council *will* end up leaving it' (MAFF source, Oct. 1996), thereby squandering much time and effort on the part of the Commission. More likely, the Commission will listen to the issues that most delegations are concerned about, and seek to make the minimum amount of adjustments to the proposal to secure acceptance by the member states on a qualified majority vote in the Council (see Chapter 7). A third mechanism by which the Commission can get support for a legislative proposal is by making undertakings that are not reflected in the text. This can be in the form of an open undertaking, such as a Commission declaration made when the text is adopted by the Council: for example, 'the Commission undertakes when considering implementation that it will do x or y, or take account of . . .'. However, in recent years the Commission has been more hesitant about making these sorts of declarations, because it binds successive Commission administrations to previous agreements and in turn effectively reduces the scope for policy entrepreneurship on the part of the Commission. More recently, the Commission has resorted to making bilateral undertakings to different national delegations that are not recorded publicly—in effect a closed undertaking. As one Council negotiator commented: 'These are of the sorts "don't make a fuss about this; why are you worried about this aspect; we assure you that, when it comes to this aspect, it's not our intention at all to . . .". So up to a point . . . the Commission can soothe people's fears' (MAFF source, Oct. 1996). Another modality to engineer consensus is for the Commission to work very closely with the Presidency of the Council (see Chapter 7). This 'tandem relationship' enables the Commission to help the Presidency frame compromises that are acceptable to the Commission and are likely to secure qualified majority approval in the Council. As a Council negotiator explained: 'when the Presidency tables compromises and amended texts, any effective Presidency will have ensured that the Commission can actually accept the amendments and the compromises—although of course they won't do so in any overt fashion' (MAFF source, Oct. 1996).

3.4. Shaping Ideas to Fit Commission Strategic Agendas: Policy Entrepreneurialism and the Agri-Environmental Regulation

The policy proposals of the European Commission are designed not solely in terms of reactions to specific economic, political, or budgetary circumstances within the Union. Crucially, they are developed according to the Commission's medium-term and long-term strategies for European integration and, specifically, the need for it to secure its existing competences, and to develop new ones, within this integration process, relative to other EU institutions and to sovereign governments. This view is supported by Majone (1992*b*: 138), who suggests that the aim of the Commission is to 'maximize, not its budget but its influence as measured by the scope of its competence . . . the utility function of the Commission is positively related to the scope, rather than to the scale of the services provided'. It is clear that, in shaping policy proposals, the Commission utilizes a number of modalities to further its integrationist aims (Pollack 1996). As we have seen, several mechanisms are used to engineer consensus over a proposal, but the drafting of the proposal itself also requires considerable ingenuity on the part of the Commission in order to ensure that, although certain responsibilities for EU policy are ceded to member states, crucial control and monitoring functions are retained by the Commission. In essence, the mechanisms used by the Commission at the policy-shaping stage aim to provide member states with sufficient flexibility (or 'ambiguity'—see Chapters 8 and 9) of interpretation in the implementation of Union legislation. The principle of subsidiarity provides a novel mechanism by which the Commission can achieve these strategic ambitions, while at the same time dampening concerns felt by member states over the escalation of the Commission's activities. In this sense subsidiarity could be viewed as a double-edged sword for a member state, where the outcome of the division of power and competence between it and the European Commission may decisively favour the latter.

Within this context of satisfying its own integrationist aims, the Commission's proposals may, on the one hand, be an immediate response to a specific policy issue or, on the other, be part of a longer-term plan. If we turn to the CAP reform process, we argue that the Commission's aims were to maintain its authority to initiate proposals in the EU agricultural policy sphere while at the same time redefining its role with regard to control, implementation, and administration of policy relative to national administrations. Within this process, the agri-environmental Regulation played a minor though significant role. As one well-placed DG Agri official commented:

The first idea [for EC 2078/92] was to facilitate reform of the CAP, and in some way compensate some options . . . by including Regulation 2078 there was a positive element which could be offered to farmers . . . 2078 was very much an element which increased the acceptance of the whole package . . . and 2078 was something which was already in the pipeline before the CAP reform started and so we made this approach an accompanying measure of the CAP reform. I think this was synergy.   (DG Agri source, Dec. 1996)

For the Commission, determining the division of competences between itself and member states for the agri-environmental Regulation was problematic. For example, across the EU there were differing levels of experience of agri-environmental policies. Some member states had highly developed agri-environmental policies that were strongly supported by political and public consensus (for example, Denmark, Germany, and the Netherlands). On the other hand, there were states (for example, Spain, Portugal, Italy, and Greece) with little or no expertise in this area. This was acknowledged by one DG Agri official:

Awareness of agri-environmental problems may be different from one member state to the other; the problems themselves are quite different from one member state to the other . . . the consciousness of the problem and the question of political priorities are sometimes quite different . . . there are member states where quite clearly economic development or rural development is much more important, and is a much bigger priority than environmental policies.   (DG Agri source, Dec. 1996)

Brinkhorst (1991) suggests that this difference of expertise between member states means that, without taking decisive action, the Commission could not guarantee that all member states would move in the same direction, with the obvious negative effects that this would have on the integration process. With regard to the agri-environmental Regulation, even if states did follow the same direction, differences in timing of implementation and the content of national agri-environmental programmes could create market distortion: hence the diversity of legislation would in effect act to divide rather than to unite the Union. This issue of market distortion in the implementation of agri-environmental policy by member states was also cause for concern for *COPA*. As their senior negotiator explained in interview: 'We became interested in the Commission's proposal because of the dangers of distortion of competition. We have examined the proposal not because of its environmental content as such, but rather because it could create distortion of competition between farmers in the different countries' (*COPA* source, May 1996).

By employing the principle of subsidiarity in the field of agri-environmental policy, the Commission believed that its strategic ambitions could be fulfilled if it was left to the local or national levels to put together the most appropriate combination of measures designed to achieve broadly defined economic and environmental objectives determined at the Union level. Such an approach would lead to member states having responsibility for the administration of national programmes, which would be controlled and monitored by the Commission. As one senior DG Agri official explained:

The legislation is based upon a new approach within the CAP . . . what this measure is designed to do is to give the member states more room to manœuvre . . . The system is that the Commission would open a dialogue with the member states on a partnership basis in order to discuss the measures it proposed to adopt. Thus the subsidiarity principle applies. It can perhaps be seen as a sort of test which might serve as an example for other measures. If this experiment stands the test, we will be able to cut down the amount of bureaucracy, by regionalizing and decentralizing.   (DG Agri source, May 1997)

As regards the all-important financial question underpinning its agri-environmental Regulation, the Commission maintained a strong line in the face of fierce opposition from all the Union's powerful northern member states (except the UK) during debates within Council (see Chapter 7). As one DG Agri official commented:

Certainly there were a number of member states (United Kingdom, Ireland, Mediterranean countries) more in favour of our approach [that is, funding from the

Guarantee section rather than the Guidance section of the *Fonds Européen d'Orientation et de Garantie Agricole (FEOGA)*] than others. I think some member states were certainly afraid because they saw that, within a given budgetary ceiling, the development of agri-environmental policy of the Regulation 2078 type would be at the expense of the traditional classical agricultural-support policy. It is not by accident that this agri-environmental proposal has been put by us under the Guarantee fund . . . this was the only possibility we had under the 1992 reforms to get a . . . relatively significant amount of money available for agri-environmental measures. There was no possibility at that time to do it under the Guidance funds, which had their own budgetary planning, and the order of magnitude [required] was I think ten or twelve times what it had been under Article 19. (DG Agri source, Dec. 1996, see also Chapter 2)

Central to the Commission's strategic vision for agri-environmental policy was that it could divest itself of certain traditional responsibilities, in particular routine administrative functions and support of the full costs of funding this policy. As Laffan (1997: 422) explains: 'The Commission's capacity for management is much weaker than its power of initiative because it lacks sizeable bureaucratic resources and largely implements policies through a shared administration with the member states.' *Contra* Laffan, we do not see this as a loss of the Commission's strategic position at the implementation stage. Rather, in the case of agri-environmental policy, it was a political and financially expeditious opportunity for the Commission to shed onerous responsibility and, at the same time, secure consensus among the member states for the policy proposal (see Chapter 9). In its initial submission to Council, the Commission proposed a uniform level of cofinancing not exceeding 50 per cent of the total expenditure of individual programmes. However, the southern member states' approval of the proposal was secured only by an undertaking from the Commission that it would reimburse them at more favourable rates for some of their poorest regions (in practice, up to 75 per cent of the costs). Notwithstanding this, there was satisfaction within the Commission that cofinancing by the Union, even at this higher level, would be effective in ensuring the financial prudence of member states. As a senior official in the DG Agri commented:

having a cofinancing option with member states or regions participating in the financing of these measures, and the Community contributing only a certain percentage, has in our eyes the big advantage that it creates a stronger responsibility on member states and regions; they're putting their own money, or some of their own money, in there and experience shows in fact that this has quite a positive impact. However, it has the inconvenience, and one has to be very honest about that, the inconvenience that, in the present budgetary situation, it is extremely difficult for them to mobilize the money they would like to in order to apply schemes which really respond to the problems they've got. (DG Agri source, Dec. 1996)

The Commission's position as chair of the management committee (STAR (*Comité des Structures Agricole*)) (see Chapters 8 and 9), responsible for approving and overseeing national agri-environmental policies, enabled it to take on the role of 'policy strategist'—that is, steering the implementation of this new policy across the member states and regions of the Union. This conceptualization of the agri-environmental proposal nests comfortably with the framework of 'renationalization' of the CAP, whereby member states receive some Union support for agricultural policies but bear fully the costs of policy implementation and administration. In fact, this trend in the management of the CAP was endorsed by the former European Commission President Jacques Santer in 1991, when he announced that logically the application of the subsidiarity principle would mean 'agricultural policy would again become national . . . such drastic change is absolutely necessary in the immediate future' (Santer 1991: 27). The development of the agri-environmental Regulation can, therefore, be viewed as a 'policy trial' and a facilitative measure in bringing CAP reform to fruition.

In this chapter we have shown the pivotal role played by the European Commission in the evolution and development of the agri-environmental Regulation in the multi-leveled polity of the EU. We have done so by highlighting the modalities by which this institution seeks to incorporate its own strategic agenda within this policy concern. We have also charted the ways in which the DG Agri drew upon expertise from a variety of national, territorial, and sectoral quarters, and fashioned the ideas on the agriculture–environment relation that emanated from these deliberative processes, to further its entrepreneurial aims and strategic ambitions.

In keeping with the MLG notion, we have demonstrated how the engineering of consensus needs to be investigated in multiple arenas, and, in particular, should not be restricted solely to the Commission–member state interface. Commission involvement in consensus building is multifaceted, and involves both *internal* (between different DGs within the Commission) and *external consensus* (among NGOs, as well as member states). With regard to internal consensus, it was imperative that some reconciliation of disparate environmental interests of the Environment Directorate needed to be made with the deeply ingrained productivist views of agricultural policy, espoused by the DG Agri. We contend that the protection and jealous guarding of traditional 'policy space' by these differently motivated, and unequally influential, Directorate-Generals offers an important explanation of the nature and content of the agri-environmental Regulation as it emerged from the European Commission.

The DG Agri's endeavours to reach external consensus on the agri-environmental Regulation demonstrate a number of key features, including careful timing and exhaustive preparation on the part of its staff, an ability to discern a common interest for its proposal among the member states (or a large number of them), and the promotion of that interest by the Commission in an effective manner by a variety of modalities (for example, 'bilaterals', 'open' and 'closed' undertakings, working closely with the Council Presidency). For the DG Agri's part, the passage of the agri-environmental Regulation through the institutional routeways of EU decision-making reflected its ability to present a policy proposal that secured the acceptance of key member states, such as the UK, Germany, and the Netherlands, on the basis of the political scope it offered. As we shall see in Chapter 7, the DG Agri was also successful in containing the relative lack of interest among other states and ensuring that this did not develop into destructive disinterest in the Council of Ministers.

Having conceptualized in this chapter the role of the European Commission, we recognize three important related issues in the modalities of EU governance. First, the ways in which the Commission interacted with the EP over the agri-environmental Regulation; secondly, the mechanisms for, and outcomes of, the consultation between the Commission and interest groups over the formulation of the Regulation; and, thirdly, the basis for, and development of, negotiating positions by individual member states in the supranational decision-making process. We investigate these issues in the next three chapters.

4

The European Parliament: The Inter-Institutional Modalities of 'Agenda Territories'

In this chapter we examine the modalities of the European Parliament (EP) in EU multi-level governance. We conceptualize these modalities in terms of 'agenda territories' and 'agenda-interlocking', and explicate them in the shaping and setting stages of the agri-environmental Regulation. Our main contention is that the environmentalization of the CAP enabled the EP to deploy these modalities in such a way as to interlink its institutional agenda with the pragmatic options and strategic preferences of the European Commission. In this way, the EP, despite formal constraints on its power in agricultural policy-making, was able to exercise significant influence on the development of the agri-environmental Regulation in the MLG system of the EU.

4.1. Introduction

The impact of EU institutions on policy outcomes has been highlighted in theoretical work on the political processes of integration in the EU (see e.g. Hix 1994; Garrett and Tsebelis 1996; Hurrell and Menon 1996; Pollack 1996). These findings have suggested that studies of EU policies must be sensitive not only to institutional relations, procedures, and changes, but also to the complexities of an integration process that often proceeds as much informally as formally (Hurrell and Menon 1996). In this chapter we take up the challenges presented by Judge *et al.* (1994: 49) for researchers to 'dive wholeheartedly into further conceptualization and detailed empirical assessment of the EP', and by Hubschmid and Moser (1997: 241), who wish 'to encourage scholars of EU decision making to focus their attention on [the] constraints and changes [facing the EP]'. To this end we investigate the various modalities by which the EP attempted to exert influence in the policy-shaping and policy-setting stages of the agri-environmental legislative process. These stages covered the period

1985–92, and, as we have discussed in Chapter 1, they culminated in a formal agreement on the agri-environmental Regulation by the Council of Ministers in early summer 1992 (see Chapter 7).

4.2. Theoretical Approaches to the Influence of the European Parliament in EU Multi-Level Governance

The recent changes to the EU's governance system brought about by the Single European Act (1986), the Treaty of European Union (1992), and the Treaty of Amsterdam (1997) have stimulated great interest among political scientists in the nature of the EP's influence in EU governance (see e.g. Tsebelis 1994, 1996; Kreppel 1999; Meyer 1999; Moser 1996). The conceptualization of this influence has wavered between two views of the institution. In the first, the EP is viewed as becoming increasingly influential in certain areas of EU policy (see e.g. Lodge 1993); whereas in the second, it is contended that the EP's overall influence in EU governance remains minor relative to other EU institutions, in particular the European Commission, the European Court of Justice, and the Council of Ministers (see Kerremans 1996). However, events in early 1999 saw the EP tabling a censure motion on the European Commission, on the basis of increasing 'fraud, cronyism and other forms of maladministration' (J. Smith 1999: 71), with the Commission responding by establishing an independent committee to tackle financial irregularity. To many observers this demonstrated that the EP had flexed its muscles effectively and had judiciously exercised its influence in the EU polity (J. Smith 1999). Aside from the EP's somewhat reluctant use of its formal powers of censure and control over the Commission, the precise modalities of influence within EU governance remain in dispute. Whilst Treaty changes have witnessed an expanded role for the EP in the elective, control, and legislative process of EU governance in some policy areas, for other policies, such as agriculture, the EP retains only a consultative role. This has led to authors espousing a liberal inter-governmentalist view, such as Moravcsik (1993), to credit the EP with little or no independent influence on EU bargaining outcomes. Others, including Tsebelis (1994), have claimed that the influence of the EP is a result of conditional agenda rights. This second position has been refuted by Moser (1996), who maintains that the EP is able to exert influence only if it is able to take advantage of changing preferences among member states in the Council for particular features of a policy proposal. Building on this point, we suggest that the EP's ability to exert influence depends on the degree to which its position(s) on specific policy issues interlocks with the pragmatic options and strategic preferences of the European Commission in that institution's own efforts to engineer consensus in the Council of Ministers (see Chapter 3).

Judge (1992) and Judge *et al.* (1994) argue that the EP's influence in EU governance must be considered both temporally and sectorally (and, indeed, in the same policy sector at different times), concluding that 'statements about the "influence" of the European Parliament should be specific rather than general and empirical rather than assertive' (Judge *et al.* 1994: 49). These authors also contend that the EP has been able to exert significant influence in policy areas, such as environment, on the basis of proactive agenda-shaping and covert and indirect exertion of influence, strengthened latterly by the introduction of 'Cooperation' and 'Codecision' procedures for decision-making (see also Tsebelis 1994, 1996; Westlake 1994). Although we would not dispute the proactive functions of the EP, nor the importance of informal modalities deployed by this institution to exert influence, we would argue against Judge *et al.*'s (1994) implication that the EP's influence in other policy fields such as agriculture has been minimal. This observation, as we will demonstrate in the context of the environmentalization of the CAP, is a misreading of the operation of the EP and the dynamics of this institution's legislative influence in the EU's MLG system.

Although EU agricultural policy-making accords only a Consultative role for the EP (see Jacobs and Corbett 1994), the ability of the Parliament to exert influence is, we argue, dependent on the EP and Commission reaching agreement—what we term 'interlock'- enabling a united front to be used in the Commission's dealings with the Council. This interlock is both time specific and proposal specific and, importantly, does not represent an enduring coalition of interests, a point confirming Kreppel's observation (1999: 534) that 'not only can and does the EP have a politically significant impact on EU policy, but [also] that this influence is not constant'.

From the position of the EP, interlock is achieved through the 'murky waters of [EP] policy influence' (Judge *et al.* 1994: 28). Whereas these authors refrain from exploring this idea, we suggest that one possible means of progressing this issue is through the clarification of these 'murky waters' in terms of different institutional modalities, such as agenda territories, operating within the EP. The concept of agenda-setting has itself found increasing appeal among researchers of EU governance (see Peters 1994; Pollack 1997). Specifically we explore the agenda territories in the EP, which arise out of the different internal decision-making structures and factions operating within this institution. These agenda territories embody the broad spectrum of political and policy interests comprising these structures and factions. We argue that, when these agenda territories are compatible with Commission agendas, their mobilization results in an increase in the EP's ability to influence EU policy outputs. In the MLG system there are, of course, many tiers of negotiation and exchange between the EP and the Commission (Marks *et al.* 1996), offering numerous modalities for the interlock of EP agenda territories and Commission preferences. By focusing upon agri-environmental policy, we are able to address the request lodged by Judge (1992: 187) for 'more detailed studies of specific issue areas, studies which examine the inter-institutional connections within the EC especially the informal flows of influence as well as the formal, treaty prescribed contours of power'. Moreover, we are also able to tackle the issue raised by Kreppel (1999: 522) that 'Little effort has been made to address the more complex, and perhaps more important, question of *when* the EP is influential' (emphasis added).

4.3. Agenda Territories, Agenda-Interlocking, and EP Influence in EU Governance

In Chapter 1 we referred to two stages in the EU policy process: 'policy-shaping' and 'policy-setting' (Petersen 1995a). Policy-shaping decisions are taken at an early stage of the policy-making process, when options for EU legislation are being formulated. For the EP, this policy-shaping stage is characterized by the institution's efforts either to place issues on the policy agendas of one or more of the different DGs of the European Commission, or to move pre-existing items up these agendas, which are often overcrowded or congested with other legislative business already. This can be achieved by the EP through formal modalities such as 'Own Initiative' reports (see below); or through informal modalities, including bringing pressures to bear upon Commission staff; or a combination of these formal and informal modalities.

For EU agricultural policy, there are numerous 'access points' (that is, nodes of communication offering the means to influence policy) in the machinery of decision-making, presenting the EP with a multitude of opportunities to bring influence to bear upon the Commission during the policy-shaping stage (see also Grande 1996). Such access points can be utilized by the EP only when the interests of relevant parties are fulfilled adequately. These relevant parties can include Commission and EP officers of the highest level, as well as individual members of EP Working Committees and Commission administrators, and can take place at different times and in formal and informal contexts.

When agenda-interlocking occurs during the policy-shaping stage, the EP exercises influence over the substance and overall direction of a European Commission legislative proposal. The EP's efforts to influence the Commission's policy preferences during this stage need to be seen in the light of the Commission occupying the driving seat in the initiation of EU policy, as the EU's formal agenda setter (Pollack 1997; see Chapter 3). In fact, the likelihood of EP–Commission agenda-interlocking is based upon the Commission's careful examination of Parliament's suggestions to see whether these would benefit DGs in their drafting of legislative proposals. Specifically, the EP's views might assist DGs in achieving any or all of the following Commission goals, which are the prerequisites for a successful Commission proposal: (1) a Commission proposal needs to appeal to pivotal players in the Council, would need to be pro-integrationist in nature, and would need to be preferred by the Council to the status quo ante; (2) a Commission proposal needs to be able to secure internal consensus in the Commission—that is, it would need to satisfy the Commission's medium-term and long-term strategic agendas; (3) a Commission proposal has to advance legislation in a policy area across all member states; and (4) a Commission proposal not only needs to secure internal Commission consensus, and external consensus among the majority of member states, but must also secure the support of the EP in plenary session.

After policy options have been developed into a legislative proposal by the Commission, there follows a policy-setting stage. In EU decision-making, 'policy-setting' refers to the political interaction between Commission proposals, EP opinions and amendments, and the Council of Ministers' Committee decisions (see Chapter 7); this stage is less well understood in terms of the theoretical literature (although see Risse-Kappen 1996). Unlike EP involvement during the policy-shaping stage, the role of Parliament in the policy-setting stage is determined by the Treaty basis of the subject under discussion. Under the Consultation procedure, as the majority of EU agricultural policy is determined (see Westlake 1994) at the policy-setting stage, agenda-interlocking is focused upon EP amendments to Commission proposals. Again, the Commission is the lead institution in determining whether agenda-interlocking with the EP takes place, as it must take into consideration what it can realistically have ratified by the Council of Ministers (Westlake 1994). Hence agenda-interlocking over EP amendments will occur when the Commission believes that an EP amendment to its proposal will: (1) serve to clarify the proposal to all affected parties; (2) enlarge the scope of the proposal, while still being acceptable to the Council of Ministers; (3) strengthen the Commission's ability to engineer consensus over the proposal among member states; and (4) serve Commission strategic agendas in the overall policy field.

For the EP, as agricultural policy falls under the Consultation procedure, agenda-interlocking with the European Commission is the only means by which it can exert influence in CAP decision-making. As one London MEP explained, 'if we haven't got the Commission in agreement with Parliament on the Consultation procedure, we're stuck really. We can be outdone by the Council of Ministers. If the Commission and the Parliament are "on-side", it means there's a certain amount of EP leverage within the Council of Ministers' (MEP source, Feb. 1998). Our interpretation of agenda-interlocking and the fundamental importance of the Commission in bringing it about is supported by Pollack (1997: 123), who suggests that 'the agenda setting power of the Commission and the location of the equilibrium policy choice depend fundamentally on both the Commission's preferences and the distribution of preferences in the Council, which the Commission must always take into account in making its proposals'.

4.4. The European Parliament: A 'Hothouse' of Agenda Territories

We suggest there exists a number of modalities by which the EP can exercise influence in EU multi-level governance. One of the most significant of these procedural forms for advancing EP interests is agenda territories. These agenda territories, as we term them, enable the promotion of (1) the EP as an institution; (2) EP political groups; (3) EP Working Committees; (4) national interests through the institution of the EP; and (5) sectoral interests and individual career ambitions. We examine these EP agenda territories in more detail below.

4.4.1. Agenda Territory: Promoting the Influence of the EP as an Institution

One prescribed procedure by which the EP promotes its institutional influence during the policy-shaping stage is by preparing what are known as 'Own Initiative' reports. In these reports policy questions facing the EU, such as the impact of EU policies on particular economic sectors, regions, or communities, are addressed. The Own Initiative report may also serve the Commission in advancing its own strategic preferences, and the EP typically produces such reports when it has discovered that the timing is appropriate for an enthusiastic reception by the Commission. The EP's Environment Committee has become well known for the number of Own Initiative reports produced on key EU topics (Jacobs and Corbett 1994), some of which have been acknowledged by the Commission as having prompted action or changed its priorities (Judge 1992). These reports have led some commentators such as Marquand (1997: 105) to note that the '[EP] probably has more influence on the "pre-legislative" [policy-shaping] phase of Community policy-making than Westminster MPs have on the UK equivalent'. However, timing is all important, and failure to sound out the Commission about its own intentions reduces the possibility of the Parliament interlocking with the Commission's agenda. Ultimately this can lead to a poor reception among Commission officials for EP Own Initiative reports. This may have coloured the opinion of MEPs over the effectiveness of the Own Initiative report in the policy-shaping stage. As one British MEP explained in interview, 'what we haven't got time to do [any more] is mess about producing tons of paper about nothing especially if the reports end up sitting on a shelf somewhere, dismissed by the DGs as a lot of hot air' (MEP source, Mar. 1998).

The key objective for the EP is to capitalize on opportunities for the advancement of influence with other EU institutions. In the policy-setting stage under the Consultation procedure, there are several other modalities by which it can further this goal. One is the power of delay. Before the EP's final vote in plenary session, the EP may ask the Commission whether it will accept certain parliamentary amendments to its legislative proposals (Westlake 1994). If not satisfied with the response of the Commission, the EP can refer a Commission proposal back to the EP Working Committee for further consideration. This delaying tactic is an important weapon in the EP's battle to secure concessions from the Commission, and to ensure that the Council of Ministers does not reach decisions without having first received the EP's opinions. This situation is summed up by a national delegate in the Agriculture Council:

> whereas in the past the Agriculture Council had been quite cavalier in agreeing on things and then saying we'll then formally adopt this once the EP had given its opinion, and the EP cheerfully went along with that . . . that stopped with the European Commission under the leadership of Jacques Santer, who refused to go along with an agreement in the Council until a European Parliament opinion had been delivered. (MAFF source, Jan. 2000)

In this respect, the EP and Commission can act together to rein in the Council.

Another modality to extend EP influence, which is open to well-placed senior members of the EP, may come about as a result of their own long-established contacts with high-ranking Commission officials and with representatives of national governments. Informal and social contacts between such individuals often not only enhance the individual's position (see below) but also enable the EP's views on a particular issue to be articulated, thus circumventing the limits imposed on Parliament by its formally prescribed legislative powers. As a former EP President commented in interview: 'Personally I work very closely with Fischler [currently the EU's Agriculture Commissioner]. I have worked very closely with him in the past, and I shall continue to do so in order to bring about EP influence. I will also talk to Santer [the then EU Commission President]—I get on very well with him—so I'll be working with well-placed members of the Commission' (MEP source, Mar. 1998). Clearly, by their very nature, such points of access will not be open to all members of the EP, though they offer the potential for senior EP officials to progress informally the EP's position in policy debates.

4.4.2. Agenda Territory: Promoting the Influence of EP Political Groups

The political groups of the EP provide another vector for the advancement of EP influence in EU governance. Informal contact between political groups in the EP and Commission staff grants the EP access to current and future thinking of the Commission over policy issues, and on this basis enables Parliament to organize in advance a substantive response to them, as well as enabling the establishment of a tactical position to further the group's objectives within the Parliament—for example, in terms of bidding for Rapporteurships (MEPs assigned to oversee and coordinate the Working Committee's response to a

Commission legislative proposal) for the item when it is presented as a Commission proposal, or mobilizing support from other interested parties (Westlake 1994).

This use of political networks to further links with individuals in the Commission is a particularly important modality for political groups both in the policy-shaping and in the policy-setting stages of a Commission proposal. As one southern England MEP explained, 'You know what's coming up, and you know what the thinking is and there's an ongoing relationship. Sometimes it'll be through the party political network: if you like, the sisterhood or brotherhood of fellow socialists will mention a name, [or] will say that a person in the Commission can be trusted' (MEP source, Apr. 1998).

The relationship between Rapporteurs and the Commission is an important one in the EU system of governance (Bowler and Farrell 1995). It could be interpreted as collusive, not only for the Commission, which is able to manipulate the Rapporteur in the phrasing of amendments, but also for the Rapporteur, who is provided with an ideal opportunity to promote a political group or a national agenda territory or indeed for career advancement. Nevertheless, it is a fundamental mechanism for the EP to interlock with the European Commission. One British member of the Agriculture and Rural Development Committee stated that: 'Providing the Rapporteur gets the trust of the Committee, he or she can do a lot of behind-the-scenes business with DGVI [now known as DG Agri] officials' (MEP source, Feb. 1998). Similarly a Danish MEP described her own experience:

If you're a Rapporteur on a piece of legislation, you find out who the Commission official is who's responsible for it. You see them and you talk to them. What are the ideas behind it? What's the Commission trying to do? Is there anything they feel has been left out—that is, that didn't get through the College of Commissioners—that the [Commission] might want in and which [the EP] might agree with? Why haven't they put in things we wanted? Generally, if it goes right, the relationship can be effective . . . although a lot of hard negotiation goes on . . . (MEP source, Feb. 1998)

The character of the Rapporteur is crucial in this latter respect, as a Dutch MEP explained: 'Some are very conscientious, and take a "European" view—they will take their [political] group's view and their Committee's view. They can overcome their personal likes and dislikes, their national sectoral interests. Sometimes, though, they take the opposite line, advancing views based on their own experience, or on data from national experts . . .' (MEP source, Mar. 1998). With the potential to exercise considerable personal influence over European policy, Rapporteurships are, therefore, much prized by MEPs. Hence the remark of an Italian member that 'some people are killing for Rapporteurships—they're stabbing each other in the back [in order] to get them' (MEP source, Feb. 1998).

4.4.3. Agenda Territory: Promoting the Influence of EP Working Committees

Working Committees of the EP are an essential ingredient in any conceptual-ization of the Parliament's influence in EU governance. As Westlake (1994: 66) notes, 'Committees take a traditionally tenacious view of their roles and pre-rogatives', developing a character that is the result 'of a mixture of factors: sub-ject matter, tradition, style of the Chairman, and attitudes/style of active members'. In assessing a Committee's role as an agency of EP influence, one has to consider not only how a Committee furthers its interests relative to other EP Committees, but also how it constructs and sustains its relations with other institutional actors in EU multi-level governance. In this second respect the Working Committee's relations with DGs in the European Commission are critical in facilitating agenda-interlocking. In several cases the Committee–DG relationship is founded upon shared beliefs and assumptions regarding the spirit, purpose, and direction of EU policy in a specific field (see Chapter 2). For example, the DG Agri and the EP's Agriculture and Rural Development Committee have built up a particularly strong relationship, with protection of the core doctrines of the CAP and the minimization of policy upheavals as its focus (Clark *et al.* 1997). This bond was alluded to by a British MEP on the Agriculture and Rural Development Committee

DG Agri and the Agriculture and Rural Development Committee . . . work . . . closely together . . . the [Agriculture] Commissioner is a good attender of the meetings of the [EP] Agriculture and Rural Development Committee, as are administrators from DG Agri who are always there, often four or five of them. If an issue of real concern [arises], and nobody from the Commission delegation can deal with it, DG Agri will ensure that somebody's there within the day to answer it.   (MEP source, Dec. 1997)

The EP's Agriculture and Rural Development Committee has itself gained a (fully justified) reputation for being dominated by farm lobbyists, well briefed and prepared to defend the principles of the CAP to all its critics both inside and outside the EP. As a former Chairman of the EP's Agricultural and Rural Development Committee explained in interview:

It has to be said that the majority of members in [the Agriculture and Rural Development] Committee were naturally on [that] Committee because they were farm lobbyists. If you take my own position, in 1979, when I was the first Chairman of the then Agriculture Committee, there were five ex-Presidents of farmers' unions on that Committee, and I suppose that speaks for itself! And of course all of us were steeped in agricultural policy. I'd also been President of *COPA* for three years before 1979. (MEP source, Dec. 1997)

One Socialist MEP from north-eastern England also admitted that 'the major-ity of members of the Agriculture and Rural Development Committee regard themselves as members of the "Farmers' Committee", speaking for farmers and safeguarding their interests as they see them. This is particularly so among the new member states of the Mediterranean . . . I have to remind them on occasion that we are not the "Farmers' Committee" ' (MEP source, Feb. 1998).

Conversely, the poor working relationship between certain EP Committees and Commission DGs actively reduces the potential for agenda-interlocking. According to some MEPs, this is because of the reluctance of the Commission to negotiate on an equal footing with Parliament, or an unwillingness among some Commission staff even to recognize the Parliament as a player in the policy process. Poor relations can also be attributed to particular nationalities occupying key posts within certain DGs in the Commission. For example, a British MEP commented in interview: 'DG Agri is a French bureaucracy basically, designed to be impenetrable, designed to block transparency—all the obfuscation [from DG Agri staff] can be very frustrating' (MEP source, Mar. 1998). This nationality bias of the Directorate was confirmed by a French DG Agri official: 'The organization of DG Agri is, of course, very influenced by the French way of managing administration. I mean it has been conceived on a French model. In the key jobs, you have people who are of the French administrative culture,' (DG Agri source, Apr. 1998). Ironically, furthering working committee interests with the European Commission in the face of such nationality-based barriers is often achieved through the establishment of 'nationality networks' between key EP Committee officers and Commission staff, structured in such a way as to favour Parliament's interests, as one Conservative MEP explained: 'you don't necessarily go to number one in the [Commission] Section or . . . Division you're dealing with—you may go to number two, or number three. Personally I might go to number three . . . because he's an English chap. He might know the Cotswolds rather well, so I'll be thinking, "Let's talk to Jim" ' (MEP source, Dec. 1997).

For some Committees in the EP, relations with the Commission may be less than harmonious as a result of the strident character that the committee has adopted or actively promotes. For example, the Environment Committee is notorious among personnel in the DG Agri, though its generally close relationship with the Environment Directorate mirrors that of the Agriculture and Rural Development Committee with DG Agri. As a British Socialist MEP on the Environment Committee explained: 'our Committee has the reputation for sending away DG Agri officials in tatters, as mincemeat. Some of them give as good as they get, some of them have a real ding-dong with us, a good battle . . .' (MEP source, Apr. 1998).

Another important consideration in assessing the EP Committee structure as a medium for EP policy influence is that, on occasions, individual Working Committees of the EP are themselves at loggerheads. The Agriculture and Rural Development and the Environment Committees provide perfect illustrative examples, demonstrating that the relationship between EP Working Committees is critical to understanding their impact on the overall influence of the EP in EU governance. On both Committees in recent years, deeply entrenched matters of principle have been reinforced by strong personalities. This has been combined with the Agriculture and Rural Development Committee's struggle to regain control of a changing agenda for agricultural policy in the face of an Environment Committee eager to overthrow the productivist principles of the CAP. In essence, these factors lie at the heart of this intra-parliamentary dispute, which is regarded by many MEPs as having led to a weakening of the EP's policy influence over the European Commission. Levels of suspicion between the respective Committees were summed up by one British MEP from the Environment Committee: 'They [the Agriculture and Rural Development Committee] have adopted a new technique now . . . we've noticed that they have sent infiltrators to the Environment Committee. There are people there now who have different interests to the majority of the Committee' (MEP source, Apr. 1998).

However, the case of the Environment–Agriculture and Rural Development Committees' relationship is perhaps the most polarized in the EP. More often, relations between Committees and the concomitant overall effect on EP influence is a product of contingent factors, as a Dutch MEP indicated:

members of the main Committee will try to attend a meeting of the other opinion-forming Committees' when it challenges their own agenda. They try and get their argument in that way. I guess the process is *ad hoc*. Sometimes [members from the different Committees] liaise very closely, sometimes they don't. Sometimes their agendas agree, sometimes they don't. It's often to do with personalities, sometimes it's to do with time, sometimes it's to do with policies.   (MEP source, Feb. 1998)

Within the above agenda territory, then, there are at least four modalities by which the EP attempts to exercise legislative influence in the policy-shaping and policy-setting stages of EU governance. These are: the nature of the relationship between the Working Committee and the Commission DG; the degree to which it is strengthened (or indeed weakened) by nationality questions; differing perceptions held by those in post of the formal relationship between the Parliament and the Commission; and the extent to which the Working Committee's goals, positions, and views have a receptive audience with relevant Commission DGs.

4.4.4. Agenda Territory: Promoting the Influence of National Interests through the Institution of the EP

The promotion of national interests by MEPs is an established though under-researched aspect of the EP in MLG. This promotion enables the EP to interlock with the Commission when the Commission seeks support for particular national viewpoints in its brokerage activities in Council. Modalities deployed for this promotion include the choice of Working Committee membership made by MEPs; the interventions made by them in EP debates and the tenor of amendments made by Working Committees to Commission proposals; and the preferential use made by MEPs of contacts in the European Commission sharing the same nationality in order to promote national interests. All these issues are reflected in a pithy comment made by an Italian MEP: 'there is the feeling that you really want to do the best for your country . . . that's obvious' (MEP source, Mar. 1998). As a British MEP also commented: 'The French and the Spanish are particularly notorious for closing ranks across political parties on certain issues, acting as lobbyists for national governments' (MEP source, Apr. 1998).

Each MEP selects one Working Committee as her or his principal Committee. In some instances, the outcome of this selection leads to quite clear national distributions. As a London MEP commented: 'Spain, Greece, Portugal, and Ireland tend to go for Agriculture and Regional Development and pack those two Committees. It's like the French nuclear experts sitting on the Energy Committee . . . there are no French socialists on the Environment Committee, they're just not interested . . .' (MEP source, Oct. 1997). South European MEPs choose the Agriculture and Rural Development Committee because, as one French MEP explained, 'they want to make sure that their country doesn't lose out, or to ensure it gets the best deal possible in the Annual Price Review or whatever' (MEP source, Feb. 1998). The outcome of this, as a Welsh MEP explained, is 'a geographical defence of policy' (MEP source, Apr. 1998).

Interventions in EP debates, either in Committee or Plenary, reflect these national preoccupations with MEPs under pressure from national administrations, sectoral lobbies (see Chapter 5), and from local constituency concerns, reflecting the MLG of the EU policy. This is verified by one north Italian MEP, who commented: 'I speak a lot with my national government, reading all the [relevant] documentation . . . and after I prepare my opinion within a political strategy, for example we have some priorities in agriculture in the Socialist Grouping, and it's within that strategic [framework] that [Socialist MEPs] work in the Committee' (MEP source, Feb. 1998). As was noted above, pushing the domestic agenda with the European Commission is accomplished through personal contacts, especially with own nationals. The setting-up and furtherance of nationality networks to promote national agendas appears to be an established, though clandestine, modality of the EP, as one Central England MEP revealed: 'It's chaotic, you wonder why is someone so disorganized and inefficient, why haven't they got the paperwork done? Well you know why, it's because it's deliberate, they don't want you to interfere. It's already stitched up between them and one of their nationals in the Commission' (MEP source, Apr. 1998).

4.4.5. Agenda Territory: Sectoral Interests and Career Ambitions

The use of the EP to further the self-interest of MEPs—in particular to progress careers outside the EP—has ramifications that are important in analysing the Parliament's influence in EU governance. MEPs must be seen not only as the focus for lobbyists, but individuals anxious to further their own careers by promoting the interests of national political elites, members of the higher echelons of other EU institutions, representatives of the European business sector, and, of course, major actors in their own constituencies. Understandably MEPs' activities, interventions, and participation in EP business reflect these personal ambitions, and can have a significant impact on EP influence in EU governance.

In succeeding sections of this paper, we use the organizing concept of agenda territories to demonstrate the modalities of EP influence in the development of EU agri-environmental policy. In doing so, we use this concept in two ways. First, we use the different agenda territories to identify precisely the mechanisms for articulating EP influence during the policy-shaping and policy-setting stages; and, secondly, with reference to detailed interview and archival materials, we tease out the substance of the five agenda territories presented to demonstrate the degree of policy influence exercised by the EP over the development of the agri-environmental Regulation.

4.5. The EP's Influence in Policy-Shaping: The Du Vivier Report on Agriculture and the Environment

From 1985 onwards, it is possible to trace clearly the involvement of the EP in the evolving debate over the CAP's impact upon the rural environment. There are several reasons for this development, not least greater impetus for progressive specification of an EU agri-environmental policy following ratification of the Single European Act (1986), which itself conferred greater powers upon the EP in EU decision-making (Lodge 1993). Also, the surge of interest in environmental issues from the mid-1980s gave greater opportunities for the EP's Environment Committee to challenge, on environmental grounds, the entire gamut of EU policies and the established policy constituencies surrounding them. The CAP, long regarded as the cornerstone of European integration efforts, was a prime target for Committee scrutiny as the negative environmental effects of this policy became increasingly apparent (among the earliest critiques being Baldock 1985; Noirfalise 1988).

In drawing attention to the growing environmental crisis in EU agriculture, the Environment Committee sought to promote its own agenda over that of the Commission's DG Agri and the then Agriculture Committee, which, over the preceding decades, had established a quasi-monopoly on problem definition and policy solution concerning the CAP. This analysis is supported by Peters' work (1994: 10) on EU agenda-setting: 'issues are a resource as well as a problem, and actors within the formal institutions can utilize problems and issues to push forward their own goals . . . organizations attempt to seize on or create (conceptually if not in reality) problems in order to enhance their own power.'

To challenge the productivist views of agricultural policy espoused by the Commission's DG Agri and the majority of MEPs on the Agriculture Committee, in 1986 the Green group within the EP's Environment Committee drafted an Own Initiative report on *Agriculture and the Environment.* The report was prepared by François Roelants du Vivier, a Belgian Green MEP, and called for a 'revision of the CAP in terms of a more integrated approach to ecological concerns and an overall policy based on quantitative and qualitative objectives' (EP 1986:6). The report continued: 'Intensive farming (the productivist agriculture which is predominant in Europe) is rather like a steamroller which it is essential to bring under control' (EP 1986: 13).

The reaction of the EP's Agriculture Committee was somewhat predictable, given the Environment Committee's interference in its traditional arena of policy. Their rejection of the Du Vivier report was based on two arguments. First, environmental claims were dismissed as overly sentimental and lacking rigorous scientific evidence, summed up aptly in the comment of the Chair of the Agriculture Committee that: 'there was no statement of the scale of the problem in quantitative terms . . . the result is a certain amount of scaremongering and exaggeration . . . this makes it difficult to discuss this topic coolly and rationally' (EP 1986: 58). Secondly, the failure of the Du Vivier report to offer a solution by which EU agriculture and environment policies could be linked was also highlighted. The sniping between these two committees, as Arp (1992: 60) has noted 'reflected repeated tensions between agricultural policy-makers and environmental policy-makers in the European Parliament', though significantly it also marked '. . . an important step by the Agriculture Committee towards at least recognizing environmental objectives'. In fact, with the Agriculture Committee's subsequent recognition that environmental considerations could be incorporated in the CAP without compromising the Committee's trenchant defence of farm interests, superficially at least a 'greening' of attitudes among its membership came about (see Chapter 2).

We have maintained that EP influence crucially depends upon interlock with the European Commission agenda. The Du Vivier report was initially of little strategic value to the DG Agri, as the relationship between agriculture and environment was still not clearly articulated; certainly, it was not accepted by the Agricultural Directorate that the relationship was necessarily negative. Secondly, the DG Agri was not under immense pressure politically to propose new legislation in this area. However, the terms of reference for the European Commission in the field of environment changed substantially under the Single European Act (1986). This, combined in the early 1990s with the expansion in several northern member states of national schemes aimed at encouraging environmentally friendly farming practice, altered the DG Agri's vision of the strategic importance of agri-environmental policy. The Du Vivier report was now deemed to be a useful basis on which this Directorate could draw up future legislation in this policy area. The view of the EP's influence on the Commission in this process is confirmed by a senior Directorate official: "A

... source for [agri-environmental policy] was a report by the parliamentarian Roelants Du Vivier in 1986, which dealt with the relationship between agriculture and the environment—let me say, for the first time. It was the first document based on this particular issue' (DG Agri source, Dec. 1996). This example demonstrates, too, that EP influence in EU decision-making must be considered both in sectoral and in temporal terms, as contended by Judge (1992).

4.6. The Influence of the EP in Policy-Setting: National Agenda Territories of Mediterranean States and COM (90)366

The publication of the Du Vivier report in 1986 did not immediately prompt the European Commission into proposing more sophisticated Community legislation, as a former Chairman of the then Agriculture Committee explained: 'When Du Vivier produced his report, it was seen by the Commission as a document which might or might not influence their thinking. They could take it or leave it' (MEP source, Dec. 1997). The Commission's decision to broaden Community policy on the agriculture–environment relationship was, instead, prompted by other factors. First, although several northern member states had introduced some voluntary agri-environmental programmes under EC regulation 1760/87 (CEC 1987*b*), the new Mediterranean states of the EU had not greeted this legislation with much enthusiasm. Secondly, the development and refinement by the DG Agri of its initial approach to agri-environmental policy, particularly the correction of the perceived northern European bias of its objectives, fulfilled the Directorate's obligations under the Single European Act to bring environmental objectives closer to the heart of the CAP (Baldock and Lowe 1996). Thirdly, this new suite of agri-environmental policies complemented other strands of EU agricultural policy, such as 'set-aside' and 'extensification', which supported the DG Agri's goal of reducing chronic overproduction in the CAP's market regimes (see Chapter 2).

Nonetheless, it was not until late 1990 that a proposal for a Council Regulation on agri-environment policy, COM (90) 366 (CEC 1990*b*), was brought forward. Drawing upon northern member states' experiences of implementing agri-environmental schemes, this document set out a range of new voluntary measures designed to encourage farmers to adopt environmentally friendly farming practices (Whitby and Lowe 1994).

The development of COM (90) 366 was an 'in-house' effort within the DG Agri, as the German Commission official responsible for EU agri-environmental policy at that time explained in interview: 'We developed the idea here in my Division without having any instructions and succeeded . . . in formulating a Commission proposal. This proposal was developed between DG Agri and the cabinet of [Agriculture Commissioner Ray] MacSharry. The final version was written one afternoon by Patrick Hennessy [responsible for agri-environment in MacSharry's cabinet], my director Mr Sevante Pinto, and me. The document came out of MacSharry's cabinet without any major modifications, and was passed by the College of Commissioners with some minor modifications having been made by the Environment Directorate' (DG Agri source, Dec. 1996; see also below, Chapter 3). This quote offers a number of key insights into the formulation of COM (90) 366. First, the DG Agri staff appear not to have undertaken detailed consultation with the full range of member states prior to drafting the document ('We developed the idea here in my Division without having any instructions . . .'); hence, there was the risk of not accurately reflecting the full spectrum of member states' agri-environmental interests. Furthermore, as the proposal was based on earlier legislation modelled on the national experiences of northern member states, it was inevitable that the national agri-environmental interests of the Mediterranean states were largely missing from COM (90) 366. Thirdly, the lack of internal consultation by the DG Agri within the Commission, especially with the Environment Directorate, is evident in the lack of 'major modifications' made to the proposal; it is also testimony to the poor working relations between the two DGs at this time (see Chapter 3). Taken together with the obligatory nature of the centrepiece of the proposal, this lack of representation of southern agri-environmental interests in COM (90) 366 led to concerted efforts by these states to redress the balance through lobbying for change, through both the Agriculture Council and the EP.

COM (90) 366 was submitted to the EP in mid-October 1990 under the Consultation procedure. The proposal was referred to the EP's Agriculture Committee as the principal committee responsible, with the subsequent appointment of Joaquim Miranda da Silva as Rapporteur. A Portuguese member of the relatively small Communist-dominated group, *Le Groupe Confédéral de la Gauche Unitaire Européenne* (*GUE*; Confederal Group of the European United Left; this group was disbanded in January 1993, though later reformed to include a 'Nordic Green Left' (see J. Smith 1999)), his appointment reflected the concerns of this group, which has traditionally been dominated by south European MEPs advocating the position of small Mediterranean producers. The GUE and southern MEPs saw COM (90) 366 as an opportunity for promoting the Mediterranean agenda territory, through increasing the budgetary allocations for agri-environmental schemes, pushing for measures to prevent rural depopulation and minimize land abandonment, and raising the specific environmental hazards of the Union's Mediterranean regions. Thus the Portuguese Rapporteur, actively promoting Mediterranean agendas, pressed the Commission 'to take into account phenomena which particularly affect the south of the Community, such as fires, soil erosion and the depopulation of certain regions. Inseparable from this and even decisive for the success of the measures . . . is obviously the guarantee of a fair income for farmers' (EP 1991: 31). The Portuguese Rapporteur believed the proposal fell short of satisfying the requirements of Mediterranean states, describing COM (90) 366 as 'inadequate . . . because it confines itself to reconsidering certain measures relating to extensification, set-aside and the environment [all northern European policy concerns] . . .' (EP 1991: 31). The forthright promotion of this agenda territory by the Portuguese Rapporteur meant that the Commission was made fully aware of the shortcomings of its proposal, and the difficulties it would be likely to face in gaining the willing assent of southern member states in Council.

Commissioner MacSharry responded on behalf of the DG Agri to EP criticisms of COM (90) 366 at the Plenary Session of Parliament on 11 March 1991. MacSharry remarked that 'the debate on the future direction of the CAP is now in progress, the present proposal . . . will be subsumed at a later stage in the broader approach and I should like to thank the House sincerely for its very worthwhile contribution to this proposal' (EP 1991: 36–7). This recognition by MacSharry of the importance of the EP's amendments motivated by Mediterranean interests within the Agriculture Committee constituted interlocking between the DG Agri and the EP. This was signalled by his declaration that 'there [would be] a very generous and substantial . . . level of financial commitment' (EP 1991: 37) available in the poorest areas of the EU for the implementation of an 'agri-environmental' Regulation.

On the basis of this agenda interlock, the Commission decided to withdraw COM (90) 366. There was also recognition that a future proposal could play a facilitating role in the painful CAP reforms that the DG Agri was having to contemplate at this time (see Chapter 2). As a senior Commission official rather defensively explained: 'It was not in any respect a question of COM (90) 366 failing. We brought it out again because [Council delegates] wanted something in the context of CAP reform, and the proposal [by then] had taken on a greater and *more essential political dimension*' (DG Agri source, Dec. 1996; emphasis added).

4.7. National and Careerist Agenda Territories in the EP and their Influence on COM (91)415

Between October 1990 and March 1991 internal and external pressures for CAP reform intensified (Swinbank 1993; Patterson 1997). With all the key policy actors in the EU involved, the stakes became extremely high, with failure to secure the desired outcomes likely to have far-reaching political consequences for all concerned. For the EP, the CAP reform process presented an opportunity for parliamentary officers, EP political groups, and Working Committees to mobilize agenda territories to ensure effective parliamentary involvement in this high-level reform debate.

Drawing on the substance of the EP–Commission interlock over COM (90) 366 (CEC 1990*b*), the European Commission submitted a new proposal (CEC

1991*c*) for a Council agri-environmental Regulation (COM (91) 415) in September 1991, to accompany the reforms of the market regimes of the CAP. COM (91) 415 was far more positive and assertive than COM (90) 366 had been about the Commission's strategic agenda for reconciling agriculture and the environment. Given the raised stakes, all the main political groups in the EP took an active interest and involvement in discussions on COM (91) 415 in the then Agriculture Committee. The importance of national and careerist agenda territories was evident, expressed particularly in high levels of MEP attendance at meetings. Whereas there were only twenty-three MEPs present during voting on COM (90) 366 in the Agriculture Committee, for the debate on COM (91)415 almost fifty members were in attendance. A further indication of the importance attached within the EP to COM (91) 415 was the protracted bidding by political groups for the key post of Rapporteur, because of the significance of the proposal to the overall symmetry of the CAP reforms. The Christian Democratic European People's Party (EPP) (the second largest political group in the EP at that time), a group championing the interests of the EU's wealthiest farmers, eventually secured this vital role, despite keen bidding from the EP's largest political group, the Party of European Socialists (PES). This group championed very different views from those of the EPP, as one of its British MEPs explained: 'If I were to describe the socialist policy [for agriculture], I would say . . . we decide in favour of the smaller farmer, the farmer from the poorer area' (MEP source, Apr. 1998). This EPP's political standing and support were thus diametrically opposed, not only to the PES, but significantly to the more parochial *GUE*, which had directed the Committee during its deliberations over COM (90) 366.

The EPP's selection of the south German Reinhold Bocklet as Rapporteur was a cleverly judged move. A senior figure within the EP, and representative of one of Germany's most influential farming regions, Bocklet was able to command the respect of DG Agri officials and was resolute in his support of German farming interests. Having a Rapporteur of German nationality was also of crucial importance, given that any agreement over CAP reform would be dependent upon German financial backing. From debates in the Council over COM (91) 415, it was clear that there were varying degrees of enthusiasm for the Commission's proposal among member states (see Chapter 7). This is verified by the admission of the British negotiator in those debates that:

Along with the UK, the Germans were enthusiastic, the Danes were too, although they had slightly different ideas about what COM (91) 415 might mean in practice. And the Dutch were pretty keen as well. I think those were the key enthusiasts. The Belgians took the view that they didn't have an environment to worry about, while the Mediterranean members saw COM (91) 415 as an opportunity to get more money going their way.   (MAFF source, Oct. 1996)

The Agriculture Committee's debate over COM (91) 415 led to thirty-eight amendments being made to this proposal. Many of the amendments served to further the national agenda territories promoted by MEPs in the Committee. There was a clear congruence between the national positions expressed in the Council, and the national agenda territories promoted in many of the interventions made by MEPs in the parliamentary debate over COM (91) 415. For example, Mediterranean financial demands were the substance of interventions by southern MEPs of all political groups. The speech made by the Spanish socialist MEP Colino Salamanca is testimony to the articulation of the Mediterranean agenda: 'My criticism [of agri-environmental measures] is not so much of the content of these [proposed] regulations as their financing' (EP1992:49). However, it was the Commission that would decide whether any of the national agenda territories expressed in the EP would enable it to broker agreement over COM (91) 415 in the Council.

In early March 1992, a week before the Agriculture Commissioner was due to address the EP on amendments to the proposal that the DG Agri was prepared to accept, the Commission received a list of demands made by national delegations in the Council. As stated in the *Document de la Presidence* of 2 March 1992, 'the Commission's proposals relative to the Accompanying Measures will need to be adapted to take into account the following points—zonal programming, conversion of arable land into extensive grassland, organic farming, extensification, maintenance of farming practices already compatible with the environment, and courses, traineeships, and demonstration projects' (CoEC 1992*b*: 1). These demands demonstrate the point made by Rometsch and Wessels (1994) that the constellation of interests in the Council is highly complex, and various coalitions—and counter-coalitions—are possible, in which the Commission must act as a promotional broker. Apprised in this way of the Council's views, the Commission was now in the position to determine how far parliamentary influence would extend on this proposal. In short, the Commission would determine the agenda interlock with the Parliament.

On 9 March 1992 in the plenary session of the EP, Commissioner MacSharry identified those EP amendments to COM (91) 415 that the DG Agri had decided to accept in its new legislative text. Of the thirty-eight amendments to the proposal, MacSharry accepted thirteen either in total or in part, which provided the basis for agenda interlock on COM (91) 415 between the EP and the Commission. These areas included zonal programming, conversion of arable land, and organic farming. Within EU governance, the EP's ability to exert influence depends on how its position(s) on specific issues interlock(s) with the pragmatic options and strategic preferences of the Commission in its own efforts to secure Council consensus. The agenda interlock between the Commission and the Parliament is well demonstrated by the issue of zonal programming. The Commission preference was to devolve responsibility to the regional or local level, with the twin aims of streamlining and simplifying administration of EU agri-environmental policy (see Chapter 3) and ensuring that local agri-environmental policy needs were met adequately (see Chapter 9). Some member states with a strong history of regional representation were especially interested in this approach—for example, Italy, Spain, and Germany. There were several important interventions on the zonal-programming issue in the debate by MEPs from these countries. For example, MEP Giulio Fantuzzi, the member from Emilia Romagna, argued powerfully that '[the Commission's proposal] must be corrected to take account of . . . the conditions of the various European farming environments, the use of more flexible parameters, and the involvement of the regional and local authorities in the implementation of programmes' (EP 1992: 45). In the same debate, the Spanish MEP Domingo Segarra maintained that a weakness in the Commission's proposal, and one that should be properly addressed, was that 'the regional and local authorities must play a part in co-defining with the governments and be involved in its implementation, above all in the evaluation of its results' (EP 1992: 52; see also below, Chapter 9). The acceptance by the Commission of the EP amendment dealing with zonal programming enabled it to put pressure on those Council members holding reservations about this feature of COM (91) 415. In this respect the Commission used the EP's opinion as a modality for bringing extra pressure to bear upon the Council for its own purposes.

A high-profile Rapporteurship, such as that held by Bocklet in 1992, also offered a perfect vehicle for furthering career ambitions. A close European parliamentary colleague of his confirmed: 'his mind was on two things; I'm not being unfair to him—he was a good friend of mine, still is. As a Bavarian, he was thinking with Bavarian interests at the forefront of his mind "if I get this wrong, my chances of becoming Minister for Agriculture in Bavaria will be nil". A bit blunt to be saying that, but you could sense this running all the way through his Rapporteurship' (MEP source, Dec. 1997). Several of the EP amendments accepted by Commissioner MacSharry favoured German interests, such as measures for the conversion of arable land into grassland. Many MEPs saw the promotion of German interests at the expense of other national agenda territories as thanks in no small part to the role played by a German Rapporteur eager to further his own career agenda. Bocklet's relationship with DG Agri officials was also singled out by several MPs for criticism, as the Dutch MEP Verbeek angrily claimed: 'Mr Bocklet bears a very heavy responsibility. He was not concerned to bring about a Community position on a really sensible reform[,] but rather to give the Commission a free hand . . . I do not know how you can look a single farmer in the eye . . . anywhere in the Community' (EP 1992: 78).

4.8. Critical Conditions for Agenda Domination in EU Multi-Level Governance

Two issues concerning the EP's influence in EU governance require further explanation. The first is why certain EP agendas, on occasions, do not interlock with those of the European Commission. Secondly, and closely linked to the first, is how one or more EP agendas dominate over others. Our argument in this chapter is that the Commission occupies the driving seat in the relationship with the EP because, if its agendas are not adequately fulfilled, it has the formal power to withdraw its policy proposal (see Chapter 3). The Commission, with the knowledge of member states' negotiating positions as a result of bilateral discussions, steers a course by which it seeks to satisfy its strategic agendas, *and* secure agreement in Council (see Chapter 7). It will frequently be the case that certain EP agendas do not interlock with those of the Commission because, as discussed above, they do not strengthen the Commission's ability to engineer consensus over its proposal among member states, and, in turn, do not serve Commission strategic agendas in the overall policy field. Numerous examples of agenda-interlocking not taking place can be found in the debates over COM (90) 366 and COM (91) 415. For example, in the case of COM (91) 415, the demand by the Mediterranean lobby for 100 per cent funding from the EU for agri-environmental measures would have required the Commission to secure German acceptance of this in the Council—an unlikely prospect, given Germany's preoccupation with the spiralling costs of German unification (see Jones 1994*b*). Moreover, this Mediterranean demand ran counter to the tight financial envelope imposed on CAP spending that the Commission itself had earlier agreed with member states. Additionally, faced with growing evidence of fraudulent activity associated with CAP expenditure, the Commission was of the opinion that a cofinancing option was the most appropriate means to minimize this risk (see Chapter 3).Within the EP, the process by which one or more agendas come to dominate over others is often a consequence of Rapporteurs and their relationships with the Commission. As one British MEP explained: 'agreements are made other than through the formal process . . . behind the scenes things between the Rapporteur and the Commission' (MEP source, Mar. 1998). The Commission will advise the Rapporteur over its thinking behind the policy proposal, apprise her or him also of its current position, and chart the likely points of interlock between the Commission and the EP in the light of the political mood and developments in Council. With this knowledge, the Rapporteur must direct the EP Committee to align its agenda(s) with those of the Commission if the EP is to exert any influence in the policy process. The modalities by which Rapporteurs can achieve this can be through formal and informal meetings with leaders of political groups in the Parliament; through skilful handling of the Committee's debate on the Commission's proposal; and through careful drafting of the Committee's report in response to it. Significantly, some agendas, which ultimately do not interlock with those of the Commission, may become allowed to dominate. Several factors may be responsible for this, including the Rapporteur failing to work closely with Commission officials; having been too influenced by the views or position of his or her own political group; or having been swayed by other motivations (including career ambition).

4.9. Evaluation of the EP's role in the Agri-Environmental Regulation

In 1992, the Council of Agriculture Ministers agreed upon COM (91) 415, which subsequently became EC Regulation 2078/92 (CEC 1992). The debate within Council saw the acceptance of several of the issues raised by the EP, including recommendations on zonal programming, provisions for extensification, and measures on training (see Chapter 7). As we have argued in this chapter, the EP's activity in this policy area began with the publication of the Du Vivier report in 1986, which signalled the Environment Committee's determination to overhaul the CAP. However, the EP's influence on EU governance is conditional upon whether agenda-interlocking occurs with the European Commission because, as we have contended, it is this second institution that is the motor of integration efforts. The Commission's reliance on the Du Vivier report as a source of ideas for its subsequent proposal COM (90) 366 is clear, though this proposal failed to secure the necessary approval from member states in Council discussions, or to generate sufficient enthusiasm among MEPs in the EP. Nonetheless, the passage of COM (90) 366 through the EP's Agriculture Committee was an opportunity for the articulation of Mediterranean national agendas, particularly the call for the DG Agri to be made more aware of, and responsive to, the needs of the EU's poorest regions.

The second effort by the DG Agri to bring forward a Regulation on agriculture and the environment, COM (91) 415, was delivered in the context of increased strains in the functioning and financing of the CAP, and worsening EU relations with its principal trading partners in the GATT round. This proposal was, therefore, deemed by all parties to be much more politically significant than COM (90) 366. Within the EP, a number of what we have termed 'agenda territories' became especially prominent, specifically the interests of political groups, the pursuit of national agendas, and the careerism of certain MEPs. A number of formal and informal procedures were invoked in pursuit of the goals. The EP's influence over COM (91) 415 was reflected in the strong agenda interlock with the DG Agri, measured in terms of the number of parliamentary amendments to the proposal accepted by the latter. Moreover, the careerist agenda territory identified was confirmed by the appointment of Reinhold Bocklet to the position of Bavarian Minister for Agriculture not long after the CAP reform package was agreed.

In this chapter, agenda territories and interlocking have been the principal concepts elaborated to cast light on the modalities of EU governance. We have argued that they provide a robust basis on which to analyse the EP's interactions with the European Commission over the environmentalization of the CAP, in both the policy-shaping and policy-setting stages of EU decision-making. Significantly, they also offer an important explanation of the ways in which the EP, despite treaty-based restrictions on its powers in the field of agri-cultural policy, can be an influential institutional actor in the MLG system of the EU.

5

The Modalities of Interest Representation at the EU Level: *COPA* and the Agri-Environment Regulation

The preceding chapters have focused on the role of EU institutions in configuring the agri-environmental Regulation, within a decision-making system characterized variously as 'multi-level governance' (Marks *et al.* 1996) or 'multi-level joint decision making' (Grande 1996). From these chapters and other studies (e.g. Bulmer 1994; Kassim 1994), it is not only clear that EU institutions are among the most important formal decision-making bodies in the evolving EU governance system, but also that their personnel are adept at exploiting more informal 'policy routeways' (Jones and Clark 1998) to shape proposals to suit the strategic agendas of these institutions. These policy routeways, or 'channels of influence' (Mazey and Richardson 1993*a*: 24), are a distinctive modality within the EU MLG system.

Often these modalities can be used to exert a decisive impact on the way in which policy decisions within EU institutions are arrived at, for, as Pedlar and van Schendelen (1994) note, a tremendous range of informal processes and procedures are constantly feeding into EU decision-making activities. These authors indicate that, within the EU polity, political 'influence' often emerges as more important than clearly delineated institutional 'powers'; that nationality networks are used within and outside EU institutions to facilitate decision-making (see Chapters 3 and 4); and that, unlike many national policy-making arenas, the different stages of the supranational policy process are typified by 'bargaining [among policy actors,] instead of hegemony [between them]' (1994: 12).

Clearly, these less formalized decision-making processes will also influence profoundly the nature, degree, and scope of lobbying activities undertaken by public and private interest groups at the supranational level. Nonetheless, despite recognition from 'all authors . . . that there is a strong need for empirical studies . . .' of EU lobbying (Andersen and Eliassen 1995: 436) to gauge these impacts, only a handful of such studies have been undertaken. Of those that have, 'few, if any, have presented a detailed empirical analysis' of the issues, and, notably, 'only limited attempts . . . have been made . . . to deal with the role of interest representation and lobbying in the total pattern of [EU] decision making . . .' (Andersen and Eliassen 1995: 436).

In this chapter we address this omission in the EU lobbying literature, by presenting a thorough analysis of the efforts of the agricultural group *COPA*[1] to influence EU institutions during policy-shaping and policy-setting of the agri-environmental Regulation. We examine, first, the historically close relationship between *COPA* and the DG Agri, how this relationship shaped *COPA*'s modalities of interest representation within the EU MLG system, and how deterioration in this relationship set the context for *COPA*'s lobbying efforts on EC 2078/92 between 1990 and 1992. We then analyse how *COPA*'s constituent membership arrived at a common position on the DG Agri's agri-environmental proposals, and the lobbying strategies and 'access points' selected by *COPA*'s Secretariat to advance the group's position on this Regulation within the system of supranational governance. The countervailing modalities adopted by EU institutions to defend those features of the Regulation representative of their strategic interests are then examined. We show that the DG Agri played an especially important role in this process, and, contrary to expectations, deployed robust tactics *against* the *COPA* viewpoint on EC 2078/92 to strengthen its *own* bargaining position with member states during the marathon CAP reform negotiations.

As the one element of the reform package popularly regarded as favouring farmers, the agri-environmental Regulation and the two other 'accompanying measures'[2] were critical to the DG Agri in its efforts to squeeze concessions from different policy actors over other, more contentious, components of the Commission's proposals. In effect, EC 2078/92 was integral to the overall symmetry of the DG Agri's plans. As we show, the importance of EC 2078/92 as a 'sweetener' to the MacSharry reforms of the CAP is demonstrated in the Commission's use of robust negotiating tactics and strategies, more in keeping with the politically contentious elements of the reform package, in its dealings with *COPA* on this Regulation. Hence, while the politics of EU agri-environmentalism are relatively new, the lobbying modalities examined in this chapter are fully representative of those encountered in more mainstream EU policy areas (see e.g. Grant 1993*a*; Stern 1994).

---

[1] *COPA*'s full title is *COPA-COGECA. COGECA* (*Comité Générale de la Coopération Agricole de la Communauté Européenne* (General Committee for Agricultural Coopertion in the European Community)) the umbrella grouping representing EU farm cooperatives, was subsumed in *COPA* in 1962. For simplicity, we refer to *COPA-COGECA* as *COPA* in this chapter.

[2] The two other 'accompanying measures' to the CAP reforms—destined to become EC Regulations 2079/92 and 2080/92 respectively—offered for the early retirement of farmers from the industry, and financial incentives for the management and upkeep of farm woodlands.

5.1. The Modalities of Interest Representation within the EU's Multi-Level Governance System

Work by Edgar Grande (1996) has contributed greatly to current understandings of how supranational interest groups ('Eurogroups' (Averyt 1975)) such as *COPA* operate within the EU's MLG system, and the concomitant impacts of MLG on Eurogroups' lobbying of EU institutions. Grande defines MLG as 'a new, multi-layered architecture of Statehood . . . a system of interest intermediation with its own specific features . . .' (Grande 1996: 321). According to Grande, MLG is characterized by its novel 'institutional configuration [and a] complicated distribution and integration of [decision-making] responsibilities and resources . . .'. In the specific case of the EU, Grande continues: 'the plurality of [EU] institutions and actors . . . offers a multitude of access points to the [EU] decision making process[,requiring of Eurogroups an] extensive repertory of complex strategies for the successful pursuit of interests' (Grande 1996: 321, 323).

Grande cites four requirements that, while not peculiar to EU lobbying, have a profound impact on whether or not Eurogroups exert influence within the EU MLG system (Grande 1996: 324). These are, first, the timing of a lobby approach: at what stage of the policy process will it be most effective for a Eurogroup to lobby? Secondly, the sequencing of the lobby approach—that is, lobbying with regard to whether all, some, or none of the EU institutions and other key policy actors have already expressed an opinion upon it. Thirdly, the inherent complexity of MLG means that identification by Eurogroups of the correct 'target structure' (i.e. those organization(s) that need to be influenced) is essential if a lobbying strategy is to succeed. A fourth requirement is fulfilling particular 'access conditions' to ensure lobby effectiveness with this 'target structure'.

For Grande, these four requirements underpin two factors critical to influential lobbying: first, strengthening the *bargaining positions* of Eurogroups relative to EU institutions; and, secondly, improving *conditions of access* for these groups to EU decision-making. Grande maintains that mastery of both factors underpins the '[EU] logic of influence', and is therefore crucial if Eurogroups are to affect EU policy-making. But control is a two-way process. A failure by lobby groups to master these factors leaves them open to manipulation by rival groups, other interests, or, indeed, EU institutions. For, just as Eurogroups can capitalize on known access points, identifiable target structures, and good timing and appropriate sequencing of their petitions, so too can the requirements of the different institutional arenas and the unique circumstances pertaining to EU policies be mobilized by personnel within EU institutions, to further the institution's *own objectives at the expense of the interest group concerned.* Grande (1996: 328) comments: 'public actors [can] purposefully use the "internal ties" and commitments produced by joint decision making to strengthen their bargaining position vis à vis [private] actors and interest groups.'

The mobilization of these institutional modalities at the supranational level offers EU institutions a most effective means of enhancing their own power positions relative to Eurogroups within the stratified, fragmented decision-making that constitutes MLG. Examination of these policy circumstances and institutional settings are central to this chapter, and we outline them briefly here.

Grande (1996: 329) asserts that particular policy circumstances may substantially weaken the bargaining positions of Eurogroups relative to EU institutions. These policy circumstances are, first, when the EU institution's own preferences, or those of affiliated private or public actors, conflict with the Eurogroup concerned. Instances exist at the EU level of organizational differences or a history of disputes prejudicing the outcome of lobbying campaigns instigated by Eurogroups—for example, the attempts during the early to mid-1980s by EU environmental lobbyists (coordinated by the European Environmental Bureau) to convince the Agriculture Directorate and the Agriculture Council to incorporate environmental considerations within the CAP (see also Hull 1993: 89).

Secondly, personnel in EU institutions may emphasize a wide range of 'limits' of one sort or another, which provide a real or counterfeit reason for limited or no action being taken over a particular lobby petition. Commonly, limits of this sort include political necessities (for example, the *force majeur* of an active coalition within the Council of Ministers militating against the lobby position) or political or economic considerations attached to policies (for example, financial limits, such as there being insufficient budget for the lobbied-for policy measure(s)). Thirdly, the institution might use its integration within the EU system of MLG not simply to weaken or reject the lobby group's claims, but to strengthen the institution's *own* bargaining position with other EU institutions and Eurogroups—for example, by exploiting contradictory signals from among the lobbying group's own constituency to unravel a supposedly 'unified' bargaining position.

A second set of conditions allows EU institutions to strengthen their own position by taking advantage of the limited *conditions of access* of Eurogroups to the EU decision-making process. As Grande (1996: 330) notes, 'a . . . characteristic feature of [the EU] multi-level system . . . [is] the temporary closure of the decision making process . . . [during] which . . . negotiations [are] not accessible to interest groups'. These 'periods of closure' can be used by EU institutions to initiate countervailing tactics against some or all of its lobbyists, either independently of, or in concert with, the actions of other EU institutions. Such periods of closure occur during different 'phases' in the EU policy formulation process. Grande distinguishes three such phases. In chronological order, these are the *preliminary phase,* the *agreement phase,* and the *post-agreement phase.*[3]

---

[3] Grande's 'preliminary' and 'agreement' phases characterize the chronological sequence of EU policy formulation, and are analogous to Peterson's 'policy-shaping' and 'policy-setting'

According to Grande, in the *preliminary phase* DGs of the European Commission will actively seek out the opinion of interest groups and other affected parties in order to refine their draft legislative texts. Grande notes that often this consultation process is undertaken specifically by DGs to reinforce their negotiating position with the Council of Ministers during subsequent discussions on the proposal.

By contrast, the *agreement phase* is dominated by policy discussions between public actors, such as negotiations between the European Commission and other EU institutions, or national/state administrations. Access conditions for Eurogroups to the EU policy-making process are markedly different: 'the various public actors dominate [policy discussions] and the negotiating process is not only inaccessible to interest groups . . . it is not even transparent to them' (Grande 1996: 331). 'Closed' meetings include EU Council sessions on proposed legislative measures, and meetings convened by the European Commission for smaller groupings of member states representing particular 'interest factions' within Council.

In the third, *post-agreement phase*, negotiations are once again thrown open to external consultation. However, unlike in the preliminary phase, the scope for influencing the proposed legislative text is very limited, as any textual alteration would involve unpicking the agreed final draft of the proposal—something that the Commission is loathe to undertake, as it places preceding negotiations in jeopardy.

We contend that Grande's framework provides important insights into *COPA*'s lobbying of the major EU institutions, in particular the DG Agri, over the agri-environmental Regulation. The rest of the chapter focuses on the two modalities of interest representation highlighted by Grande as determining the '[EU] logic of influence'—namely, the bargaining position of a Eurogroup, and the points of access to EU decision-making used by it. We analyse *COPA*'s lobbying of EU institutions on EC 2078/92 in these terms. We argue that a major determinant undermining the effectiveness of *COPA*'s bargaining position with the EU institutions over the agri-environmental Regulation was its deteriorating relationship with the DG Agri. To identify why the DG Agri might choose to use countervailing tactics against *COPA* aimed at weakening its bargaining position on EC 2078/92, we need to examine the historical relations between the two organizations up to 1992, and the agricultural policy situation confronting the DG Agri at that time. However, before doing so we look briefly at *COPA*'s origins, structure, and functions.

---

stages (Peterson 1995*a*: 73–74). By contrast, Grande's 'post agreement' phase refers to the initial stage of EU policy implementation.

5.2. *COPA*'s Origins, Structure, and Internal Decision-Making

COPA was founded in September 1958 as an extension at the supranational level of the agricultural unions that were then represented nationally in the EU–6. The organization's objectives remain the same in the twenty-first century as they were in the 1950s: 'to study [agricultural] questions that arise as the EU develops'; 'to closely monitor and influence the way reforms to the Common Agricultural Policy are implemented'; and 'to defend the interests of farmers, and do whatever necessary to guarantee their income [is] comparable to those of other professional categories' (*COPA* 2000: 1).

In essence, *COPA* collates and coordinates the opinions of its membership to present to the EU institutions a united and coherent view on any supranational policy proposal affecting agriculture. *COPA* policy is based on detailed consultation with the membership in *Working Parties* (WPs), of which there were fifty-five in 1998. Once discussion is completed in WPs, the conclusions are forwarded for further consideration by *COPA*'s *General Experts* group. Where the General Experts consider these conclusions to be particularly important, they may decide to draft a discussion paper for submission to the *Praesidium*, which is the official policy-making body of *COPA*. The Praesidium draws one representative from each of *COPA*'s constituent unions, and in 1998 had thirty-one members. WPs, the General Experts, and the Praesidium are assisted in their tasks by *COPA*'s *Secretariat*, servicing all levels of the *COPA* administrative hierarchy.

Critically, at each stage of *COPA*'s internal policy-making, decisions are made on a unanimity basis, rather than by using majority voting. Consequently, as a very senior *COPA* official confided in interview, 'the difficulty is not only getting a common position, but getting it together in good time . . . With thirty member organizations, agreement to be reached in the Working Parties, then among the General Experts, [and finally] in the Praesidium, very often we've fired after the battle has ended' (*COPA* source, May 1997). At the time of writing the institutional mechanisms do not exist to speed up or bypass this unanimity requirement. Hence the cumbersome nature of *COPA*'s internal decision-making means that, on occasion, the passage of a proposal from a WP to the Praesidium may take more than a year to complete.

To influence the DG Agri's thinking has always been at the heart of *COPA*'s efforts to shape EU farm policy. In Grande's terminology, the DG Agri has been *COPA*'s principal 'target structure'. This emphasis has arisen for two reasons. First, traditionally there were strong ties between the two organizations, alluded to by *COPA*'s current Strategy Director in his description of the Eurogroup as an 'institutional lobby'. This phrase requires clarification. Established by one of the architects of the CAP, Sicco Mansholt, to facilitate the dialogue between the DG Agri and national farming unions, *COPA* has always benefited from strong representation on the Directorate's advisory and management committees (Tsinisizelis 1990). Even in the late 1990s, *COPA* maintained a powerful presence in the EU's Economic and Social Committee (ECOSOC) through its member organizations; enjoyed regular meetings with the Agriculture Commissioner, although these no longer took place as regularly as they once had; and continued to benefit from cross-subsidization of its activities by the DG Agri, with the Directorate paying for *COPA*'s national agricultural experts to travel to Brussels to sit on Commission committees, and *COPA* often organizing sittings of its *own* panel of General Experts—in practice the same persons—to follow these meetings.

Secondly, *COPA* has always sought to influence the aim, objectives, and scope of EU legislative measures—that is, the drafting of supranational policy proposals, a task assigned under the Treaty of Rome to the European Commission. Clearly, such 'pre-emptive' lobbying is ambitious, requiring the careful cultivation of contacts within DGs during the 'preliminary phase' of EU policy formulation (Grande 1996), rather than more broadly based lobbying during later phases.

Hence *COPA*'s Secretariat has not only specified the DG Agri as its pre-eminent 'target structure' for lobbying. Within this EU institution, it has also precisely identified the 'points of access' needed to influence the policy-making processes underwriting the CAP. These formal and informal linkages explain *COPA*'s status as an 'institutional lobby', in theory giving this Eurogroup channels of influence with the DG Agri that are denied other lobby interests.

5.3. Setting the Context for EU Deliberative Policy-Making: *COPA*'s Deteriorating Relationship with the DG Agri

As Grande notes, a vital ingredient for Eurogroups seeking to exercising influence over EU institutions lies in the strength of their bargaining position. Specifically, if a Eurogroup is to exert policy influence there is a need for its organizational agenda *and* that of the targeted EU institution to be advanced by this bargaining position, even if this advance represents only a minor gain for both parties (see Chapter 4; see also Jones and Clark 1999).

If this overlapping of organizational agendas does not take place, Grande suggests that EU institutions are likely to disregard, attempt to neutralize, or 'adapt' the demands made by Eurogroups, through some form of counter-lobbying strategy. As we have seen, according to Grande two other circumstances increase the likelihood of such 'counter-lobbying' by EU institutions. These are when wider political-economic conditions framing EU policies militate against the bargaining position; and when dissent within a Eurogroup's own constituency effectively discredits the bargaining position. Unfortunately for *COPA*, during the 1990–2 period all three circumstances applied in the organization's lobbying of the DG Agri over the EC 2078/92, damaging severely its authority with the Agriculture Directorate. We examine each of these circumstances in turn.

5.3.1. From Overlapping Agendas to Incompatible Agendas

For many years, *COPA*'s organizational agenda (embodied in its bargaining position on different policy issues) was closely compatible with the DG Agri's strategic agenda for the CAP. This was certainly the case during the 1950s and 1960s, when there were many instances of 'agenda-interlocking' (cf. Chapter 4) between the DG Agri and *COPA*. But the *COPA*–DG Agri relationship has been unusually volatile, with a marked deterioration since *c.*1975 in relations between these two organizations over the need for CAP reform. Following lengthy interviews with former senior *COPA* officials who were in office after 1975, there appear to have been three stages in this deterioration.

1958–74: COPA *as EU 'policy insider'.*   This period was characterized by a very close working relationship between the DG Agri and *COPA* as a result of mutual organizational interests, which centred upon developing the CAP and ensuring the policy adequately served national, regional, and local agricultural interests.

1975–85: the souring of the COPA–*DG Agri relationship.*   According to interviewees, between the mid–1970s and the mid–1980s the mutual interest of the earlier period began to break down. The commonality between the two organizations was placed under pressure for the first time with the build-up of surpluses in CAP commodities. The situation worsened as these surpluses became chronic, exposing substantial, conflicting interests between the DG Agri and the national farming unions represented by *COPA* over the need for CAP reform. However, in the words of a DG Agri official, 'the unions were still powerful and they represented something. They had political weight, they could put pressure on the [European] Parliament, [and] on the Commission itself . . . [it was] more [a case of] strength shared between two organizations . . . *COPA* could still put the pressure on, and have things pushed through' (*COPA* source, May 1997).

1986–92: the marginalization of COPA *by the DG Agri.*   The third stage identified sees *COPA* losing its coherence and distinctiveness of 'voice', chiefly as a result of its growing membership. 'In the late 1980s, it [was] getting hard for COPA to reach consensus and cracks [were] appearing in the producers' united front' (Gray 1989: 222). This had severe consequences for the lobbying powers of the umbrella group, lessening its influence on agricultural policy: 'especially when you see the . . . CAP reform in 1992, where COPA hammered on the table, but nothing came through' (DG Agri source, May 1997). More gravely, *COPA*'s administrative hierarchy seemed unable, or unwilling, to acknowledge its diminished lobbying influence. From the DG Agri's perspective, by the early 1990s the quasi-corporatist relationship that some observers (Gardner 1987; M.J. Smith 1990; Fearne 1991) ascribed to the Directorate and *COPA* had long since gone. There were two reasons for this change.

First, the EU agricultural sector had suffered the vicissitudes of economic and social restructuring during the 1970s and 1980s, losing much of the strategic political and economic importance it had once enjoyed, and obliging the Commission actively to broaden its canvassing of opinion to include prominent groups outside EU agricultural policy networks. It was during this period that for the first time non-farm groups—for example, those representing consumer, environment, and animal welfare interests—were included in European Commission consultations on its agricultural policy proposals, some of which argued vociferously for 'environmentalization' of the CAP (see Chapters 2 and 6).

Secondly, by the late 1980s *COPA*'s protracted internal decision making began severely to limit the organization's intrinsic value to the DG Agri within supranational governance. In particular *COPA*'s secretariat faced insuperable problems in representing the farming interests of new members, while ensuring *COPA* policy precedents were respected. As a senior figure in *COPA*'s Secretariat commented, 'We define the policy . . . we say to new members, "You can't have your own policy—*COPA* policy is a compromise of a compromise of a compromise"' (*COPA* source, May 1996). But within the DG Agri, there was growing awareness of the shortcomings of *COPA*'s approach, which proved especially damaging. As one highly placed DG Agri official explained, 'If I take the 1992 *COPA* position [papers], most of the time I can be sure of finding one thing and the contrary thing [expressed] . . . *COPA* has lost its dominant position with us because of its archaic decision-making, the archaic way it has of deciding things . . .' (DG Agri source, May 1997).

Hence, the organization's traditional worth to the DG Agri as a litmus test for the likely outcome of negotiations in other EU institutional arenas also declined. This failing was keenly felt by the DG Agri staff, especially in their dealings with the Agriculture Council: 'COPA . . . used to help us to . . . negotiate a compromise in Council. *COPA* would discuss a proposal, we'd take the results, and we'd draw up positions to cover the alternatives likely out of Council. But with so many unions and so many different points of view, how can you reach a compromise with such complexity?' (DG Agri source, May 1997).

5.3.2. The Global Agricultural Policy Context and the Need for CAP Reform

Crucially, during the 1986–92 period, other systemic factors unconnected with the vagaries of the *COPA*–Commission relationship further undermined

COPA's status with the DG Agri. These factors included the EU's need to respond to global trade requirements, including those pertaining to agriculture as set out under the GATT and the increasing budgetary pressures on the EU.

However, undoubtedly the most important consideration was the decision taken by the DG Agri in the early 1990s to undertake what was then perceived as a radical reform of the CAP. Within Commission circles, *COPA*'s reluctance to accept far-reaching reforms of the sort envisaged by the DG Agri was already well known. As Gray (1989: 223) commented at the time, 'For many [Commission] officials, COPA's arguments have remained unchanged and do not show that they are dealing reasonably with the reality of oversupply, budgetary crisis, and the demand for lower prices for agricultural raw materials'.

Certainly the DG Agri staff were aware that *COPA* was highly unlikely to offer its support for any proposed reforms. But the bitter hostility of national farm unions to the MacSharry reforms, which were selectively leaked by the DG Agri to the media during 1990 and 1991, inevitably led to a hardening of attitudes on the Directorate's part, with staff viewing *COPA* as largely unconstructive and a potential liability in negotiations, rather than the trusted ally it had once been. Initially, the condemnation of the EU farm lobby extended even to the 'accompanying measures' to MacSharry's proposals, introduced largely to mollify agricultural opinion. By the time the reforms had been tabled in 1991, the Directorate recognized the need to neutralize the potentially powerful destabilizing effect of the disenchanted EU farm lobby upon the sensitive reform process.

Hence we contend that, during the 1992 reforms, the *COPA*–DG Agri relationship was characterized by a new development. Not only was the Directorate willing to capitalize on *COPA*'s diminished influence to provide it with greater margin for manœuvre in drafting the CAP reforms. For the first time, the DG Agri was minded to use countervailing policy modalities to neutralize *COPA*'s disruptive effect on the CAP reform process.

The DG Agri's knowledge of *COPA*'s internal decision-making difficulties proved important in this respect. Increased dissent among *COPA*'s constituent membership, and the failure of the organization's administrative hierarchy to address these difficulties adequately, were cleverly exploited by the DG Agri to weaken *COPA*'s bargaining position on the agri-environmental Regulation. These ingredients offered ample scope for the DG Agri staff to undermine *COPA*'s bargaining position. As a senior member of the DG Agri's negotiating team reflected in interview, 'we used these different national positions against *COPA*. For us, it was an ideal position—these unions were so divided, expressing views which were so diverse' (DG Agri source, May 1997). In the following section we examine the way in which these internal divisions were manifested among the *COPA* membership; and the manner in which the organization's Secretariat sought to resolve them.

5.3.3. Different Drummers, Different Tunes: National Farming Positions on the Agri-Environmental Regulation

COPA was confronted with a variety of opinions from its membership on the MacSharry reforms and, more specifically, the agri-environmental proposals. These opinions reflected the caution, uncertainty, and, in some cases, deep hostility of farming unions towards the prospect of an 'environmentalized' CAP, represented by EC 2078/92. Drafting a response to the Commission's original proposals for the Regulation, COM (90) 366 (CEC 1991*b*) in January 1991, the *COPA* Secretariat had few areas of substantive agreement to draw upon, as the following extracts from previously restricted documents show.

The *Deutscher Bauernverband (DBV)* position on the proposal was that implementing the agri-environmental Regulation must be obligatory for all member states; national agri-environmental programmes should not create distortions of competition; participation by farmers must be on a voluntary basis; and the level of EU cofinancing of the Regulation must be set at 75 per cent, to ensure that all states could participate on an equal footing. The *DBV* broadly supported all the Commission's proposals for the Regulation, with the important proviso that 'the very extensive [national] programmes [envisaged under the proposed Regulation] for the protection of nature, water, and the environment will need to be financed separately from the common market organizations' (*DBV* 1991: 4)—that is, from the Guidance, rather than the Guarantee section of the CAP budget.

By contrast, the French union the *Fédération Nationale des Syndicats d'Exploitants Agricoles (FNSEA)* described the MacSharry package as a 'masterful error', insisting that '[farmers'] income must be derived from crops produced, and not from some form of social income' (Graham 1991). One *FNSEA* official commented contemptuously of the agri-environmental Regulation, 'no one wants to be turned into a glorified civil servant, paid to cut hedges' (Graham 1991), although, significantly, the *FNSEA*'s official response was more conciliatory: 'in order to accompany rural and environmental policies . . . compensation [to farmers] . . . will have to be reinforced and enlarged' (*FNSEA* 1991: 2).

The Irish Farmers' Association (IFA) was similarly doubtful about the direction for the CAP posted by the 'accompanying measures': 'creation of a social agriculture in the EC as opposed to a commercially viable agriculture would be no more than a one-generation solution . . . it would . . . perpetuate a non-viable farm structure . . . lead[ing] to the devastation of the rural economy in the next generation' (IFA 1991: 2). The IFA was prepared to accept that the priority aim of agricultural policy in the EU had changed from increasing output to new objectives such as environmental compatibility, a modest degree of extensification, and improved product quality. However, in tune with the rest of the *COPA* membership, its fundamental position was that 'environmental problems relating to agriculture can be solved by farmers only if farming is profitable' (IFA 1991: 9).

Greek affiliates, meanwhile, were convinced that radical reform of the CAP was necessary, since regional inequalities in income across the EU had been accentuated under the policy. In this respect, Greek opinion was representative of the rest of southern Europe in wanting a reform that encompassed the principle of a 'social' agriculture. From the Hellenic viewpoint, policy measures for the agricultural environment should be specified '. . . according to the problems of . . . regions and the influence on the environment of each type of product or farm practice' (Paseges-Gesase 1991: 4).

There was also fierce disagreement among the *COPA* membership over what the precise causes of environmental degradation by agriculture might be, with one Spanish union branding north-west European agriculture largely responsible: 'it is . . . these . . . farms with a high degree of intensification which cause grave damage to the environment, provoking also an excess . . . in nitrates which then pollute ground water sources. . .' (*LUPA* 1991: 2).

From this disorganized and often conflicting set of opinions *COPA*'s Secretariat had to formulate a unified response. At first, only one issue could be agreed upon, the need for farmers to be compensated for the introduction of environmental standards into agriculture. However, even here the rationale for payments was perceived differently by members. For some unions, such as Luxembourg's *Centrale Paysanne Luxembourgeoise* (*CPL*), payments merely represented 'recompense . . . for loss of revenue . . .' (*CPL* 1991: 3). For others, such as the UK's National Farmers' Union (NFU), the proposed incentives played a crucial role in a longer-term strategy for adapting farming to the new 'post-productivist' agriculture (see Chapter 6): 'If the CAP is to be re-established on a more secure and durable basis, a new justification for agricultural support must be found . . . this ought to be sought in . . . benefits increasingly valued by society: the countryside [and] protection of the environment . . . the principal question is how to reward farmers for these other activities' (NFU 1991: 1).

An interrelated point was that, with the exception of unions from Denmark and the UK, *COPA* affiliates agreed that the source of funding for the agrienvironmental Regulation should be the Guidance section of the CAP budget, rather than the Guarantee section as proposed by the DG Agri. Two reasons account for the convergence of opinion among the unions on this point.

First, many considered the Regulation's focus to be socio-structural, rather than market related, hence strongly identifying the Regulation's objectives with existing EU policy initiatives funded under the 'Guidance section' of the CAP's budget, including previous EU agri-environmental measures. But this reason was secondary to the grave reservations of many unions to the precedent established by the Commission's proposed funding source. If the Regulation was implemented widely in national settings, the potentially very high financial costs of national agri-environmental programmes would be borne by the agricultural, rather than the socio-structural, budget line of the CAP. Inevitably, such costs would lessen the funds available to the policy's traditional 'productivist' focus, the Common Market Organizations.

From an early stage, therefore, the funding issue became the decisive element in *COPA*'s lobbying of the DG Agri on EC 2078/92. It represented an area of fundamental difference between *COPA* and the Commission, and was, significantly, one of the few points on which virtually the entire *COPA* membership could unite. However, to find a consensus position on other issues arising from the proposed Regulation required the Secretariat to pursue a much more proactive role in negotiations.

5.4. *COPA*'s Secretariat and the Modalities of Interest Representation: (1) Forging or Forcing a Bargaining Position on EC 2078/92?

COPA's unanimity principle left the Secretariat with considerable difficulties in reaching a common position among its membership on the CAP reform package. But the politically charged nature of the MacSharry proposals made this imperative. In fact, the high political stakes attached to the reform meant that there was a temptation on the Secretariat's part to create the semblance of unity on elements of the package where little, or none, existed.

Certainly this was the case with in-house discussions on the agri-environmental Regulation. As a senior *COPA* official recollected, 'it became very difficult to make the [*COPA*] consensus position from [the] forty working papers [submitted] by our member organizations. So we in the Secretariat tried to shape this consensus . . . because . . . often the [membership were] not following the same line at all' (*COPA* source, May 1997).

A subgroup of the 'Environmental Questions' Working Party was convened as the official *COPA* forum for talks on the two separate Commission proposals for the agri-environmental Regulation. *COPA*'s Secretariat provided the Secretary for this subgroup, while its Chairman, a specialist in agri-environmental relations, was drawn from the farming union *Land en Tuinbouw Organisatie-Nederland* (*LTO-Nederland*). In interview, the former Secretary was frank about the *dirigiste* role he played in shaping *COPA*'s common position:

I was preparing all the files, and drafting everything . . . I'd always draft the first paper [presented to the subgroup], and in the [drafting] process I'd try to be as provocative as possible [to] draw out discussions, so that farming unions would reach the compromise *COPA* wanted. The Secretariat knew . . . where the compromise would be . . . when unions were discussing, we could set about forming a position which was acceptable. (COPA source, May 1997)

Undoubtedly, this approach marginalized the role of the Dutch Chairman. As one national delegate recalled, '[the Chairman] agreed on the [Secretary's] provocative way of presentation . . . I guess it was then easy for him to pick up the right things—*the things the Secretariat wanted included . . .*' (NFU source, May 1997; emphasis added).

Meetings between January and April 1991 allowed the Secretariat to drive forward internal negotiations on COM (90) 366. This process was assisted by the DG Agri's publication of a second revised proposal in mid-April (CEC 1991*d*), resulting from the Directorate's initial consultations with member states on COM (90) 366. With its advocacy of a 'zonal approach' to agri-environmental policies, this revised text represented a clear break with earlier drafts, and, in its application of the EU principle of subsidiarity to agri-environmental policy, the text answered many of the Secretariat's questions concerning the implementation of national agri-environmental programmes. The DG Agri refined this proposal over the summer and consequently further debate within *COPA* was postponed until October 1991, when the new text was formally published as COM (91) 415 (CEC 1991*c*).

In the subgroup, discussions on COM (91) 415 were once again orchestrated by the Secretariat. In the words of the subgroup's Secretary:

[COM (91) 415] was the only positive part of the [MacSharry reform] package . . . What we did appreciate in this proposal was that you had voluntary schemes; money was being granted for those farmers who wanted to do something. Nearly everything in the Regulation was in the farmer's favour, and that was the reason why we reached an agreement . . . Regulation 2078 wasn't, thank goodness, yet another constraint. (*COPA* source, May 1997)

However, with hindsight, the Secretariat's approach to negotiations on COM (91) 415 produced a ragbag of compromise rather than a unified bargaining position. We contend that, while *COPA*'s failure to provide its European constituency with a common position reflecting the different subtleties and nuances of national opinions was problematic, in its presenting this fudged compromise to the DG Agri as a 'unified' position *COPA* severely damaged its credibility with the Directorate. Furthermore, this approach triggered independent lobbying of the Commission and other EU institutions by unions dissatisfied with the fudged outcome, including national delegations in the Agriculture Council. Crucially, the higher-profile farming unions from Germany and France, the *DBV* and *FNSEA*, were particularly active in this regard. As we show later, a joint pact between the respective national delegations of these countries—struck without *COPA*'s cognisance in the Agriculture Council—effectively scuppered *COPA*'s lobbying efforts on EC 2078/92.

The last meetings of the Environmental Questions subgroup took place in January 1992, and provided the basis of an 'Observations' paper drawn up by the Secretariat (*COPA* 1992). Towards the end of that month, this document was forwarded to *COPA*'s panel of General Experts, and latterly to the Praesidium. It was this 'Observations' paper that provided the basis for *COPA*'s lobbying of EU institutions on the agri-environmental Regulation.

The main points of the 'Observations' paper were as follows. First, that funding of the Regulation should come from the Guidance, rather than the Guarantee, section of the CAP budget; secondly, that the Commission should clarify its intention for programmes introduced under the Regulation to be compatible with a new EU 'Code of Good Agricultural Practice'; thirdly, that the amount of premiums offered farmers in mountain areas and LFAs of the EU be increased by 20 per cent; fourthly, that the proposed rates of reimbursement for reduction of inputs used by farmers be raised; and, fifthly, that the overall EU budget assigned to the proposed Regulation be considerably increased.

Outwardly this list represented an ambitious set of demands, yet one that an 'institutional lobby' such as *COPA* should have comfortably secured for its membership. Nevertheless, while the broad contours of the final Regulation were highly favourable to farming interests, *COPA*'s lobbying efforts did not secure a single objective listed.

The explanation for this lobbying failure lies not only in *COPA*'s flawed bargaining position, which, as we have seen, was easily undermined by the DG Agri. To unravel the full explanation of *COPA*'s lessened influence, examination must be made of the impact of Grande's second modality underpinning the EU 'logic of influence'—namely, *COPA*'s partial access to CAP decision-making processes during the different phases of EU policy formulation.

5.5. COPA's Secretariat and the Modalities of Interest Representation (2): 'Points of Access' and 'Closure' within EU Decision-Making

Grande (1996: 330) notes that, while there are numerous access points for Eurogroups within the EU MLG, 'the temporary closure of the decision making process' is a sizeable obstacle to their ever exercising decisive influence on EU policies. Indeed, these periods of closure 'seem . . . to be an important precondition [in] lead[ing] to agreements and [ensuring] negotiations are not blocked by the special interests of [Euro]groups . . .' (Grande 1996: 330). If *COPA*'s bargaining position on EU 2078/92 was already weak, these closed decision-making sessions—particularly in the Agriculture Council—ensured that the organization's influence on the Regulation was minimized.

The Secretariat attempted to circumvent *COPA*'s exclusion from the decision-making process by employing the following lobbying strategy:

We canvassed reactions from the EU institutions on the 'Observations' paper, and tried to stay in contact all the time with [the DG Agri] *fonctionnaires* at points up and down the hierarchy, including discussing the paper with the Director-General [Guy LeGras] and members of his cabinet. Then we tried to put pressure on the orientation of the funding for the Regulation . . . in Parliament and in Council. (*COPA* source, May 1997)

This strategy was based on the Secretariat's misplaced belief that the special relationship with the DG Agri still existed. In fact, it is evident that DG Agri staff were using these 'closure periods' to exploit the weaknesses in *COPA*'s bargaining position, to the benefit of the Directorate. Two sets of counter-lobbying modalities were employed by the DG Agri to undermine *COPA*'s supposedly 'unified' bargaining position. First, the Directorate gave tacit encouragement to farming unions from among *COPA*'s membership to meet the DG Agri and express their own national concerns on the Regulation to the Commission. Documentary evidence indicates a number of unions took up this offer, including the *DBV*, the *FNSEA* and the NFU.

Secondly, as part of the Directorate's efforts to facilitate the passage of the overall CAP reform package through Council, DG Agri negotiators struck a deal with French and German delegations over the budget line for funding the Regulation. In exchange for the Commission dropping its requirement that an EU-wide 'Code of Good Agricultural Practice' be introduced under the Regulation, which threatened to ratchet up environmental stipulations in all member states's agricultural sectors, the German and French delegations accepted that the Regulation should be funded from the FEOGA Guarantee section. At a stroke, *COPA*'s principal lobby goal was put beyond the organization's reach.

We argue that the effect of these counter-lobbying strategies, pursued by the DG Agri during periods when the decision-making process was effectively closed to *COPA*, had a decisive impact on the influence exerted by that organization on the reform negotiations.

5.5.1. Target Structures and Access Points used by *COPA* during the Preliminary Phase: the DG Agri and the Environment Directorate

Rightly or wrongly, *COPA*'s Secretariat regarded the DG Agri as the most important 'target structure' during the preliminary phase of lobbying on the agri-environmental Regulation. Other institutions within the EU governance system were regarded by *COPA* as less able to alter the format of this and other elements of the 1992 CAP reform package. Hence the opinion of a leading figure in the Secretariat that 'we had to act at the Commission's level if we wanted to have any of our points through. Once it was with the Parliament or the Council, it would be too late: [influencing] the basic strategy behind the [Commission] proposal was the most important thing . . .' (*COPA* source, May 1997).

Naturally the Secretariat had numerous access points within the DG Agri through which to advance its case on EC 2078/92. In the first instance, *COPA*'s 'Observations' paper was sent to all relevant personnel in the Directorate—that is, to those directly involved in the Regulation's drafting. Secondly, a two-person delegation from *COPA*, consisting of the Secretary of the Environmental Questions subgroup and the subgroup's Dutch Chairman, met with these personnel to discuss *COPA*'s position paper; these meetings took place either on an individual basis, or with small groups of *fonctionnaires.* Thirdly, the precise sequencing of these meetings, and the identity of interviewees, was timed to coincide with the progress of the proposal through the bureaucratic machinery of the Directorate. In interview, the former Secretary to the sub-group emphasized the time-consuming nature of *COPA*'s lobby effort:

First we spoke to the civil servants and the Head of Division directly involved [with the agri-environmental proposal], that was Mr Anz; and when the [agri-environmental] file went up to the Director-General's [Guy LeGras's] level, we came back [for further discussions] to try and drive our A-points through. And then we came back again when we knew it was with staff in Commissioner [MacSharry's] cabinet . . . (*COPA* source, May 1997)

These meetings with the DG Agri were complemented by a similar sequence of meetings with staff from the Environment Directorate (DG Env.). Such meetings were not only used to discuss the proposal; they also had a vital intelligence-gathering function for *COPA*, as an ex-*COPA* official who had moved to work in the DG Agri explained:

what we used to do was to play off the competition between the two DGs—they were always one against the other. So when we wanted to have information about what was going on with the Regulation in DG Env, we came here to DG Agri; and when we needed information about DG Agri, we went to [the Environment Directorate]. All the time we were trying to assess the positions of each Directorate [on the proposal] from the other. (DG Agri source, May 1997)

Hence, while *COPA*'s lobbying of the DG Agri during the preliminary phase was very intensive, it can be judged largely a failure, although, of course, the broad contours of EC 2078/92 did not inconvenience the EU farming community unduly.

5.5.2. Target Structures and Access Points used by *COPA* during the Agreement Phase: The European Parliament

By contrast, the relative unconcern of *COPA* staff in their lobbying of the EP is demonstrated by the Secretariat's adoption of a very much less onerous strategy towards this institution. Partly this reflected Parliament's truncated formal powers in the sphere of agricultural policy, with the CAP falling under the Consultation procedure (see Chapter 4).

Consequently, as the former Secretary of the subgroup recalled in interview, *COPA*'s lobbying of Parliament was less intensive than its lobbying of the Commission:

at that time, MEPs were keen to receive people from *COPA*. I went there with the Chairman and we saw many MEPs. We tried to [devise] as many positions as possible to convince MEPs [that financing of the Regulation] should come from the Guidance fund and we had very strong support for that option. And we made presentations both at the EP Environment Committee and the EP Agriculture Committee. (*COPA* source, May 1997)

In lobbying these two prominent committees, *COPA*'s aim was to advance its preference for financing the Regulation through the FEOGA Guidance Fund, in contrast to the Commission's preference for Guarantee as a source of funding. The outcome of these negotiations was positive, with both committees supporting *COPA*'s preferred funding option.

5.5.3. Target Structures and Conditions of Access used by *COPA* during the Agreement Phase: The Agriculture Council

COPA's goal of financing EC 2078/92 from the CAP Guidance fund was lost in winter 1991 as a result of political bargains struck between the DG Agri and two national delegations during closed sessions of the Agriculture Council. And yet, during autumn 1991, reports from *COPA* sources within the Council were broadly optimistic regarding the likelihood of its securing this crucial point. A very senior *COPA* official closely involved with these negotiations recalled: 'we nearly succeeded: at an early stage in [Council] discussions, this idea was in favour. We had the reports from the discussions of the [Agriculture Structures] Working Group of the Council and they were encouraging. We thought we had a pretty good chance of getting this funding arrangement through' (*COPA* source, May 1997). However, it is likely that, even had the DG Agri not struck an agreement with the French and German delegations, the two modalities underpinning Grande's 'logic of influence' would have militated against a successful outcome.

First and most significant, *COPA* policy precedent meant that lobbying of Council delegations was within the jurisdiction of individual national unions, rather than *COPA*. As *COPA*'s Director of Strategy noted, 'Our member organizations like to be masters of their own countries, they don't like very much for *COPA* to [interfere]' (*COPA* source, May 1997). In saddling itself with this precedent, undoubtedly the Secretariat seriously weakened its case on the finance issue by permitting its membership complete autonomy in their lobbying of national delegations. Secondly, wider systemic factors, relating to shifting national goals in the ongoing GATT negotiations, rather than the concrete detail of the reform proposals themselves, recast the parameters for discussion within the Agriculture Council, and led to a febrile atmosphere among delegations (see Epstein 1997: 362–3). Even at a very late stage in negotiations, the mood among national delegations regarding the CAP reform package was unusually volatile.

The deal brokered by the DG Agri, whereby the Directorate shelved its plans for an EU 'Code of Good Agricultural Practice' in exchange for French and German delegations dropping their opposition to FEOGA Guarantee funding for the agri-environmental Regulation, exemplified the feverish politicking ongoing in Council. Reflecting on this point, *COPA*'s Director of Strategy at the time explained:

we failed to control the situation in the Council . . . I received the biggest surprise from the French delegation, when suddenly Mermaz [then French Agriculture Minister] changed his funding policy at the end of the Council negotiations. What we'd assumed they'd refuse, they went ahead and accepted. I think it was an agreement, a trade-off with Kiechle . . . [then German Federal Minister of Agriculture]. (*COPA* source, May 1997)

Ratification of this 'trilateral' decision by the rest of Council was eased somewhat by the realization among other delegations that, without Guarantee funding, only those member states with the political will and the necessary funds would implement the Regulation. A senior DG Agri negotiator recalled that 'the Cohesion countries didn't want to be the ones in the slow lane of a two-speed Europe. Under the Guarantee Fund, it would be mandatory for all states to put the Regulation into practice. So everybody came out on the same level' (DG Agri source, May 1997).

Hence, *COPA*'s singlemost important goal for EC 2078/92 was blocked, even though promising soundings had been taken by the Secretariat on this issue only weeks before. As *COPA*'s Director of Strategy reflected ruefully: 'When you see the game is lost, it's lost . . . we'd lobbied for it, but on the day the Council had refused it. At these times, you have to remember that you can't succeed on all the files' (*COPA* source, May 1997).

5.6. Conclusions

In this chapter we have used Grande's analytical framework to examine the limits imposed by the supranational system of governance on *COPA* in its lobbying on the 1992 CAP reforms. We have done so by applying the policy modalities that Grande claims underpins the EU 'logic of influence' to the case of the agri-environmental Regulation.

Our contention is that the diminution in policy influence experienced by *COPA* in its lobbying on EC 2078/92 can be understood only with reference to the institutional architecture of the EU MLG, in particular the modalities and sequencing of decision-making among EU institutions, especially the DG Agri, and the 'closure periods', when access to the CAP decision-making process was effectively denied to *COPA*. We have argued that *COPA*'s lobbying effort was fundamentally flawed by the Secretariat's preoccupation with the DG Agri as the Eurogroup's most important 'target structure', an assumption based on the organizational closeness it had once enjoyed with the DG Agri. In fact, confounding the Secretariat's expectations, such ties as existed proved to have a deleterious rather than a beneficial effect. Once a pivotal member of the supranational policy community of the EU–6, by the early 1990s *COPA* was merely one of a number of relatively important actors in a fiercely competitive policy community. Consequently, when faced with the overwhelming need to push the 1992 CAP reforms through Council, and confronted by a European farm lobby bristling with hostility, the DG Agri utilized to the full the fragmented, diffuse structure of EU governance to play off the disparate views of *COPA*'s own policy constituency *against* the organization's formal bargaining position. This fatally damaged the credibility of *COPA*'s negotiating stance, preventing this group from destabilizing the overall CAP reform process.

COPA's lobbying of EU institutions on EC 2078/92 provides a number of valuable insights into the nature of supranational governance. In the first instance, it demonstrates that portrayals of the EU as an open, accessible, and relatively permeable decision-making structure are only partially correct. In fact, the dynamics of this MLG structure contain as many pitfalls for Eurogroups as opportunities, not least in the formidable battery of counter-lobbying possibilities open to those EU institutions that choose to capitalize on the limited access conditions of Eurogroups to the EU decision-making process. If the findings of this chapter are not atypical, it suggests that 'counter-lobbying' by EU institutions is more common than previously thought. Indeed, the very nature of the EU MLG makes such counter-lobbying by competent institutions relatively easier to instigate at the supranational than at the national level.

This chapter also demonstrates the complex nature of policy influence within EU MLG, and the almost military levels of regimentation and discipline required of Eurogroups and their constituencies in order to exercise it. It seems only appropriate that longer-term, targeted lobbying activities are labelled 'campaigns', since, as we have indicated, separate engagements in different EU negotiating arenas must be fought and won successively by Eurogroups if decisive influence is to be secured. In this example, at least, *COPA* was comprehensively outmanoeuvred by the DG Agri.

Among highly placed *COPA* officials and commentators alike (see Grant 1995; Coss 1997; Clark and Jones 1999; Nugent 1999), there is recognition that this organization's influence within the EU's MLG system has declined further following the events of 1992. At one level, this decline can be attributed to the continued growing division and disunity among its membership, and the Praesidium's relative lack of appetite for facing down the most prominent, and vocal, of its affiliates. Hence, commenting on the reaction of *COPA*'s membership to the Agenda 2000 proposals (CEC 1998*a*), Maitland (1998) observed: 'Far from a united position, the reactions [of farming unions] are many and conflicting ... *COPA* ... acknowledges that th[is] lack of a unified front strengthens the hand of the European Commission in pushing for reform.' But, while this comment recognizes the division in *COPA*'s ranks, it also acknowledges the powerful role of the European Commission in driving the supranational policy process forward, and, implicitly, this institution's mastery of the modalities of MLG.

We have also shown in this chapter the degree of opposition from EU producer groups to the environmentalization of agriculture. In Chapter 6, we look at the activities of groups at the opposite pole of the ideological spectrum, environmental NGOs, and how these organizations pushed forward the 'environmentalization agenda' for agriculture in a constituent member state of the EU, the UK.

6

National Modalities of Agri-Environmental Policy-Making in the United Kingdom

Having examined the activities and motives of supranational actors in policy-making on the agri-environmental Regulation, we turn in this chapter to the national arena. The MLG perspective attributes importance to all tiers of political administration within the diffuse polity of the EU, but few MLG theorists would disagree that the national level remains one of the most significant arenas of Union decision-making (see Chapter 1; see also Borzel 1999; Jeffrey 2000). However, while the level of our examination shifts here from the supranational to the national scale, the substantive analytical themes strongly complement those of previous chapters. Our aim is to provide a study of the CAP's environmentalization from a domestic perspective—that of the UK—which offers important additional information on this dynamic process, by characterizing its interrelationship with state-specific modalities of agricultural policy-making. In this context, the UK provides a compelling case example, as this member state was among the first in the EU to capitalize on the political opportunities presented by the EU's MLG structure to develop its national agri-environmental policy. Ultimately, though, the interdependence of agri-environmental policy actors and processes within the EU MLG transcends the different arenas and scales at which they operate. As the chapter shows, in the UK's case the evolution of agri-environmental policy has depended vitally on the involvement of, and creative synergies between, subnational, national, and supranational actors and institutions.

The chapter is set out as follows. We begin by developing the argument of Chapter 2 that socio-cultural traditions have profoundly influenced the historical evolution of EU agri-environmental policy. We do so by examining the national policy context within which deeply ingrained socio-cultural traditions in the UK, relating to farming's 'trusteeship' of the natural environment, have been mobilized by policy elites in the MAFF to legitimize agri-environmental programmes to the agricultural community and the general public alike. We contend this strategy has been pivotal to the MAFF's attempts to control the environmentalization of national agricultural policy since the early 1980s.

We then sketch out the historically close association between the evolution of these socio-cultural traditions, or *agrarian beliefs*, and the activities of UK NGOs. We show how certain of these NGOs sought to manipulate these beliefs to hasten the environmentalization of national agricultural policy-making. (There are interesting parallels and contrasts here between the actions of these NGOs and their commitment to environmentalization, and the resistance to 'greening' of agriculture exhibited by EU farming unions, examined in the preceding chapter.) We maintain their activities culminated in an unprecedented politicization of the agricultural debate in the UK, which contributed to the MAFF's decision to take the agri-environmental policy issue to the supranational level.

The impact of 'hegemonic' agrarian beliefs on the formulation of the UK negotiating position towards EC 2078/92 is then examined. A synopsis follows of the national and subnational changes instituted under the agri-environmental Regulation and the RDR, and we conclude by speculating to what extent environmental and other NGOs have been able to build upon these changes, and to capitalize on their ground-breaking involvement in UK agri-environmental policy.

In order to contextualize our argument, we address two questions in the first part of the chapter. First, how are socio-cultural traditions mobilized in the UK agricultural policy community, and why have they been actively sustained by the MAFF? Secondly, how do the activities of the UK agriculture departments, NGOs, and sectoral constituencies configure the evolution of these traditions, and how, in turn, are their actions conditioned by them?

6.1. Socio-Cultural Traditions and the Modalities of UK Agricultural Policy-Making

Pioneering work by Benson (1975, 1980) identified the fundamental importance of 'shared assumptions' and beliefs in structuring interrelationships between organizations situated within 'activity networks'. These networks 'consist of a number of distinguishable organizations having a significant amount of interaction with each other' (Benson 1975: 230). Benson's conceptualization can thus be applied to a range of organizational activities, including the formulation and implementation of agricultural policies, which is the application used here.

Benson notes that activity networks may be diffuse with intermittent interactions between all actors, or be highly clustered around one or a number of influential organizations. However, regardless of the precise morphology or degree of interaction within these networks, two resources are critically important to policy elites seeking to control network operation: amassing financial assets, and securing power and authority. Elites strive continually to augment their existing quota of these two resources.

Securing new sources of finance is vital to achieving organizational ambitions, and, while it may not be easy to accomplish, the procedures involved are relatively unambiguous. But the means of acquiring inter-organizational authority are less clear-cut. In this context Benson indicates that 'shared assumptions' and beliefs are critically important, as they legitimize activities, such as policies disseminated by organizations, that in turn define areas of administrative competence:

Shared assumptions . . . [are] employed primarily to provide continuing ideological legitimation for ongoing activities . . . Authority refers to this legitimation of activities, the right and responsibility to carry out programmes of a certain kind, dealing with a broad problem area or focus. *Legitimated claims of this kind are termed domains. The possession of a domain permits the organization to operate in a certain sphere, claim support for its activities, and define proper practices within its realm.*   (Benson 1975: 231–2; emphasis added)

By their inculcation into 'administrative cultures' (that is, departmental procedures and daily routines within the workplace) beliefs may shape, or even dictate, options available to policy elites (see also Friedrich 1989). Referring to this process, Benson (1975: 237) notes that 'ideology asserts a connection between assigned tasks and chosen policy procedures', an observation with which Swidler (1986) concurs. Similarly in related work on the impact of national 'economic cultures' on elites in their formulation of policy, Plaschke (1994: 126) remarks that 'economic cultures . . . exercise an independent . . . role by defining the legitimate policy alternatives available [to elites] at a given moment of time'. Work by Schein (1996) also alludes to the potency of beliefs in shaping policy formulation within organizations, noting especially their effect on the higher echelons of management: 'norms held tacitly across entire organizations [are] much more likely to change leaders than to be changed by them . . . such taken-for-granted, shared tacit ways of thinking, perceiving and reacting [are] one of the most powerful and stable forces operating in organizations' (Schein 1996: 231).

Clearly beliefs are of tremendous importance within organizations with formalized policy-making powers. Lowndes (1996: 185–6) dubs such organizations *mythic institutions*, 'having a shape and style reflect[ing] the "myths" of the institutional environment instead of the demands of specific work activities . . . [for these organizations] determining the character of institutional myths and symbols may be as important a power resource as control of material factors like budgets and buildings.' We contend that this situation—where elites mobilize beliefs, and orchestrate them through formalized decision-making procedures, and the discharging of organizational activities—is exhibited in the managing of UK farm policy. The responsible territorial departments are the Scottish

Executive's Rural Affairs Department (SERAD), the Welsh Office Agriculture Department (WOAD), the Department of Agriculture and Rural Development in Northern Ireland (DARD), and, pre-eminent among them, the MAFF.[1]

The application of Benson's' and Plaschke's theories to the UK farm sector suggests that 'agrarian beliefs'—that is, ingrained socio-cultural traditions relating to UK agriculture—have a major influence on the intra- and inter-organizational working practices of the agriculture departments. It implies, for example, that certain policy issues are perceived by elites within these organizations in particular ways, and that these elites prioritize the use of specific instruments over others to ensure 'favoured' policy issues are treated 'appropriately'. Crucially, these beliefs also underpin the administrative domains (Benson 1975) each agriculture department commands. These administrative domains have grown incrementally since the Second World War, and are zealously defended. As a result, historically each department has come to enjoy a degree of policy discretion relative to the other arms of government, enabling a certain freedom of action to be exercised. This 'sectoral freedom' (cf. Whitby and Lowe 1994: 6) has been bolstered in the post-war period by the development of permissive corporatist ties (Cox *et al.* 1988) between agricultural departments and farming unions especially, recasting the loose-knit UK agricultural policy network as a tighter, ideologically focused policy community (M.J. Smith 1990; Marsh and Rhodes 1992), favouring agrarian interests and effectively monopolizing policy-making in this sphere. Indeed, the engine of agricultural policy formulation in the UK since 1945 has been fuelled more by the collective action problems confronting organizations within this emergent policy community than by more objective national agricultural needs.

Agrarian beliefs have played an important role in the creation of this agricultural policy community. Over time, these beliefs have been subtly redefined to reflect more closely the requirements of both policy elites and producer groups. In turn, these requirements have changed in response to the prevailing political-economic situation confronting UK agricultural markets. Thus the ideologies of policy elites and producer groups have traditionally been strongly complementary, cementing their close working relations. In Benson's formulation, this complementarity of beliefs provides the basis of *cooperative strategies* (Benson 1975: 241) in which the MAFF and the UK's pre-eminent producer groups, the NFU and the Country Landowners' Association (CLA), have participated principally. Powerful representation by these two producer groups across the spectrum of agricultural policy issues has ensured the marginalization of other NGOs.

---

[1] Following the programme of constitutional devolution launched in the UK in 1997, both SERAD and WOAD have acquired new powers from the MAFF, and have begun to develop their own distinctive approaches to certain policy issues. However, in the short term at least, this development is unlikely to threaten the MAFF's dominant position within UK agricultural policy-making

By controlling financial, legal, and jurisdictional resources within UK agriculture, the MAFF has been able to pressure other organizations to subscribe to the resulting interpretation of agrarian beliefs favoured by the core policy community. We term these interpretations the *hegemonic* interpretations. In promulgating these hegemonic agrarian beliefs, the MAFF has used a variety of rhetorical devices. Majone's notions of *rationalizations* and *feasibility arguments* are particularly useful explanatory tools in this respect (Majone 1992*a*), as they clarify the role and scope of beliefs in shaping UK agricultural policy development. Majone contends that these two discursive forms provide the principal means of mobilizing beliefs in policy deliberation. 'Rationalizations' explain problems confronting policies in terms of their underlying 'principles' (see Chapter 2). By contrast, 'feasibility arguments' are forward looking, setting out how actors believe policies must develop in relation to the constraints—principally ideological (that is, the underlying evolutionary logic of the policy dictated by its principles), but also social, economic, and political—that impinge upon policy sectors. We employ these two concepts in the context of agri-environmental policy later in this chapter.

Typically, in its formulation of agricultural policies, the MAFF has placed far less importance on concerns voiced by what Jordan *et al.* (1994: 511) describe as *externality groups*—that is, 'groups challenging the dominance of agricultural interests on matters such as food safety and [the] environmental impact of farming methods'. Chiefly environmental NGOs and consumer interests, these groups are excluded from the core policy community, and until recently were confined to the peripheries of agricultural policy-making. Historically, the relatively muted roles of the UK's Department of the Environment (DoE; after 1997 (the Department of Transport, Environment, and the Regions (DETR)) and the statutory agencies for nature conservation (until 1990 the Nature Conservancy Council (NCC)) and for landscape recreation (until 1999, the Countryside Commission (CC)) in shaping agricultural policy are also explained by these organizations being excluded from the UK agricultural policy community. This was confirmed by the relatively poor working relations that existed between the MAFF and the DoE, with the Ministry often contriving to minimize the Department's influence in its administrative domain (see e.g. Cloke and MacLaughlin 1989).

The distinct identities of the NCC and the CC also enabled producer interests to portray UK environmental opinion as apparently divided, to the advantage of the farm lobby. The specific responsibilities of these organizations often proved problematic. While the NCC and the CC were leading advocates in the evolving national debate over the environmentalization of agricultural policy, their impact was curtailed because of their advisory rather than legislative remit. This remit tended to distance both organizations politically from the Whitehall decision-taking process. Hence, in order to exert any influence on environmentalization, rather than on more general environmental policy debate, both organizations were at times obliged to uphold hege-monic interpretations of agrarian beliefs.

Nevertheless, in the process of beliefs becoming more widespread and uni-versalized during the agricultural policy-making process, they are exposed to redefinition by externality groups. Traditionally, these groups have advanced arguments opposed to agricultural productivism (Chapter 2), and at times have pursued what Benson characterizes as *disruptive strategies* (Benson 1975: 242)—that is, 'the purposive conduct of activities which threaten the resource-generating capacities of a target agency', for example, challenging beliefs underpinning the MAFF's productivist policies, and the carefully guarded administrative domain these policies constitute.

We contend that by pursuing disruptive strategies, externality groups can seriously undermine policy positions, especially if they can demonstrate incon-sistencies and anomalies between the policies of executive agencies, ministries, and so on, and the espoused beliefs these outputs are founded on. Plaschke (1994: 118) alludes to this process in noting 'at any moment of time beliefs are the result of specific historical developments in the form of confrontations, struggles, alliances, and compromises between social interest groups'. Clearly this has implications for 'mythic institutions', such as the MAFF, which are heavily dependent on these discursive motifs to underwrite policy legitimacy, and to defend administrative domains. As a result, UK agricultural elites are engaged in a continuous struggle to maintain hegemonic interpretations of agrarian beliefs, as these provide the cornerstone of the MAFF's administra-tive culture: 'Perpetuation of [administrative] culture is . . . dictated by organ-izational self-interest . . . and by continuous adjustment and maintenance. [Policy] elites have to work at maintaining the system' (Wilks 1990: 150).

UK agrarian beliefs and the policies with which they were associated were put under intense scrutiny for the first time by externality groups during the late 1970s and early 1980s, as a result of chronic overproduction and an esca-lating budgetary crisis in the CAP (see Chapter 2). But debate over agriculture and the environment—in effect, the precursor to environmentalization of domestic agricultural policy—predates this period, and has evolved over time. At a superficial level, in the 1960s–1970s debate focused on increasing levels of farm profitability and productivity in marginal farmed areas, where environ-mental conditions were not suited to the adoption of intensive agricultural practice. In the late 1970s–1980s, debate shifted to the environmental impacts arising from government- and EU-subsidized agricultural policies. From the late 1980s onwards, agri-environmental discourse began to specify a range of public expectations and societal responsibilities that farmers should fulfil if the sector was to retain its historic policy entitlements (including price support, intervention purchase, and export refunds).

At a deeper level, the evolution of environmentalization of UK agriculture is explicable in terms of contested meanings and varied interpretations of UK agrarian beliefs, in particular those relating to environmental protection and the management of the countryside. For example, in the post-war era the age-old notion of the farmer as 'trustee' of the national agricultural estate, maintaining high levels of productivity in the 'public interest', has been used by producer groups to justify agricultural 'improvements', such as the wide-spread practice of wetlands drainage, and the ploughing of semi-natural pastures. But, from the early 1980s, reinterpretations of this belief provided the basis around which agri-environmental 'advocacy coalitions' (Sabatier 1988) coalesced. In conclusion, the national modalities of UK agricultural policy-making have ensured that farm interests are well placed to configure agrarian beliefs, especially as these relate to the environment.

6.2. UK Agrarian Beliefs

Prior to 1880 much of the UK's agricultural land was managed as estates, often with a number of compatible land uses including farming, forestry, and hunt-ing (Mingay 1981). Although this situation no longer pertains, the principle of 'estate management' and the agrarian notions it engendered (for example, maintaining functional 'tidy' landscapes through good husbandry, and keep-ing land in 'good heart') has proved surprisingly durable (Lowe and Bodiguel 1990; Lowenthal 1991). Following piecemeal agrarian reforms in the late nine-teenth century, these traditional notions, rather than lapsing or being repudi-ated, met with an unspoken but generalized acceptance among tenants and owner-occupiers, embuing UK agriculture with a set of pervasive agrarian beliefs. However, in common with other EU states, the basis of UK agrarian-ism can be traced to 'the symbolic importance that agriculture has occupied in political and cultural organization . . . plac[ing] the rural at the centre of national consciousness' (Hoggart *et al.* 1995: 93). In the UK's case, a crucial feature explaining this incorporation of agrarian beliefs into the national polity is their explicit recognition and quasi-legal status as a core element of post-war countryside planning controls (Buller 1992).

Discussing agriculture's responsibilities towards the environment, Street (1937: 1–2, 4) refers to one of the most enduring of these agrarian beliefs, the per-ceived role of farmers as 'trustees' of the countryside, both providing environ-mental management and imposing a sense of ecological order in rural areas: 'The . . . farmer has done his duty as trustee of [the] land . . . the beauty of our countryside is largely due to farming . . . in an unfarmed state our valleys would be impassable swamps and the lovely patchwork quilt which has clothed our countryside for hundreds of years would give place to an ugly jungle . . .'.

As Street implied, the basic concept underlying 'trusteeship' in the inter-war years was to master 'unruly' natural landscapes, rather than to inform land management in any ecological sense. In other words, 'trusteeship' was steeped in agrarianism. In an early conservationist account, Stapleton (1935: 1, 5) con-curs with this view, asserting that

Whatever may be said for the . . . culture of the British [farmer] . . . it cannot . . . be claimed that it . . . demands an all-pervading spirit of carefulness and of respect for the way in which our limited natural land surface is used . . . the revolution that is . . . taking place in the national attitude towards nature and the countryside is . . . being fostered in the towns[,] rather than the rural districts . . .

There is, in short, no steadfast environmental or conservationist credo informing UK agrarian beliefs. Instead, alongside other notions, the farmer as 'trustee' has been respecified by landholding and production groups and legitimized by the MAFF to suit the sector's own goals—goals dictated chiefly by the prevailing political-economic situation confronting UK agriculture. Other than having strong cultural resonances, these beliefs are no more than vectors for the advancement of farming interests within the agricultural policy making process (cf. Chapter 2; see also Clark *et al.* 1997; Clark and Jones 1998). It is power relations that emerge as the animating substance shaping UK agrarian beliefs, and typically landscapes have reified these relations by bestowing upon them a tangible value. However Mabey (1987: 22) notes that these agricultural landscapes have also had a tremendous symbolic importance:

the countryside's enormous potential as a symbol has been repeatedly commandeered and redefined by powerful minorities. In the late 18th and 19th centuries, the 'Age of Improvement' in the countryside was used by the aristocrats to display their wealth and taste and authority. In the [Second World W]ar, the countryside was equated with 'The Country' and used as a symbol of national unity. Since the War it has mostly been defined as the workplace of the farmer, some of whom have the temerity to say they 'created' it . . .

This observation demonstrates the ascendancy of the UK's landholding classes in determining the character of hegemonic agrarian beliefs, and implies that in the post-war period this mantle was assumed by the MAFF, which in its capacity as a 'mythic institution' continues to use beliefs as a resource for legitimizing policies in much the same way as it does financial or material assets.[2] In doing so, hegemonic interpretations of agrarian beliefs have been defined with two express aims: first, to underpin the 'sectoral freedom' of the Ministry—that is, guaranteeing autonomy for its elites to develop agricultural policy; secondly, to underwrite the 'territorial freedom' expected by UK farmers—in other words the necessity for farm activities to be relatively unfettered by regulation, and for compensation from the state where this is not the case.[3]

---

[2] For example, a wartime promotional report from the agriculture departments, exhorting farmers to produce more, commented: 'Land is a pretty good mirror of Man's state of mind. It reflects his outlook, his way of life, his standard of civilization. A countryside of weeds and broken hedges will point surely to the demoralization of the community living upon it, just as well-ordered cultivations will show its self-confidence and power' (MoI 1945).

[3] Cox, Lowe, and Winter (1988: 330) define 'territorial freedom' as 'maximiz[ing] politically feasible autonomy for the individual farmer and, where policy initiatives are deemed to have compromised that autonomy, [exacting] some form of compensation . . . for the associated infringement of property rights'.

In policy terms, this 'territorial freedom' has been articulated most power-fully on behalf of farmers by producer groups, such as the NFU and the CLA. In response to growing environmental concerns over the post-war trend towards intensifying agriculture, these groups made increasing use of 'trustee-ship' as a notion that seemingly could reconcile landscape and nature conser-vation with modern farming practice. During the 1960s and 1970s, this rhetorical usage became increasingly generalized in UK agricultural policy, prompting a CC representative to remark: 'farmers believe . . . that a func-tional landscape which reflects modern, efficient agriculture is visually pleas-ing. With this notion are strongly-held . . . views . . . that farmers automatically pursue conservation policies and that the future of the landscape is safe in their hands . . .' (Davidson 1978: 96). It was this elaboration by production groups of 'trusteeship' to encompass *environmental*, as opposed to merely *agrarian*, objectives that became the focus of the UK agri-environmental debate during the mid-1980s.

For the UK's agricultural bureaucracy and farming community, these 'sec-toral' and 'territorial freedoms' have remained sacrosanct. While the MAFF was obliged in the 1980s to respond to arguments put forward by externality groups that expressly targeted 'trusteeship', the agricultural policy community has not surrendered its right to these two freedoms. Instead, they have been used to structure the Ministry's response to environmentalization of agricul-tural policy, by shaping its political and policy antecedents.

6.3. The Politics of 'Collective Consumption' and the Environmentalization of UK Agriculture, 1981–1987

In understanding the development of the UK's agri-environmental politics and policies, the starting point is to recognize the status of the agricultural environment as a complex assemblage of 'public goods' (Hagedorn 1985). According to Grant (1993*b*: 68), in the EU from the 1980s onwards public goods were swept up in a 'politics of collective consumption',

concerned with the outcomes of the policy process . . . [and] generat[ing] a form of pol-itics which [was] far less amenable to corporatist solutions because it [was] not possible to resolve the problems that ar[o]se through a system of elite bargaining . . . Decision making mechanisms which ha[d] worked well in resolving problems of economic distri-bution [could not] cope with the challenges provided by these new issues.

We contend that during the early 1980s in the UK, a politics of collective consumption emerged around the agricultural environment. As Plaschke inti-mates, the new politics had its roots in the actions of interest groups intent on reinterpreting the hegemonic agrarian beliefs espoused by the MAFF. In the agricultural sphere, collective consumption politics began to unfold around the activities of environmental groups, and was largely a response to their experience of the acrimonious passage of the Wildlife and Countryside Act in 1981 (Cox and Lowe 1983). It was characterized by the deployment of novel tactics by these NGOs, including their coordinated lobbying of both Houses of Parliament; their widespread use of media coverage to illuminate policy issues; and their development of 'issue-led' environmental campaigns that, with hindsight, all targeted hegemonic agrarian beliefs. Taken together, these modalities constituted the main elements of an 'alternative' environmentalization strategy for UK agriculture, one that challenged the mainstream ideological approach.

These campaigns focused on the negative effects of intensive agricultural practice on valued habitats and landscapes, such as that organized in 1981 by the Council for the Protection of Rural England (CPRE) over the drainage of the Halvergate Marshes in Norfolk (O'Riordan 1985). Contesting the hegemonic interpretation of 'trusteeship' promoted by the MAFF was an unspoken but key feature of the Halvergate campaign. Certainly the CPRE was aware of the tremendous cultural resonance of challenging this conception. As Robin Grove-White (1987: 24–5), CPRE's Director throughout this period, reflected, 'Conservation concern in Britain is part of our continuing culture . . . the British nerve on environmental questions is more likely to be touched by threats to long-established . . . landscapes or hedgerows, than by . . . such "continental" concerns as . . . soil protection . . . And CPRE knows how to touch these [cultural] chords.'

Through its adroit campaigning at Halvergate, with other environmental groups the CPRE demonstrated the hollowness of claims made by the UK farm lobby that the traditional notion of 'trusteeship' could encompass both agrarian *and* environmental goals for farmland. By doing so, the CPRE's activities showed the fallibility of this hegemonic interpretation. As Benson notes, once new interpretations of beliefs have popular support, organizational elites cannot afford to ignore them without risking policy legitimacy and endangering the stability of administrative domains. Combined with demands from the Treasury for savings in the sizeable UK agriculture budget, in 1983 the MAFF recognized its untenable policy position by abolishing agricultural production grants subsidizing agricultural 'improvements', including drainage. As Grove-White (1987: 24) concluded, 'Working closely with the news media to direct well-aimed fire at particular targets . . . sen[t] reverberations through the Whitehall policy machine . . . Our narrow campaign on Halvergate Marshes . . . helped undermine the whole agricultural grants system.'

The CC also played a significant role in the Halvergate saga. With the MAFF's agreement, in 1983 the CC proposed to offer indemnity payments to farmers who were prepared to forgo either draining or ploughing of wetlands under a new Broads Grazing Marsh Conservation Scheme (BGMCS). The precedent for this measure had been set by the Wildlife and Countryside Act. The BGMCS addressed the requirements of an agri-environmental policy based upon 'territorial freedom' perfectly, as the new policy mechanism was distributive, and did not threaten UK farmers with environmental regulation. And by controlling moneys disbursed under this new measure, the MAFF ensured that the CC's encroachment into its administrative domain was minimized.

Notwithstanding this, from the point of view of producer groups the MAFF's approach to Halvergate seemed dilatory. This hesitancy can be explained in terms of an organizational dilemma facing the Ministry. While the MAFF's hegemonic interpretation of 'trusteeship' was under intense pressure from environmental NGOs, it still legitimated much of the MAFF's administrative domain. A reinterpretation of 'trusteeship' might have offered the Ministry extra responsibilities focused on agriculture and the environment—but there was no guarantee that it might not also destabilize flagship agricultural policies, thereby endangering the Ministry's overall executive competence, as the production grants issue had done.

For environmentalists, on the other hand, the policy response to Halvergate was heartening. In 1984–5 the CPRE followed up its activities in Norfolk with a highly successful parliamentary campaign aiming to 'twist . . . the Minister of Agriculture's arm . . . to get him to put a new conservation dimension into the [EU's] farm grant proposals . . .' (Grove-White 1987: 26). Potentially this made the agricultural environment a subject for action at the supranational level. But this was made a certainty only by the Ministry's willingness to pursue agri-environmental issues through EU, as opposed to domestic, decision-making channels. This decision was testimony to the highly politicized nature of domestic agricultural debate, and the way in which externality groups, in particular environmental NGOs, had forced a reinterpretation of agrarian beliefs. The CPRE's activities not only demonstrated that the legitimacy of these beliefs had been questioned. For the first time, through effective parliamentary lobbying, national agricultural policy modalities had been successfully challenged on explicit environmental grounds. In taking the issue to the EU level, as much as anything else the MAFF was seeking to prevent any further unravelling of agriculture's special status within the UK polity.

The MAFF's actions at the EU level brought about Article 19 of EC Regulation 797/85, whereby member states could designate ESAs within which payments could be made to farmers for adopting low-intensity farming practices (see Chapter 2; see also Whitby and Lowe 1994). Seemingly, UK environmental groups had won a considerable triumph at the Ministry's expense. Paradoxically, however, the ESA initiative offered the UK's farming community a welcome respite from criticism, and the means to restore its threadbare public credibility. Critically, it provided the MAFF with a new policy instrument with which to legitimize activities in a novel administrative sphere, enabling the Ministry to enlarge its administrative domain, and to transform the UK agricultural community into 'stewards' of the countryside. Initially, both the NFU and the CLA took the lead in this process (Cox *et al.*

1985). But only the MAFF was able to legitimize this new environmental responsibility both to farmers and to the general public. In doing so the Ministry enhanced its own organizational status as well as that of the farming community. As Boehmer-Christiansen (1994: 71) notes: '[Agri-] Environmental threats . . . are mental constructs created from a mixture of knowledge, experience, ideology and culture . . . Like all threats, they invite defensive action and redistribute power to those who . . . claim to be able to protect and defend.'

It took some time for the impact of Halvergate and other environmental campaigns to be reflected in the MAFF's recasting of agrarian beliefs, a process given greater emphasis in the Ministry following assumption in 1986 of a new environmental mandate under the Agriculture and Food Act. Subsequently, policy elites lost no time in transforming Street's 'agrarian trustee' into the more dynamic notion of the farmer as 'steward', notions structured around the industry's 'sectoral' and 'territorial freedoms'. Although the terms 'custodian' and 'steward' had been in circulation for many years, they had been used before by commentators chiefly in a descriptive sense. By contrast, the MAFF's deployment of these rhetorical devices in ministerial speeches, press releases, and official documents was novel and noteworthy, signalling the Ministry's willingness to redefine the hegemonic interpretation of beliefs underpinning UK agricultural policy. This redefinition provided the MAFF with the means of wresting control of the environmentalization agenda for agriculture away from interest groups, through the development of a UK agri-environmental policy.

6.4. Environmentalization and the MAFF's Recasting of Hegemonic Agrarian Beliefs, 1988–1990

Although the Ministry had been slow to acknowledge the political importance of the agricultural environment, by 1988 senior officials recognized that substantial political capital could be made by promoting an 'environmentalized' UK agriculture. This objective was part of the MAFF's goal of repositioning UK agriculture to suit a countryside increasingly dominated by consumption, rather than production-oriented demands (Marsden 1993) through realigning the Ministry's traditional competencies. So, in a speech delivered on 26 May 1988, the Minister of State at Agriculture, John Gummer, noted:

With modern transport systems . . . more and more people from the cities can visit the countryside. And when they do so, they will be able to see visible signs of the steps [the MAFF is] taking to bring agriculture into the 1990s and cater for the new demands of urban man [*sic*]. [For example] we have introduced eighteen Environmentally Sensitive Areas . . . where aid is offered to farmers . . . prepared to . . . preserve the natural beauty of the area . . .   (MAFF 1988: 2)

Yet while this statement acknowledged the changed political priorities within UK agriculture, the Minister of State was still being briefed by the MAFF's policy elite to respond to environmental critiques of the CAP in terms of *feasibility arguments* (Majone 1992*a*), founded upon UK agriculture's two 'freedoms'. So, in the same speech, Gummer argued that radical reform of agricultural policy was to be avoided, chiefly on ideological grounds: 'management of . . . traditional farming . . . has always exercised so much fascination for the nation at large . . . A farmed countryside is an attractive countryside . . . Of course we want CAP reform and a more rational institutional price framework . . . but we cannot do this suddenly, removing virtually all support from agriculture. This would only bring rural dereliction . . .' (MAFF 1988: 1–2).

Instead, following the success of the ESA precedent, the Agriculture Minister John MacGregor promoted the vision of a diversified UK agriculture, capable of responding to market conditions and of producing a variety of niche products, including 'public goods', provided these were assigned 'prices . . . to which our farmers can respond'. In a speech at the 1989 Oxford Farming conference, this line of thinking was evident in the Minister citing agri-environmental schemes as 'a strand of policy for the 1990s which will provide additional sources of income' to farmers, offering them a challenge that they would 'recognize [in] their role as custodians of the countryside' (MAFF 1989*a*: 18). MacGregor also noted the addition of the Farm Woodlands Scheme and Farm Diversification Grant Scheme to the emerging suite of UK agri-environmental measures, concluding that, together with ESAs, they 'demonstrate, if this were needed, the commitment of the industry to its custodianship role' (1989*a*: 18). Whether the UK agricultural community was committed to this role or not, this 'custodianship' placed no obligation on farmers to participate in the flotilla of new measures. And even for scheme participants, environmental requirements were largely discretionary, and were remunerated relatively favourably. Clearly the 'territorial freedom' required by UK farmers had cast a long shadow over the specification of UK agri-environmental policy.

At the same time as recasting the farmer as 'custodian', the MAFF also sought to neutralize possible future infringement by environmental groups of its 'sectoral freedom'. With this in mind, in April 1989 the Ministry's Permanent Secretary emphasized 'the need for environmental protection in agriculture to be securely based on scientific understanding of the issues involved, as environmental decisions without such a basis can lead to confused priorities' (MAFF 1989*b*: 1). Such a strategy drew the teeth from the highly successful culturally based critiques of intensive agriculture mounted by environmental NGOs, and restricted severely their capacity to dictate the environmentalization agenda as they had in the early 1980s.

Rather than disenfranchising these groups the MAFF's strategy aimed to restrain their influence in agricultural policy by depoliticizing UK agrarian beliefs. It also enabled environmentalization of domestic agricultural policy to occur only on terms of the Ministry's own choosing. Hence, by the late 1980s, a consensus has emerged between policy elites and environmental NGOs over farming's new 'green' mandate, exhibited most clearly in the MAFF's more considered approach towards these groups. While farming and environmental interests had worked together before—most notably in securing Article 19 of Regulation 797/85—by August 1990 the new Agriculture Minister John Gummer felt confident enough to speak of 'conservation and farming working together . . . The ESA scheme shows that it is possible to farm in a way that benefits wildlife . . . I am sure that it is recognized that the countryside we regard as natural owes much to the work of generations of farmers . . . And it is farmers who will continue to manage those features' (MAFF 1990*a*: 1).

With the environmental lobby broadly supportive of farming's attempts at reform, and the ESA initiative garnering public approval, the Ministry could portray agri-environmental policies as integral to the agriculture sector's future: 'Farming in Britain is facing changes but those farmers who face these changes fairly and squarely will see not a problem, but an opportunity to reposition farming as a benign and positive force in the stewardship of the countryside' (MAFF 1990*b*: 1).

This subtle cultural repositioning from custodian of the countryside to environmental steward was indicative of the MAFF's increasing confidence in the public legitimation afforded the farming industry by agri-environmental measures, and reflected the Ministry's wish to bestow on farmers a more active role in environmental management—providing it remained on the MAFF's terms. In short, this was a policy that the MAFF felt comfortable seeing elaborated at the EU level.

6.5. UK Hegemonic Beliefs and the EU's Agri-Environmental Regulation 1990–1992

By the late 1980s the CAP was in profound crisis. This had a concomitant effect on the policy's socio-structural measures, including EC 797/85, the Regulation giving legal force to Article 19 (ESA) schemes. EC 797/85 was subject to repeated amendments and additions during 1985 and 1986, and, in the interests of administrative simplicity, was superseded in 1987 by a new Regulation, EC 1760/87. This Regulation also introduced EU cofinancing of Article 19 schemes (see Chapter 2), and obliged the European Commission to review the Article's implementation by member states after three years (Baldock and Lowe 1996).

As discussed in earlier chapters, the result of this Commission review was published in October 1990 as COM (90) 366, on 'agricultural production methods compatible with protection of the environment and maintenance of the countryside' (CEC 1990*b*: 11; see also above, Chapters 2, 3, 4, and 5).

Broadly the report noted that, aside from a clutch of north European countries, few member states had implemented Article 19 or related extensification schemes. Faced with this result, the DG Agri proposed that the Article be included as part of a wider policy approach, embracing more comprehensively member states' environmental interests in the field of agriculture (see Chapter 3; see also Jones and Clark 1998).

The most prominent of the new measures outlined in COM (90) 366 final was to offer payments to farmers for making a 'significant reduction' in their use of fertilizers and pesticides. Understandably, the UK's response, advanced by the MAFF's principal negotiator in the Agriculture Council in a series of meetings between August 1990 and February 1991, was founded on the Ministry's experience of administering ESAs, and piloting Nitrate Sensitive Areas (NSAs). Crucially, in crystallizing the UK's position, the MAFF's policy elites grounded their response in terms of hegemonic agrarian beliefs; as Plaschke (1994) notes, beliefs structure social action through their legitimization of a range of policy alternatives. This was most evident in the position adopted by the Ministry towards eutrophication,[4] which was the focus of COM (90) 366 final. As one of the MAFF's negotiators commented in interview:

We were coming at this proposal from a different national perspective . . . based on countryside and the natural environment, which was not what COM (90) 366 was about at all . . . it wasn't driven by a British view of the landscape, or a British view of wanting more farmland birds or more wild flowers. I don't think these beliefs had been acknowledged at all. They were probably not understood at the time by the Commission. Our view was that such a policy, seemingly driven by eutrophication concerns, wouldn't be very meaningful in Britain, because MAFF's position is and always has been that a eutrophication problem doesn't exist here. We also didn't want a proposal that could lead to a country disadvantaging its farmers: that's what COM (90) 366 threatened to do in its enforcing fertilizer restrictions.   (MAFF source, Dec. 1996)

This response demonstrates the impact of British agrarian beliefs on the formation of the MAFF's negotiating position. In the first place, it confirms that environmental concerns *per se* such as eutrophication were not easily made supportive of UK farm interests, and so were perceived as 'second-order' considerations by the MAFF. But as important was the MAFF's acknowledgement of avoiding regulatory policies at all costs, an obligation imposed by 'territorial freedom'. This freedom had to be observed, if agri-environmental measures were to be made politically acceptable to UK farm groups. Hence, 'because we felt that COM (90) 366 didn't represent our interests . . . we formulated a line of questioning focused on [eutrophication]. I don't recall the Commission giving any decent answers . . . And that's why in its initial stages

---

[4] Enrichment of water nutrient levels (chiefly of nitrogen or phosphorus), often arising from human activities, which can result in loss of biodiversity.

this proposal came all unstuck. We went through it Article by Article, and just tore [the proposal] to pieces' (MAFF source, Dec. 1996).

This comment is indicative of the MAFF's leverage over other delegations, including the Commission, in these Agriculture Council discussions, which derived from the UK's relative expertise in agri-environmental policy. This expertise seems to have placed the MAFF team at a considerable advantage, as the Ministry's principal negotiator of the time explained:

The idea of having a national agri-environment programme was a novelty for a lot of member states. I think we were pretty much out on our own, and were far better placed to advance what we thought would work and why. The German Article 19 approach was similar to our own. The Danish scheme was quite different—more like our SSSI [Site of Special Scientific Interest]. I remember also that the French were thinking very much along the lines of our ESA scheme. So we knew there was some commonality in terms of the ESA approach, although at that time there weren't a great number of member states with experience of it. Certainly no groups had got experience of dealing with large areas of land and channelling money through environmental land management contracts to farmers. We'd got that experience, and based on evidence . . . had convinced ourselves that it delivered conservation benefits. We were able to dominate Council discussions and steer them because nobody else had this experience.   (MAFF source, Oct. 1996)

Assuming this proposal would form the blueprint for a European Community Regulation targeted at the agricultural environment, the MAFF used the new policy modalities offered by its improved relations with UK environmental groups. Staff in the Ministry approached certain NGOs to press the UK case with other member states through their sister organizations in these countries. Within the MAFF, responsibility for this task was given to a Grade 5 administrator:

We knew the agri-environment was an idea that was catching on. We talked to the Royal Society for the Protection of Birds (RSPB) at the time, telling them it was very important to do as much lobbying in other countries as possible to get other national delegations on board. In Spain RSPB worked through SEO [*Sociedad Espanola de Ornitologia*, the Spanish Ornithological Society]. I recall the Spanish delegation taking it on quite whole-heartedly in subsequent discussions, declaring they were going to do all sorts of wonderful things along ESA-type lines.   (MAFF source, Dec. 1996)

However, in the words of this MAFF official, by late February 1991 'things had gone very quiet' on COM (90) 366 final. For reasons discussed earlier (see Chapter 3), this policy area had become embroiled in the Commission's strategic plans for the reform of the CAP ongoing at the time (Jones and Clark 1998). During summer 1991, the Commission embarked on a significant reworking of COM (90) 366 final, which seems to have met with an unfavourable reaction from national delegations generally. A new proposal, COM (91) 415, more accommodative of member states' environmental and political concerns, emerged in October 1991 (CEC 1991*b*).

The publication of this new Commission proposal coincided with a desire on the MAFF's part to extend the suite of agri-environmental measures at its disposal. However, a crowded UK parliamentary agenda gave no prospect for the time needed to enact the necessary legislation. Hence the MAFF entered negotiations on COM (91) 415 with a 'profound interest in getting a decent Council Regulation through' that which would meet the UK's domestic requirements (MAFF source, Nov. 1996). Through diligence and good fortune a number of UK additions were made to COM (91) 415 between the proposal and final draft stages. Of these additions, the inclusion at UK insistence of an access clause in the last throes of negotiation on the Regulation demonstrates the fundamentally political basis of 'stewardship' in UK agriculture:

We were very concerned to get provision of access payments in, because at the time [1992] there was increasing public interest in widening access in the countryside. Ministers didn't want there to be a 'right to roam' on farmed land, that would've been politically explosive. But they *did* want financial encouragement for farmers to open up suitable farmed land, for example places linking existing footpaths.   (MAFF source, Nov. 1996: emphasis in original)

As Benson indicates, beliefs can provide the basis for *cooperative* or *disruptive strategies* adopted by organizations. An instance of the MAFF pursuing a *disruptive strategy* during negotiations over COM (91) 415 occurred when the UK delegation was confronted with a proposition from the Commission's Environment Directorate-General that the Regulation offer incentives to farmers for maintaining or reintroducing endangered livestock breeds. This suggestion conflicted with the MAFF's reformulated conception of environmental stewardship in the UK's 'post-production' countryside. The Ministry's response was unequivocal:

the whole Regulation was about farming landscapes in an environmentally sensitive way, then [the Environment Directorate] wanted to add this thing about making payments to keep rare breeds of farm animals . . . we thought it wasn't the place for it at all, and we couldn't see a reason to start paying farmers to do it . . . it was a completely unhelpful contribution, reflecting [that Directorate's] lack of grip, but we didn't succeed in getting it knocked out. But we made sure it wasn't . . . obligatory . . . (MAFF source, Nov. 1996)

The impact of this reformulated hegemonic interpretation of environmental stewardship on the MAFF's treatment of agri-environmental issues was evident throughout the early 1990s. During the UK's EU Presidential term beginning in July 1992, agricultural speeches and statements made by the Presidency were clearly couched to take advantage of common notions of rurality inherent in *all* member states, around which Council compromises could be struck (see Chapter 2; see also Clark *et al.* 1997). The then Agriculture Minister, John Gummer, typified this approach in addressing a conference in the Netherlands on the subject of the 'European Countryside'. But, while emphasizing at this conference the commonality of this notion among EU member states,

Gummer's distinctive interpretation of stewardship was firmly rooted in UK agrarian beliefs:

the environment of Europe is the heritage of all Europeans. We in Britain have a real interest in the protection of the historic countryside here in the Netherlands . . . The European [Union] will not be forgiven if it does not ensure that all the governments of Europe protect their heritage . . . No Member State can opt out of the duty to conserve Europe's landscape for future generations. We are all stewards.   (MAFF 1992*b*: 1–2)

6.6. Changing Modalities of UK Agri-Environmental Policy-Making?

During 1993, the MAFF consulted with some ninety NGOs on its plans for implementing the agri-environmental Regulation (MAFF 1993), although this was undertaken at a very late stage in the policy-setting process; interested parties were given barely eight weeks to provide the Ministry with formal replies. Despite there being four agriculture departments, the UK's national response to the Regulation was drawn up chiefly by MAFF personnel, reflecting the hegemonic position enjoyed by the Ministry over the formulation of national policy.[5] The Regulation's 'zonal approach' (see Chapter 1) was largely eschewed in this response, with the MAFF choosing instead to delimit the four countries as separate 'zones', each with its own agri-environmental programme, 'for reasons of administrative simplicity' (MAFF 1996: 3). While, therefore, there were some minor differences in content between the UK's four territorial programmes, in essence each mirrored the MAFF's own submission.

In common with the UK stance during negotiations on EC 2078/92, the MAFF viewed implementation as an opportunity to advance the hegemonic notion of 'environmental stewardship' by expanding the scope of its existing schemes, rather than to introduce new measures (cf. the French and Spanish experiences, Chapter 9). A core element of the English agri-environmental programme thus focused on expanding the area of farmed land in NSAs and ESAs, by proposing the designation of six new ESAs and thirty new NSAs.[6] The MAFF also confirmed its dominant position in national policy-making by retaining overall responsibility for liaising with the DG Agri over general coordination of UK agri-environmental policy.

These developments demonstrated the UK's rigid top-down approach to the implementation of EC 2078/92, and the MAFF's attachment of relatively

---

[5] In formulating this national response, the Ministry also consulted with the then DoE and the government's statutory advisers English Nature, English Heritage, the then CC (now part of the Countryside Agency) and the then National Rivers Authority (now subsumed within the Environment Agency).

[6] The NSAs scheme was wound up in 1998, and replaced by a new designation, Nitrate Vulnerable Zones.

little importance to the subsidiarity element implicit within the Regulation (see Chapters 1, 3, and 9). Certainly, in the four territorial programmes submitted by the UK to the European Commission, there was little to indicate that the modalities of national agricultural policy-making had been changed by adoption of the Regulation, or, indeed, by the range and scope of NGO activities over the preceding decade.

However, subsequent events in England have painted a slightly more equivocal picture. In 1995, the White Paper *Rural England* (DoE/MAFF 1995) introduced a number of new deliberative forums for agri-environmental policy, designed 'to promote effective consultation on agri-environment schemes at both national and local level' (MAFF 1996: 7). These included a 'National Agri-Environment Forum', providing an arena for environmental NGOs and producer groups to contribute to the development of existing and new agri-environmental schemes; and nine 'Regional Agri-Environment Consultation Groups', one established in each of the MAFF's national administrative regions, to review the operation of local schemes, and to reflect local opinion and expertise in the policy process.

Secondly, the introduction by the DG Agri in 1996 of new administrative, monitoring, and control arrangements for EC 2078/92 under the 'Implementation' Regulation (CEC 1996) also tidied up some of the ambiguities of the original measure. Whether intentionally or not, the Implementation Regulation also greatly increased the potential for externality groups to act as 'whistle blowers' for the Commission on issues of policy infringement and 'implementation deficit' at national and subnational levels (Richardson 1996*b*).

Thirdly, the MAFF has rationalized the number of English agri-environmental measures, in an attempt to slim down the considerable financial costs and administrative burdens imposed by the proliferation of different schemes established since 1992 (HoC Agriculture Select Committee 1997). Gone are the much maligned Moorland and the rather inconsequential Habitat schemes, with their goals retained as options within an enlarged Countryside Stewardship programme, available to farmers across the country. Scheme rationalization has provided some simplification of national agri-environmental policy, but falls far short of addressing the demands of both producer and externality groups for a more integrated and unified mechanism of policy delivery (the so-called 'one-stop shop').

These events, and the policy changes they instituted, were complemented in 1999 by the assimilation of EC 2078/92 as the 'centrepiece' legislative measure (CEC 1999*b*: 1) of the RDR (CEC 1999*a*). The RDR has been the subject of far greater consultation by the MAFF within the agricultural policy sphere than the agri-environmental Regulation, prompted by the continuing political prominence of agri-environmental issues. Furthermore, in a preamble to its proposed framework for the English 'Rural Development Programme' under the RDR, the Ministry acknowledged: 'Th[is] framework builds on the fact that the greatest benefit is achieved where the approach to implementation is integrated rather than piecemeal[,] and is developed as far as possible by and with local interests rather than being imposed from the centre' (MAFF 2000: 2). The English 'Rural Development Programme' (which during the summer of 2000 was awaiting approval by the DG Agri), as it applies to agri-environmental policy, seeks to prioritize the use of the most appropriate policy instruments in the nine MAFF regions, on the basis of their economic, social, and environmental characteristics. The likely intention is also to complement and consolidate the work of Regional Agri-Environment Consultation Groups by ensuring greater local influence over the trajectory of local policies. The agri-environmental component of the RDR, therefore, could mark an important step change by the MAFF towards a less prescriptive approach to this policy.

These changes suggest there *is* flux in national modalities of agri-environmental policy-making, with the MAFF attempting to be more proactive in policy terms, by setting the agenda rather than being obliged continually to respond to it, as was the case in the 1980s. Implicitly, the MAFF has recognized the politics of collective consumption (Grant 1993*b*) surrounding the agricultural environment, and the failure of its traditional 'command and control' approach to policy-making to deal with this new reality. It is, however, still too early to assess the precise effects of environmentalization on the MAFF's departmental ethos and working culture, and whether these effects will be of an enduring or more transitory nature.

A closely related issue is the difficulty that UK environmental groups have experienced in building on their ground-breaking involvement in the environmentalization of agriculture. Militating against their greater involvement in agri-environmental policy-making (and, indeed, against the expansion of the policy itself) is the UK Treasury's reluctance to make additional national 'match' funding available, as a result of the 1984 Fontainebleau Agreement. This accord, struck between the Thatcher government and the EU, provides the Treasury with a rebate from the UK's budgetary contribution to the EU, by cutting the level of cofinancing available from the supranational level on EU policy measures implemented in the UK.[7] The rebate is calculated annually, with the amount depending upon spending by the national exchequer on 'match' funding of EU policy measures, deterring government departments, such as the MAFF, from developing ambitious EU programmes, as this would jeopardize interdepartmental relations with the Treasury.

Similarly, while new consultative arrangements were introduced in 1995, it could be argued that these mechanisms represent an attempt by the MAFF to 'steer' the environmentalization of UK agricultural policy, rather than being genuine efforts to embrace it. As the analysis in this chapter has shown, in the

---

[7] Under the terms of the Fontainebleau Agreement, EU cofinancing of agri-environmental schemes of 50% (offered in all territories that are not designated under any EU socio-structural policy 'Objective') is closer to 30% in the UK.

recent past the Ministry has proved itself quite adept at co-opting externality groups, such as the CPRE and the RSPB. Arguably, the National Agri-Environment Forum and the nine Regional Agri-Environment Consultation Groups are more sophisticated mechanisms for co-optation, enabling the MAFF to control the speed and direction of policy change by implicating directly these groups in the policy process, thereby making 'hegemonic' interpretations of agrarian beliefs more defensible. Certainly, the first five years of operation of these forums have not brought about a noticeably more environmentally sensitive UK agriculture.

However, the potential for further, deeper environmentalization of UK agriculture can be judged only by taking into account the revitalized political and administrative context of its four constituent countries. Through the WOAD and the SERAD respectively, the National Assembly and the Scottish Parliament have already begun to flex their muscles in terms of signalling new environmental approaches to agriculture. At the same time, in England, the introduction of Regional Development Agencies (RDAs) charged with 'the economic development of rural areas, [including] remoteness, [and] integrating town and country' (DETR 1998: 44) should create positive synergies with the less prescriptive policy structure introduced as part of the English Rural Development Programme. A major unresolved issue here is how the MAFF's Regional Service Centres will work with the RDAs in developing agricultural policy objectives attuned to regional needs. The fusion of the CC with the Rural Development Commission as the new Countryside Agency could also potentially benefit the scope for environmentalization of agriculture in the regions, by alloying the separate and historically successful extension efforts of these two organizations. Taken together, these factors augur well for the future development of a 'regionalized' agenda for UK agriculture that is more sensitive to locally specific environmental goals.

It would seem that, with the RDR's introduction, agri-environmentalism is spilling out of the MAFF's administrative domain, into the realm of territorial policy-making.[8] New political configurations and new forms of political engagement between the subnational, national, and supranational scales are likely to emerge in the twenty-first century, with their precise specification conditional on local territorial endowments, informal institutional identities, and local power coalitions. The era of stable and predictable agricultural policy-making appears to be drawing to a close. Nor is this process confined to the UK. In Chapters 8 and 9 we sketch out what some of these new local territorial modalities of political engagement in agri-environmental policy might be, with reference to France and Spain.

---

[8] This is evident from the proliferation of government policy initiatives targeting rural areas, including the creation in 1999 of the Cabinet Office 'Ministerial Group on Rural Affairs' to oversee the development of more integrated and coordinated delivery of rural policies by all government departments.

6.7. Conclusions

The national arena emerges as a tremendously important locus of decision-making and decision-taking within the EU polity. We have shown in this chapter that it is a highly dynamic activity space for mobilizing different actors, different territorial and sectoral identities, and different socio-cultural traditions and beliefs. In particular, we have sought to locate UK 'agrarian beliefs' in their proper political setting of the domestic agricultural policy community. Defined by a particular equilibrium of power relations between its constituent organizations, this policy community has been dominated during the post-war period by the MAFF.

We have argued that fundamental to post-war agricultural policy has been the dissemination by the MAFF and producer groups of 'hegemonic' interpretations of agrarian beliefs. These 'hegemonic interpretations' are fashioned to suit the MAFF's own organizational goals and ambitions. They are critically important as they serve to legitimize new policies to the farming community and the general public, by rationalizing them in terms of the established architecture of UK agricultural policy. By legitimizing policies in this way, these 'hegemonic' interpretations have also anchored in place the MAFF's bureaucratic responsibilities in the form of an extensive administrative domain (Benson 1975). This manipulation of agrarian beliefs by elites has sought to safeguard the Ministry's 'sectoral freedom' and the largely complementary 'territorial freedom' of the UK farming community, a process masked by the MAFF's output of 'legitimate' public policies. Hence agrarian beliefs have also underpinned the Agriculture Ministry's administrative culture, a key characteristic of 'mythic institutions' (Lowndes 1996).

Nonetheless, agrarian beliefs are also routinely contested by interests external to the core agricultural policy community, prompting their gradual redefinition. As we have shown, in exceptional circumstances these 'externality groups' (Jordan *et al.* 1994) have demonstrated major inconsistencies between underlying agrarian beliefs, and the agricultural policies they legitimize. In these situations, policies can be overturned, as evidenced by the withdrawal of UK agricultural production grants in 1983. Hence we argue that agrarian beliefs have provided a modality for agricultural policy formulation by dictating the range of policy instruments available to elites for addressing particular problems. In turn, policy formulation and implementation have redefined agrarian beliefs, shown here in the MAFF's incremental redefinition of the environmental responsibilities of the UK farmer since 1981.

Agrarian beliefs have thus provided the MAFF with a modality through which policy debate with a wide spectrum of externality groups has been kept within clearly prescribed parameters. While environmental NGOs have debated and contested 'hegemonic' agrarian beliefs, obliging the MAFF to substantiate its rhetorical claims by introducing policies supportive of 'environmental stewardship', in practice these policies have been most effective in furthering the ambitions of the UK agriculture departments and their affiliated producer groups.

Not surprisingly, the prospect of environmentalization of domestic agricultural policy has been perceived by the MAFF and UK NGOs in a radically different light. We have shown how this had determined their respective approaches to EU initiatives in the field of agri-environmental policy. The MAFF's stance has been one of studied caution and only partial engagement, with the Ministry seeking in 1985 a European 'solution' to the agri-environmental 'problem' for purely pragmatic political and financial reasons. Not the least of these was to restrain the influence of environmental NGOs on the domestic stage, so enabling environmentalization of the sector to occur more on terms of the Ministry's own choosing (that is, preserving sectoral and territorial 'freedoms'). However, the Ministry has also made use of the new modalities of agri-environmental policy-making offered at the EU level. For example, by cementing its relations with the RSPB in the 1990s, the MAFF accessed multi-level agri-environmental policy networks in Spain to suit its own organizational purposes.

By contrast, environmental NGOs such as the CPRE and the RSPB have capitalized on the 'multiple points of access' within the EU polity for altogether different reasons. Consistently throughout the 1980s and 1990s, these externality groups have sought to widen and deepen the domestic environmentalization agenda through pushing for European initiatives and legislation on the agricultural environment, culminating most recently in the RDR.

We have argued that the late 1990s witnessed further change in the external circumstances impinging on UK agriculture, including greater pressure for continued environmentalization of farm policy. In turn this has created flux in the national modalities of agri-environmental policy making. Since 1992, the MAFF has made efforts to be more proactive in policy terms, seeking to set the policy agenda rather than being obliged continually to respond to it, as was the case in the 1980s. The Ministry has done so by introducing new agri-environmental policy mechanisms, including the institutionalization of consultation arrangements for this policy. On balance, these would appear to constitute an attempt by the MAFF to retain some measure of control over the increasingly vocal calls for local representation in agricultural policy-making. However, we have suggested that, in trying to control the policy agenda in future, the MAFF's elites may face a much more difficult task than they have so far experienced. With the introduction of the RDR, environmentalization has become conflated with a wide range of rural issues to create an enlarged policy agenda for the UK territories. Effectively, policy-making has spilled out of the MAFF's and the other agriculture departments' exclusive domains, into the wider realm of territorial politics. Actors at a variety of politico-geographic scales—supranational, national, and subnational—are likely to become increasingly involved in these new forms of territorial policy-making.

In this chapter, we have examined the intersection between national and supranational modalities of policy-making. As a 'knowledgeable advocate' with prior national experience and expertise in the agri-environmental field, the UK enjoyed a privileged working relationship with the European Commission, and with other members of the Agriculture Council, in the formulation of EC 2078/92. Important corollaries flow from this analysis. How did this unique relationship compare with that enjoyed by other member states? And how did the DG Agri engineer policy consensus from among the diversity and polarity of positions around the Council table? We investigate these issues more fully in Chapter 7.

7

Concordance Systems, Multi-Level Governance, and the Negotiation of the Agri-Environmental Regulation in the EU's Council of Ministers

Despite its pivotal position in the institutional tapestry of the EU, the Council of Ministers remains a largely under-researched decision-taking forum. There are several reasons cited frequently for this, though paramount is the cloak of secrecy that has surrounded member state behaviour at this level of EU governance (Hayes-Renshaw and Wallace 1997). The Council of Ministers has come to embody a recurrent tension between supranationalist and inter-governmentalist views of the development of the EU, with the Council perceived as a block to the supranational ideas and ambitions of the European Commission, or as a forum for reconciling the distinctive goals and powers of the individual member states that make up the Union. The overall result of this academic jousting has been that writings on the Council are 'commonly full of lacunae, often contain[ing] errors about basic facts and lack[ing]nuance' (Hayes-Renshaw and Wallace 1997: 3). It is against this backcloth that we examine the negotiation of agri-environmental policy in the EU Agriculture Council.

From the MLG perspective, member states' executives, while powerful, are only one set among a variety of actors in the European polity (Rosamond 2000). Significantly, states do not monopolize the link between domestic politics and inter-governmental bargaining in the EU, nor do their actions and preferences alone fully explain the outcomes of supranational decision-making. Consequently, as we have shown in Chapter 1, MLG theorists posit a set of overarching, multi-level policy networks, whose operation results in a structure where political control is variable across policy areas (see Chapters 8 and 9; see also Marks et al. 1996). This undermining of nation state bias

(Eriksen and Fossum 2000) in conceptualizations of EU decision-making can be usefully explained through the analytical context of the EU's Council of Ministers. For inter-governamentalists, the Council of Ministers is the primary forum for bargaining between governments in the EU system, with national representatives there to articulate and defend their interests and to negotiate from this basis in a particular policy area. However, as Rosamond (2000: 6) explains, 'there is a lot going on besides. Ministers have to attend to the problems of coordinating their position with those of their colleagues . . . have to engage in calculus about the appropriate way to present significant policy outputs to domestic constituencies.' Moreover, 'Meetings of Councils are not without their institutional memories. Many Councils have evolved distinctive working practices and bargaining styles over time . . . the member state holding the Presidency of the Council has issues of agenda management and brokerage to contend with as well as the conventional representation of national preferences.' The multi-dimensionality of the Council's activities, and, not least, the significance of non-state actors such as the European Commission in setting the nature of Council business through its legislative proposals, have strengthened the opinion that processes of EU decision-making are best investigated through a broader theoretical lens that incorporates a variety of analytical concepts (Peterson 1995*a*). In this chapter, we suggest that new institutionalist perspectives offer a valuable means to unpack the modalities of Council activities in EU governance. To this end, we draw on the notion of concordance systems, which was first elaborated by Puchala (1972) and is widely regarded as in keeping with MLG perspectives on EU governance. Indeed, Puchala is credited with 'prefigur[ing] some of the themes of multi-level governance and new institutionalist approaches by the best part of two decades' (Rosamond 2000: 89). Our view is that concordance systems provide a valuable approach for understanding the behaviour of state and institutional actors in the governance forums of the EU's Council of Ministers. The Council is a good example of a 'concordance system', which is defined as: 'an international system wherein actors find it possible consistently to harmonize their interests, compromise their differences and reap mutual rewards from their interactions' (Puchala 1972: 277). There is thus an obvious congruence with recent MLG conceptualizations of the EU polity. For example, Meyer (1999: 635) notes: 'EU is a multi-level system of governance driven by negotiation and geared towards compromise among experts, civil servants and politicians.'

The concordance system, while according importance to the state, does not accredit it primacy. The system is based upon consensus, with conflict when it occurs, stemming from divergent views about ways to cooperate, rather than from fundamental incompatibilities in the interests of the various actors. As a result, what Puchala (1972: 280) calls 'primitive confrontation politics' seldom occur in the system; thus an atmosphere of high mutual sensitivity and responsiveness between actors prevails. By treating the Council as a concordance system, we can show how the Council 'locks' national ministers and their departmental officials into permanent discussion about their 'evolving cooperation and about a shared and enlarging policy agenda' (Hayes-Renshaw and Wallace 1997: 2).

7.1. Concordance Systems in EU Integration

Four key elements constitute concordance systems.These are: complexity of structure; novelty in process; actor bargaining; and attributes of atmosphere. The first of these has been the focus of much recent work in European governance (see Hix 1998, 1999), with several authors highlighting the constant deliberative and cooperative processes occurring between multiple levels of state and non-state actors (Mazey and Richardson 1993*b*; Peterson and Bomberg 1999). These processes are based upon and facilitated by what Puchala (1972: 279) termed 'organizational networks' (though what some writers have termed policy networks; see, e.g. Peterson 1995*a*; see also above, Chapter 1). These networks are conceived as arenas for the mediation of the interests of the state executives and interest groups. As Peterson (1995*b*: 391) maintains: 'The term 'network' implies that clusters of actors representing multiple organizations interact with one another and share information and resources. Mediation is suggestive of the network as providing a setting for the playing of positive sum games: they facilitate reconciliation, settlement or compromise between different interests which have a stake in outcomes in a particular policy sector.' For Puchala (1972: 279): 'conflict is regulated and cooperation facilitated via institutionalized . . . precedential or . . . standardized, patterned procedures which all actors commit themselves to use and repeat.' Therein lies the novelty of process.

Bargaining among actors in the concordance system is based upon exchanged concessions and ultimate compromises. Importantly, coercion and confrontation are not respected in the system, which is organized in a way that rewards participants for their cooperative behaviour and tends not to be respectful of rogue conduct. As Puchala (1972: 281) suggests: 'In short, there is no premium on secrecy and deception in the politics of the concordance system.'

The prevailing atmosphere in the concordance system is that of pragmatism. Actors regard the range of politico-economic problems as both real and resolvable. Such problems are dealt with by actors with due sensitivity to others' goals, objectives, preferences, and needs. Puchala (1972: 282) observes: 'it is precisely this atmosphere of shared compulsion to find mutually rewarding outcomes, this felt and shared legitimacy in concession making, and this reciprocal sensitivity to needs' that characterizes the atmosphere of the concordance system.

These assertions regarding the concordance system offer a number of important avenues for empirical investigation—a detailed analysis of its decision-making structure; the tactical and strategic dimensions of decision-making within it; and the illumination of the attitudinal environment within which this occurs. Significantly, such analyses should be able to shed light on the pragmatism, mutual sensitivity, perceived interdependence, and systemic legitimacy that are critical features of the behaviour of actors within the concordance system. In the context of Council negotiations over the agri-environmental Regulation, in this chapter we consider the modalities deployed by actors in association with these particular systemic attributes. In doing this we progress the views of Hayes-Renshaw and Wallace (1997: 18), who comment that:

The whole system [of the Council] depends on a crucial assumption that there is give and take between the positions of the Member States and that, whatever the starting positions of the members, there is both scope for those positions to evolve and a predisposition to find agreement. Thus atmospherics, mutual confidence and trust are important ingredients [of Council activities].

7.2. The EU's Council of Ministers as a Concordance System

As discussed in Chapter 1, MLG theorists have looked to institutionalist perspectives to assist their explanations of EU political processes. The compatibility of these perspectives with the MLG agenda is regarded as particularly close, as Rosamond (2000: 114–15) suggests: 'The EU, with its rich mixture of formal and informal institutions is often seen as an ideal testing ground for the various forms of institutional analysis', further adding 'that the fact that [EU] institutions may be defined as systems of norms gives the institutionalist a fairly wide remit'. Importantly, no single version of institutionalism can provide a comprehensive account of EU institutional behaviour. Explaining political processes in the EU's Council of Ministers is no exception to this.

Earlier discussion has highlighted the major distinctions within the institutionalist literature, and has particularly focused upon that between rational-choice institutionalism and historical institutionalism (Bulmer 1994). In short, the rational-choice school argues that institutional rules regulate the behaviour of actors in their rational pursuit of political gain, and as a result actors must quickly learn more accommodative norms and accept institutional values if they are to be successful in those institutions (Peters 1999). Historical institutionalism, on the other hand, argues that institutions cannot be considered as mere 'passive' arenas within which political action is played out. Rather, the arenas are embedded with particular 'beliefs, paradigms, codes, cultures and knowledge' (March and Olsen 1989: 26; Clark *et al.* 1997; Clark and Jones 1998; Jones and Clark 2000). As such, then, the institution can be interpreted as a 'carrier of history', imbuing its current members with views, beliefs, and ideas from earlier periods in the institution's political history.

Transposing these institutionalist perspectives to the context of the EU's Council of Ministers offers crucial interpretative opportunities. For example, Hayes-Renshaw and Wallace (1997: 275) maintain that 'in the recurrent bargaining that characterizes the Council many factors beyond concrete interests come into play; symbols count as well as substance; and values and norms often make an identifiable difference to what outcomes emerge'. Furthermore, they argue that analyses of the Council that are devoid of institutionalist considerations inevitably lead to false accounts of EU political process, contending:

We reject the notion that Council negotiations are exclusively interest based. The games played are about the nature of cooperation, as well as about specific policy decisions . . . Models of decision making that fail to take this wider context into account fail to characterize accurately the patterns of negotiation, overemphasize a constricted set of interest-based preferences and produce seriously distorted explanations of decision outcomes.   (Hayes-Renshaw and Wallace 1997: 278)

Below, we develop the notion of the Council as a concordance system through the lens of historical and rational-choice institutionalism. We treat the Council not as an inter-state body but rather, as Wessels (1991: 137) maintains, 'a body at the supranational level'—a critical distinction respected by several other writers (see Edwards 1996; Nugent 1999), and one that ensures that other important actors in EU MLG, such as the European Commission (see Chapter 3), are not excluded from analytical discussion of Council activities.

7.3. The Council's Structure and Agricultural Policy-Making

The EU's Agriculture Council is, in terms of the amount of legislative work it handles, one of the principal councils in EU governance. The Agriculture Council is reliant on a pyramid of preparatory committees, the most important of which is the Special Committee on Agriculture (SCA), a body comprising senior officials from the agriculture departments in each member state. Specialized working groups prepare the work of the SCA by discussing the technical aspects of Commission proposals, before passing the dossier up to the SCA for approval or further discussion (Wessels 1991; Grant 1997; Hayes-Renshaw and Wallace, 1997; Rometsch and Wessels 1997). In this respect, the Council's decision-making takes the form of a clearing system, with each stage of the committee process witnessing a filtering of decision-taking (van Schendelen 1996). As a consequence, almost three-quarters of Agriculture Council business is decided well before it reaches the negotiating table of the agriculture ministers. This point is summed up by a member of the SCA:

The process of Council decision making is a simple one for CAP measures, that is a proposal by the Commission, an opinion of the EP, and a decision by the Council by qualified majority. The job of the SCA is to narrow down the areas of disagreement and focus down the issues which would enable the Council to reach an agreement, so it's part of a hierarchy. Once you've got a Commission proposal, Council Working Group experts would chip away at the proposal, identify the common ground, identify the difficult areas, and the theory was that you would have these wise men on the SCA who faced with the result of this process . . . would tackle the real issues and narrow down the points yet further to a stage where the Agriculture Council had something which it could comprehend and do deals about . . . (SCA source, Jan. 2000)

The SCA and the Working Groups are chaired by a rotating Presidency among the member states of the EU, and are attended by senior officials from the European Commission's DG Agri. The Commission role is to articulate and defend its proposal, and it must exercise its judgement on what tactics are best deployed to secure its own strategic interests (see Chapter 3). The Commission can be made to withdraw its proposal only if there is unanimity among the member states in the Council. This Commission–Council relationship is clarified by a Council official:

The Commission's role through the negotiating process is to defend its proposition. Once they've made the proposal that's what they defend until they decide that something is going to provide an opportunity for an agreement which is acceptable to them. If the Commission isn't flexible enough except in those unusual situations where they've got unanimity against them . . . if the Commission isn't flexible about its proposal, you're not going to get agreement. So Commission flexibility is important. They'll be thinking of all sorts of other factors such as is it going to get any better if we stick out now and wait for whoever it might be in the Presidency. Their role through a long part of the process is a defensive role, and sometimes publicly an unhelpful role, and sometimes really an uncomfortable role to a Presidency. (Council source, Jan. 2000)

The SCA reports on Commission legislative proposals to the Agriculture Council, which also receives reports on their financial aspects from the Ambassadorial-ranked members of the Committee of Permanent Representatives (COREPER). Each member state maintains a Permanent Representation in Brussels whose role is to articulate her or his government's views on policy issues, gather intelligence on Commission thinking and negotiating positions, and report these back to the national capital. The Permanent Representation is crucial to the concordance system; its members are conscious of the need to reach agreement, and predisposed to seek compromise solutions that take the interests of other states into account. For one former UK Minister, the UK's Permanent Representation in Brussels was 'Totally Europhile. [Its] sole objective . . . [was] to "expedite business" [and in the process] . . . not make a fuss about anything, however monstrous' (A. Clark 1993: 138–9).

Contact between the Permanent Representations in Brussels is frequent and based upon mutual trust and understanding that 'facilitate the construction of coalitions and compromise solutions to common problems' (Hayes-Renshaw and Wallace 1997: 82). This *esprit de corps* between Brussels-based national representatives is confirmed by a British member of the SCA: 'One of the reasons [the representation is there] . . . at considerable expense to the tax payer . . . is to help develop contacts and oil the machinery of Brussels decision-making. For example, if the Head of the crops division in the Commission was a Dane, you didn't go to the Brit in the next office, you went to the Head of the Danish Permanent Representation' (SCA source, Jan. 2000; cf. above, Chapter 4).

Within the Agriculture Council, member governments have differing endowments of political weight. The largest states (France, Germany, the UK, and Italy) have been accorded the most votes, which may provide power to carry the argument, as is often the case for France and Germany, or the power to prevent agreement, a feature of UK behaviour (see Hayes-Renshaw and Wallace 1997). However, this is not to suggest that those states accorded fewer votes do not possess the ability to disrupt the dominant agendas of the larger states. Member states in the Agriculture Council, as Hayes-Renshaw and Wallace (1997: 187) make clear, 'look at most issues with an intense but narrow focus on their relevance, cost-benefit and impact for the individual Member State. They look at the concerns of other Member States primarily to assess the negotiability and sustainability of particular outcomes.' In this respect cooperative behaviour is the corollary of Council participation.

7.4. Institutionalist Explanations of the Council's Concordance System

Several scholars have advanced the merits of the historical institutionalist approach for the analysis of political and policy activity in EU MLG (Bulmer 1994, 1998; Pierson 1996). This approach regards institutions as intervening variables governing the wider context within which political actors operate. As Thelen and Steinmo (1992: 9) suggest: '[institutions] structure political situations and leave their own imprint on political outcomes.' For Rosamond (2000), the key aspect of this approach is that political actors are not perfectly knowledgeable about the full implications of their participatory actions in institutional venues. Of secondary importance is that institutions tend to lock into place and create path dependencies—that is, decisions taken at particular times while context specific, can shape the nature and content of political agendas over a longer period. As Rosamond (2000: 117) further explains: 'evolved norms of behaviour . . . persist beyond the short term occupancy [membership] of institutions by particular actors. In short, subsequent actors have to operate within these self-reproducing institutional scripts.' Consequently, institutions are to be perceived as 'normative vessels' embodying various beliefs, knowledge, understandings, values, and established ways of doing things. Institutional cultures are thus conceived as important factors in shaping the behaviour of political actors. As Peters (1999: 71) argues: 'the structural elements of an institution may establish conditions that make certain [policy] outcomes much more likely . . . [though] individual decision makers [must] translate those constraints into action.'

The Agriculture Council comprises several decision-taking forums, from the technical Working Groups to the SCA (and the COREPER), to the sessions of the agricultural ministers from each member state. Each decision-taking forum, within this concordance system, is founded upon bargaining and consensus-building; indeed, national actors participate on the critical assumption and long-established understanding that there is give and take between the positions of the member states. Council actors uphold the deeply etched Council values of membership, terms of participation and expected individual deportment. These institutionally embedded values and codes of conduct have a significant bearing upon actor behaviour and influence in the Council's arenas; in particular they make it difficult for Council participants to renege on their commitments to each other. Council actors are thus compelled to operate within institutional settings created in the formative years of the EU and whose *modus operandi* has largely remained unchanged. As a senior Council official explained: 'One thing that a lot of people have a deal of difficulty getting to grips with is that the significance of any bit of the Council depends upon not the powers or the abilities of the people who are there but what it has been set up to do normally by the Treaties' (Council source, Jan. 2000). The shared culture of participation, with actors holding a mutual commitment to the collective arena, has an important influence upon the atmospherics of the Council's concordance system. This is summed up by a senior Council delegate, with five years' active involvement in Council negotiations, who declared in interview:

There is a feeling of mutual trust in the Council. The Community is a well mannered institution . . . you don't tell blatant lies . . . you don't go back on what you've said . . . and once you've agreed to something that's, in general, 'pocketed' . . . you don't renege on that. So that trust and the concept of the *acquis* are the bits of glue that hold the Community together, and you would only go back on something that you'd agreed earlier at a personal considerable political cost. The people who are most regarded as the most effective in the SCA are the ones who can deliver their governments [that is can negotiate in the knowledge that their actions will be supported by their government] . . . if you say 'I believe that this thing is something my government can support', and it turns out to be true, then you fit into the atmosphere of the Committee better than those who hit the table a lot and ultimately can't do a deal. (Council source, Jan. 2000)

Whilst consensus and conciliation are the mainstays of the Council's concordance system, the means by which these are achieved varies between parts of the Council apparatus, and crucially depends upon the ways in which the architects of the EU designed the 'institutional scripts' for particular committee roles and activities. For example, the contrast between the COREPER and the SCA is marked in this respect, as a Council delegate explained:

You can see a clear contrast between the SCA and COREPER. In the SCA, what you're doing is identifying areas of disagreement so that you can focus the members of the

Council on the areas of disagreement and get them to thrash them out. In the COREPER you're trying all the time to dismiss the areas of disagreement and establish what the areas of agreement are. The mission of the COREPER is to avoid things coming to the Council, whereas the mission of the SCA is to recognize that things have got to go to Council and isolate the issues which the Council has to decide upon. They've both got something to say for them, they both can be very time-consuming, they can both be quite quick. The SCA method tends to produce more viable workable decisions with less inclination to fudge than the COREPER method.   (Council source, Jan. 2000)

Institutional roles within the Council develop in terms of a combination of these historically based treaty obligations and normative components of actor participation. For example, members of the Council's SCA see their role as protecting the core principles of the CAP from both endogenous and exogenous forces, as explained by a senior Council official in interview: 'in the SCA we act as guardians of the CAP—that is, guardians of the decision-making process of the CAP' (Council source, Jan. 2000). The picture is further complicated by the normative components of actor participation (Bulmer 1994). For example, the UK Agriculture Minister William Waldegrave, commenting in 1995 on this normative behaviour in the Agricultural Council, declared:

you will not persuade the Germans or the others that it is wicked to support Bavarian farmers or who ever because it cost money; they know that, believe that they can afford it, and are qute happy to go on doing it. And they cannot see why we have convinced ourselves that we are so poor that we cannot tolerate the support of our smaller farm sector at a lesser cost than many of them.   (Waldegrave 1995, cited in HoC 1999: 42)

Actor behaviour in Council is also a function of historically embedded national participatory styles, to the extent that even new Council delegates become locked into long-established patterns of national contributions to Council debates. As a Council delegate from the UK explained:

We have a style, the Brits characteristically have a style in Brussels, of having sorted out our position rather early and rather firmly, which is not always all that helpful. The Italian style is quite legalistic, often based on a careful analysis of texts but not upon practical effects of issues as they might hit those people who are affected, but often though bringing a lot to the party because they can often uncover legal problems which if they are not uncovered at that sort of level can cause an awful lot of difficulties later on. On the part of the French, always an ability to take some maximalist positions . . . to say that ten things are essential and not really to judge which of those ten is the sticking point before it comes clear what's available and what's not.   (MAFF source, Jan. 2000)

The application of rational-choice institutionalism (or actor-centred institutionalism (see Scharpf 1997)) to the concordance system of the Council leads to its conceptualization as a collection of rules and incentives that establish the conditions for what has been termed 'bounded rationality' (Ostrom 1990). Council arenas are therefore 'political spaces' within which interdependent political actors can function (Peters 1999). Such actors seek continually to maximize their personal utilities, though at the same time they recognize that their political options may be constrained by institutional rules, or by long-established and accepted codes of procedure and behaviour in the Council. Rational-choice institutionalist approaches to the Council directly focus upon the ways in which actors interact with the Council's treaty bases, rules, and operational procedures in order to create political preferences. Vitally for the integrity of the concordance system, this interaction requires actors to adopt accommodative positions and be respectful of the Council's institutional values. The system's actors accept this position in the knowledge that all actors in the Council are similarly faced with the same set of institutional constraints. The net outcome of this situation is that Council decision-making is seen to be both highly stable and essentially predictable in terms of the range of possible decisions available to Council members—the principle of collective rationality. Moreover, it enables actors to view decision-making in a pragmatic, standardized, and routinized fashion—the hallmarks of Puchala's concordance system (1972). The system's collective rationality is also sustained by the particular voting rules in the Council, with most areas of agricultural policy subject to QMV. Consensus is thus implicit in this voting procedure, and as a consequence what has been referred to as a 'structure-induced equilibrium' (Shepsle 1989) characterizes Council activities. Moreover, the system's operational procedures reward those actors who respect the Council's institutional values and penalizes those who do not. Council actors are, therefore, in calculative mode—that is, abiding with Council rules whilst concurrently searching for maximum benefits from their participation. Given the regularity of Council meetings, actors are engaged in positive sum games (Puchala 1972); as Peters (1999: 49) makes clear, '[since] members [of the Council] will participate in a number of decisions, they can make up for losses on one round in subsequent iterations of the "game" '.

7.5. Actor Strategies for Securing Maximum Benefits in the Council's Concordance System

Operating within the concordance system of the Council, we suggest that there are five key ways open to national actors to secure maximum benefits from their participation in Council decision-making. These have become familiar features of MLG in the EU and routinely part of the game plan of member state engagement with supranational decision-making. They are the modalities by which national delegates attempt to maximize benefits whilst working within the historically embedded rules and accepted codes of procedure and behaviour in the Council of Ministers.

7.5.1. Effective Briefing

Policy information is critical to member states in their Council dealings. There are a number of methods by which member states ensure a regular supply of information on policy and political developments in Brussels to assist them in the formulation of negotiating positions for Council. Of crucial importance is the Permanent Representation that each member state maintains in Brussels, which enables intelligence to be gathered on shifts in Commission thinking on particular policy proposals, other states' views on policy developments, and possible scope for concessions and deals between Council players. In conjunction with the stream of information reaching national capitals from the offices of the Permanent Representations, government departments keep a close eye on EU political business so that a national negotiating position can be constructed for the relevant official or minister in Council discussions. In the UK this negotiating position arises from inter-ministerial meetings coordinated by the Cabinet Office, as a MAFF official explained in interview:

The UK's highly developed system of preparation for Committee negotiation is run by the Cabinet Office . . . and this manifests itself in a fairly regular process on the weekly cycle that's followed by an SCA and the Agriculture Council . . . MAFF prepares formal written briefs for the SCA spokesman on the basis of the way in which the position is developing, on the basis of agreed Whitehall positions coordinated if necessary by the Cabinet Office, and often it doesn't have to be because of bilateral/trilateral discussion between interested departments, and often on the basis of advice from the spokesman about what's achievable and where we really ought to be going. I suspect the last of those elements is probably the most important, though other people might say different, but that's in addition to more or less continuous telephone contacts that are sorted out at a regular meeting on a Thursday before each meeting of the SCA or Agricultural Council. You have a brief which is set out in fairly formalized terms which tells you what the [Commission's] proposal's all about, what would be nice to have . . . it would be nice if they all said what would be nice to have, what you must avoid, what possible compromises might emerge, how you should cast your votes if a proposition looks likely to . . . Very often, this happens right across Whitehall, right across the major subjects you get a guide to what you should say to defend the UK's ideal position, which is great except *that's not what you're supposed to do* . . . that's not what the job is and you therefore have to make it up as you go along in a sense. One of the justifications of having a relatively senior bod as your spokesman is that you're in a position to make judgements when there's a gap between what you've been told to say and what it is it seems likely you're going to get is acceptable.   (MAFF source, Jan. 2000; emphasis added)

This official's comments reflect clearly the need for Council delegates to seek compromise solutions based upon their own judgements of what will be acceptable both to their own national administrations and to those of other delegates. In this way, the concordance system has a distinctive working practice. Council delegates can, therefore, find themselves severely hindered by briefings that restrict their ability to harmonize their interests with delegates from other member states. This subscription to the tenets of the concordance system is explained by another MAFF official:

The combination of the Permanent Representation's input and the preparation that my colleague was talking about left us in a better position than most of our partners to get what we wanted out of a discussion. We never found ourselves voting symbolically against things. However, I think sometimes though our domestic arrangements risked boxing us in and sometimes we employed a bit of energy to ensuring that you're not left with an utterly indefensible position.   (MAFF source, Jan. 2000)

According to Hayes-Renshaw and Wallace (1997: 213): 'By the time [Commission] texts are being negotiated in Brussels . . . each member state normally aims to have a well-defined national position.' Often, however, this is not the case, since, in practice, the prevailing political situation or arrangements for decision-making in member states can militate against early formalization of negotiating positions for Council meetings. In Germany, for example, the constitutional requirement for the Bund to consult with the Federal States (*Länder*) over EU policy-making creates a diffuseness in the German negotiating position for Council. As Hayes-Renshaw and Wallace (1997: 231) emphasize, this makes it 'difficult for its partners to predict what the German position will be on any given point and diminishes the utility of advance negotiations with German officials'. This has been significant for Council decision-making, as a Council delegate explained: 'the fact that the Germans come to their internal decisions about the positions they're going to adopt quite late is an important factor in the way in which a discussion will go . . . another member state from time to time might find themselves in that position too . . . you could find yourself in negotiations without knowing what your negotiating position is' (Council source, Jan. 2000). Compromise settlements readily flow from such Council situations.

Many national delegates regularly find themselves less well briefed than their peers in Council meetings, often because of limited personnel resources in domestic ministries and the increased workload associated with EU Council activities. As a senior MAFF official declared:

Many delegations were systematically less well briefed than us [the UK], though whether it made much difference so long as they know what they want. The delegations which appeared to be shortest on resources, I think you'd say, were the Greeks, the Belgians, Luxemburgers of course, but shortage of resources sort of shades into lack of agility, which could hit the Nordics from time to time and could hit the Germans on occasion, but everybody on various occasions is caught out by knowing less than their 'oppos'. I suppose the French were those caught out the least often, because they put a lot of resources into that area [agriculture], which is very important to them.   (MAFF source, Jan. 2000)

When delegates find themselves 'out briefed' in Council discussions, the consequences are less serious than they may at first sight appear. The Council stage of decision-making is not about 'primitive confrontation' (Puchala 1972) but about how a national delegate intends to cast his or her votes. As a Council negotiator explained:

it doesn't move so quickly that you can't get on to the people back home and say 'look this isn't going to fly . . . the following is' and surprisingly often people don't recognize that you're not there to argue, you're there to . . . you're not there to convince the other side . . . which you never will . . . *I can't think of a single occasion where argument has changed anything* . . . you're there to indicate what is the price of the vote. Certainly in the past remarkable amounts of energy had been expended in Whitehall on trying to think of clever ways to convince people it was a good idea for them to be hanged in the morning . . . you never will. The effective brief is the one by making clear how you will sell your votes gets you the maximum amount of what you want.   (Council source, Jan. 2000; emphasis added)

7.5.2. Forceful Intervention

Council actors have different endowments of political weight in EU governance. However, in addition to the numerical weightings accorded to member states, implicit 'qualitative' weightings are recognized by, and for, delegates in certain EU policy areas. Most obvious, in the context of the Agriculture Council, are France and Germany's pivotal positions (Grant 1997; Guyomarch *et al.* 1998). Indeed, the Franco-German axis in European agricultural policy has been a central aspect of EU governance. Interventions by delegates in Council debates are a function not only of their absolute weightings but also of these more 'qualitative' endowments. Spanish interventions in Council discussions over Mediterranean agricultural issues provide a germane example of this point. These 'qualitative' aspects of delegates' participation, and the sensitivity that others show in respect to them in the Council's concordance system, must not be viewed as separate to the absolute weightings accorded to delegations. Moreover, while delegates may be able to articulate these 'qualitative' powers convincingly over particular policy issues in Council, it is important not to underestimate the significance of the absolute weightings. As a senior Council negotiator candidly explained: 'What matters most in the Community is how you are going to deploy your votes, and the idiot with ten votes is going to have more influence in the way in which the thing runs than Einstein with two votes' (Council source, Jan. 2000). However, this is not to suggest that the Council is not consensual in its operation. The dynamic of the Council is a pragmatic search for consensus achievement. This is confirmed by a Council delegate:

There is scope for a well-timed, well-thought-through pointful intervention to make a difference but that doesn't happen every week. Mostly, what people are on the look-out for are not blinding flashes of inspiration but indications of where the *concessions* are going to be made and where the agreements are going to come. Delegates' priority in Council is to get their points across, make it clear to the other delegates what the member state is searching for, what *concessions* from other delegates will need to be offered to bring the delegation on side.   (Council source, Jan. 2000; emphasis added)

As another Council official explained: 'if you don't get your points across no matter how heartfelt they are, they are likely to be forgotten' (Council source, Jan. 2000).

The effectiveness of interventions by Council delegates can also be a function of language. As a British delegate explained:

French being a simple well-ordered language makes it easier for them to get their points across than happens in Greek or Finnish and that's a simple matter of the language which can give a particular negotiating advantage . . . it also obviously gives you the advantage that you can get your points across and the nature of the French language makes it easier for them to do that than it does for other member states to do it. (MAFF source, Jan. 2000)

7.5.3. Deals with Other Council Members

Essential to the concordance system is bargaining, reciprocity, and consensus achievement (Holland 1994). Coalition-building is a critical element in Council decision-making, as Hayes-Renshaw and Wallace (1997: 251) make clear: 'Coalitions may be recurrent or ad hoc, strategic or tactical, issue-specific or widely based, predictable or unpredictable. The longer established a negotiating forum is the more likely that coalitions will take on some repetitive characteristics and in turn become an embedded feature of the forum.' Between some member states there may well be long-standing arrangements not to impede, frustrate, or negate one another's activities (Wright 1996); the Franco-German relationship provides a good example of this (Morgan and Bray 1986). Contacts between member states can take place in a number of ways, a variety of settings, and at various stages of the EU decision-making process, reflecting the modalities of EU governance. Bilateral discussions between member states are a feature not only of the policy-shaping stage, when Commission legislative proposals are being formulated, but also of the policy-setting stage, when the Council's Working Groups, COREPER/SCA, and national ministers are engaged in debate about them. At this stage the purpose of bilateral discussion is to identify both common ground and major areas of disagreement, and to explore possible ways of resolution through inter-state compromise. The ability to reach compromise on these occasions is determined by the scope for flexibility on the part of each member state, which may reflect electoral issues, sectoral concerns, parliamentary cycles, and public unease over EU activity. Flexibility, as we have seen, may be restricted when a member state has reached a negotiating position for Council at a relatively early stage, and then finds itself unable to be more accommodating and receptive to coalition-building (Wright 1996). On the other hand, flexibility may be increased when there is scope for issue linkage, side payments, and package deals. Whilst these features have been highlighted by a number of EU scholars, their importance should not be overestimated in the concordance system, as a Council negotiator explained:

Issue linkage is not important. Very occasionally you will get direct links established between two sets of issues, often unrelated ones. I can't remember all that many during my 4½ years there where two delegations would say 'well all right I'll give you that on x you give me that on y'. It did happen very infrequently and that's one of the misconceptions about how business is done. In the Agriculture Council you're building up a kind of portfolio of outcomes which will enable you to go back home and say 'overall the outcome here is all right', so these aren't based on specific linkages; it's based upon a recognition that all delegations have got a list of things they say they've got to have ... they've got to be given most of those ... enough of those to deploy their votes in a way that leads to a necessary majority being reached and enables the Commission to sign up to it. So the concept of the 'horse-trade' isn't that important [in Council decision-making].   (Council source, Jan. 2000)

Coalition-building is often regarded as unpredictable, time-consuming, and occasionally unhelpful to member states in their quest for maximum benefits from their participation in Council sessions. Pragmatically, the priority of Council negotiators is to articulate a domestically coordinated position and achieve their negotiating objectives. Analyses of Council decision-making do, however, reveal recurrent behavioural stances of individual member states or collections of member states. For example, collectively the Mediterranean delegations in Council frequently request increased EU budgetary allocations to sign up to particular Commission proposals, while other member states, such as the UK, adopt more austere fiscal positions. As a MAFF official explained: 'We (the UK) were always looking to cut the cost of everything ... our votes were always on the conservative side of the spectrum ... [while] the net [budgetary] beneficiaries were always looking for ways of increasing spending on things that would benefit them' (MAFF source, Jan. 2000).

Achieving compromise in Council is not restricted to highly formalized sessions. Informality is also an essential part of the fabric of the concordance system. This is summed up by a Council delegate: 'Sitting around a table is not normally the situation in which you do detailed negotiating business. You have to stop the discussion and disappear into a corner with someone to sort that out. What sitting around the table is useful for is demonstrating publicly where there is flexibility' (Council source, Jan. 2000). The recurrent nature of Council discussions increases the incentive for Council delegates to cooperate and socialize, and as a consequence establish productive working relations. As one Council delegate explained:

if you spend a bit of money on lunch you might well have found yourself understanding each other a bit better and be able to calculate more easily what you needed to do in order to participate in something which was acceptable to you and acceptable to him or her ... quite often what will happen is a delegation might say 'I've got a real problem about this, I insist on having that ...' and you will say 'I'm happy with this but that would be utterly unacceptable' ... You talk to them and you discover you can meet both your needs by having that instead. So that's really important in understanding of positions ...   (Council source, Jan. 2000)

As another delegate confirmed: 'Talking to people outside the Council meeting is very important mostly in order to ensure that you've been clear and to demonstrate that their concerns are met by what you've said' (Council source, Jan. 2000)

7.5.4. Occupancy of the Presidency of the Council

Council of Ministers' meetings are normally convened by the country holding the Presidency—a position that rotates between the member states on a six-monthly basis. The Council Presidency involves several main tasks, including the chairing of all Council meetings (including those of COREPER/SCA and Working Groups); launching and building consensus for initiatives; ensuring continuity and consistency of policy development; and representing the Council in dealings with outside bodies (De Bassompierre 1988; Nugent 1999). These responsibilities bestow tremendous control and opportunities for the Presidency over the agendas of meetings and their outcome. Within limits, the Council Presidency offers a member state a platform to make its own mark on the nature and speed of EU integration. For new EU member states it is an opportunity to demonstrate not only political capability and efficiency but also regard for the EU integration process. For other member states, occupancy of the Council Presidency may provide scope for correcting what it may consider as undesirable integrationist agendas, for setting out ambitious programmes, or for promoting a particular 'vision' of Europe. Indisputedly, the Presidency offers a clear opportunity for a member state to imprint a particular style on the Council. Undoubtedly, each Presidency has a particular style. For example, the Italian Presidency has been likened to 'a bus trip with the Marx brothers in the driving seat, [while] the Luxembourg Presidency has all the signs of being driven by a sedate couple who only take to the road on Sundays and then infuriate other motorists by respecting the speed limit' (*The European*, 28–30 Dec. 1990, quoted in Edwards 1996).

While the Presidency has grown in significance throughout the history of the EU (see Edwards 1996), there are important constraints upon individual Presidencies, and these include greater use of rolling programmes between Presidencies (formalized in the 'Troika' system of policy programme coordination between the current, previous, and prospective Council Presidencies (see Hayes-Renshaw and Wallace 1997), unforeseen politico-economic events that disrupt Presidency work programmes, the administrative burden of the Council Presidency, which may restrict the political ambitions of the smaller office-holders, and the dependency of the Presidency upon a flow of Commission legislative proposals. This latter issue is raised by a former negotiator in the SCA, who claimed that:

Although the role of Presidency is crucial it's not primordial. You can't do anything as a Presidency unless, going back to the Treaty, you've got a proposal from the Commission and an opinion from the EP. It doesn't matter what might have been the ambitions of the Presidency they have got to depend upon the material they've got available to reach conclusions on . . . Many Presidencies come unstuck, when I say come unstuck . . . many Presidencies have ambitions which if you listen to their rhetoric would suggest they were going to change the world by sheer effort and will, and at the end of their six months because you didn't have any proposals to work on there was no agreement in the process.   (SCA source, Jan. 2000)

For the last British Presidency of the Council, the decision to go for an ambitious agricultural package was largely dictated by the strength of the legislative proposals from the Commission in this sector, and the realisation by MAFF officials that they were sufficiently advanced to be agreed upon in Council. Commenting on the Council–Commission relationship in the EU MLG, a senior MAFF official stated: 'We knew when we started that we'd be getting a very important proposal from the Commission on bananas, a very important proposal on olive oil, an important proposal on tobacco and a series of other important proposals . . . the Commission proposals were good and they identified pretty well where the ultimate agreement was going to emerge' (MAFF source, Jan. 2000). In this way the UK Presidency acted as the facilitator of the Council's concordance system.

Making a Presidency successful is also about investing resources in the search for compromise between member states in Council over Commission proposals—a key feature of the concordance system. As a Council member explained: 'A lot of energy has to go into the timetabling of discussion . . . you've got to go through the bureaucratic hoops . . . to collect in opinions, to have time to float out possible compromises, to have sorted out possible compromises with the Commission' (Council source, Jan. 2000). The President has to negotiate, persuade, manœuvre, cajole, mediate, and bargain with, and between, the member states and with the Commission (Nugent 1999). The key goal is to reach agreement so that a majority can sign up to a proposal but not by sacrificing the Presidency's own preferences nor by alienating the Commission. As a former President of the SCA declared:

If (as a President) you've got a vague feeling that [say] the Greeks have got a concern, but you're not quite sure what it is, you try and construct your majority elsewhere . . . The Presidency role all the time is to try and 'smoke out' an individual delegation in terms of what they think is really important to them and in terms of what they might be prepared to sign up to.   (SCA source, Jan. 2000)

7.5.5. Synchronizing the National Position with that of the European Commission

Member states invest tremendous efforts in ensuring the Commission's proposals take due consideration of their political preferences. It is in the interest of the Commission to deliver proposals to the Council, and in the Council's interest to have Commission proposals that accord with the Council's own views (Rometsch and Wessels 1997)—a mutual dependence between the two institutions, which is fundamental to the concordance system. As we saw in Chapter 3, the Commission holds bilateral discussions with member states before launching a proposal, and this provides an opportunity for both parties to identify areas of agreement and disagreement. Within Council, the Commission is mindful of the concerns of member states, though its major purpose is to muster resources in defence of its legislative proposal. As a Council negotiator confirmed:

The Commission's role throughout the negotiating process is to defend its proposition. Once they've made the proposal that's what they defend until they decide that something is going to provide an opportunity for an agreement [between member states] which is acceptable to them. If the Commission isn't flexible enough about its proposal, then if you've only got a majority for the proposal no matter how powerful, you're not going to get agreement . . . [The Commission's] role through a long part of the process is a defensive role, and sometimes publicly an unhelpful role, and sometimes really an uncomfortable role to a Presidency. (Council source, Jan. 2000)

Some member states may benefit from this Commission inflexibility. The Commission, for example, may prefer on occasions to be less flexible in the knowledge that political agreement is best stalled in order to serve more usefully its own strategic agendas in particular policy fields. For example, the Austrian government took over the EU Presidency from the UK in the late 1990s, only to find that in the agricultural sector the Commission was demonstrating a reluctance to pursue compromise, as the then UK Council delegate explained: 'The Austrians got pretty fed up with the Commission following our Presidency where they were starting to launch discussion on the Agenda 2000 dossier . . . but the Commission didn't show any manœuvre at all . . . Sensibly they knew that the final agreement was going to be a great package and it was going to come under the German Presidency . . . why bother to . . .' (Council source, Jan. 2000). This example not only demonstrates the complexity of the concordance system but also how member states' ambitions can be hindered by other institutional actors in the MLG of the EU.

7.6. Negotiating Agri-Environmental Policy in the Concordance System of the Council

In this section we examine the functioning of the concordance system and, in particular, the ways in which the above modalities of actor participation fashioned the negotiation of the agri-environmental Regulation. Concessions and compromise are intrinsic to the concordance system of the Council of Ministers, reflected in a shared compulsion among Council delegates and the European Commission to find mutually rewarding outcomes from successive rounds of negotiations in Council decision-making forums. As we saw in Chapter 2, at the turn of the 1990s pressures upon the Commission, and the

DG Agri in particular, to embark upon a major overhaul of the CAP were immense, as budgetary excesses and growing member state disagreements over levels and impacts of farm support coincided with renewed international anger over EU agricultural policy. Politically, the Commission was fully aware that member states would not be supportive of any reform proposals that would antagonize sectoral constituencies. In this troubled context, the Commission regarded agri-environmental policy as a convenient political instrument by which the alienation of the European farm community as a result of market reform could be limited (see Chapters 2 and 3). As a proposed 'accompanying measure' to the CAP reform package, agri-environmental policy not only offered the Commission a timely vehicle for harnessing the growing pressures for a more transparent environmentally friendly agricultural policy in the EU and as a sweetener to the bitter pill of price cuts, but also a means to transfer budgetary resources to the poorer southern states of the Union. Tactically, therefore, agri-environmental policy was perceived by the Commission as both multi-intentional and multi-dimensional.

With a view to easing the passage of its agri-environmental proposal through Council, the Commission's DG Agri worked closely with three member states—the UK, Germany, and the Netherlands—countries with practical experience of, and keen political interest in the agriculture–environment relation. For the Commission, they represented not only a source of political and practical reference for its proposal, but also a clutch of potential supporters in Council discussions. However, these states held very different views and interpretations of agri-environmental policy and its aims. The Dutch, for example, were in favour of a regulatory rather than a voluntary agri-environmental policy and pressed the Commission to introduce stringent taxation measures for polluters, as well as an EU-wide code of good agricultural practice on which any payments to farmers should be based. The Commission knew, however, that this would be unacceptable, not only to the UK, with which it was consulting, but, importantly, to the majority of the Union's membership. For the Commission, too, the Dutch plan would be administratively costly and bureaucratically complex. Despite Dutch protestations throughout the Council's working group discussions and meetings of the SCA, as well as a memorandum on this issue to the President of the Council, the Commission refused to alter its position on the matter, preferring to work towards a Council outcome that would enable the Dutch to implement the Regulation in line with their own national priorities and rationale for agri-environmental policy.

The German position was based on the view that only those farmers who were to practise farming methods to a higher standard than set out in existing codes of good agricultural practice should benefit from agri-environmental funds (a view also supported by the Danish delegation). The Commission, in its own defence, argued (CoEC 1991*b*) that any measure included in the aid scheme should have 'beneficial consequences for the environment' and in this respect therefore the policy 'caters for the introduction and maintenance of farming practices compatible with the environment'. This compromise statement appears to have placated the German and Danish delegations.

The UK delegation was, as we saw in Chapter 6, eager to see a 'decent' agri-environmental Regulation agreed in Council. This 'decency' encapsulated conservative spending plans, limited Commission interference in policy implementation, and provided an opportunity to enhance through the policy the dominant tradition of stewardship in UK agrarian beliefs. Several of these underlying goals were in line with the Commission's perspective for the policy, albeit for different reasons. For example, while the UK delegation was keen to stem the tide of what it perceived to be Brussels meddling, the Commission was fully aware that it did not possess sufficient administrative resources to interfere in the implementation of the policy in member states. Pragmatically, a ringing endorsement of the concept of subsidiarity satisfied both camps.

The French position on the Commission's proposal was somewhat muted. There is no doubt that the French Permanent Delegation in Brussels had intimated to the Commission early on its likely displeasure with any agri-environmental Regulation that would impinge upon the nation's export-oriented farm sector. This concern appears to have found a great deal of resonance with the Commission, who throughout labelled the proposal as an 'accompanying measure' to market reform. The French delegation argued consistently in Council meetings that market reforms to the cereals and livestock sectors would result in a disincentive to farmers to produce, with knock-on positive environmental benefits. Agri-environmental policy should, therefore, be firmly associated with farm income adjustment rather than with promoting environmentally friendly farming *per se*. The Commission's proposal therefore refrained from policy precision in environmental outcomes, so adding to the mist of ambiguity surrounding the policy and ensuring the French delegation stayed 'on-side' (see Chapters 8 and 9).

The Commission's 'own goal' in earlier experience of formulating agri-environmental policy (see Chapter 3) by neglecting the interests of the Union's Mediterranean constituents was, by and large, not repeated in its new proposal. The Commission's wordsmiths had ensured that the text of the proposal enabled Mediterranean delegates to articulate broader rural development issues in Council discussions over agri-environmental policy. The Spanish delegation took up this role, seemingly from Council minutes, on behalf of the other southern delegates. Rural decline, marginality, and small-farm predominance thus feature heavily in Spanish interventions in Council debates. For the Commission, tempering the 'northern bias' of the proposal and acknowledging the concerns of the Mediterranean delegations, without signing away large budgetary amounts, appear to have been the principal tactics in Council debates.

After the Commission's proposal had been through the technical mill of the Agricultural Structures Group (ASG), it was the turn of the political scrutineers of the member states to discuss it at the SCA. The SCA met on two occasions (25 November and 2–4 December 1991) in order to narrow down the points of disagreement for the agricultural ministers in the Council. The SCA, in its report to the Agricultural Council (10061/91, 6 December 1991), focused upon three elements: the nature and range of the agri-environmental proposal; its financial aspects; and specific questions by national delegations. The document produced by the SCA sets out the parameters by which the Agricultural Council could reach agreement.

The agri-environmental Regulation was packaged as one with multiple objectives, in order to secure the agreement of member states, as the SCA document reports: 'à renforcer les buts principaux poursuivis par la réforme, à savoir, l'équilibre des marchés, la stabilité des revenus des agriculteurs et le respect des équilibres naturels et environnementaux'. This wording, through its ambiguity, enabled delegations to support the principle of agri-environmental policy, whatever their particular attitudes, beliefs, and conceptions of the environment, and agriculture's place within it. As an SCA official explained: 'You need ambiguity, if that is where you get agreement. Very often ambiguity is part of the requirement to get something agreed . . . in the process of EU decision-making you quite often get things which are deliberately ambiguous so that there are two possible ways of reading it, and it is read in the way in which each side want to read it' (SCA source, Jan. 2000).

The Commission had also been able to convince most delegations that the measure, once adopted by Council, should become obligatory on member states to implement, though voluntary for farmers. The German delegation preferred the measure to be optional, while the UK delegation required the Commission to be more precise over the degree of flexibility that member states would enjoy in the implementation of the policy. The Greek delegation was also worried that implementation of a rigid proposal from the Commission would be difficult in the Greek context—a point the Greeks had raised at earlier stages in Council discussions. To avoid the proposal falling at this hurdle, the SCA document includes a statement from the Commission suggesting that it would leave to member states 'la flexibilité nécessaire pour permettre la meilleure adaptation des mesures proposées aux réalités nationales et régionales', though the Commission preferred not to outline any precise parameters for the policy's implementation. The Irish delegation, somewhat rightly confused by this, sought clarification on whether an entire country could be a 'zone' for policy implementation. The Commission response was that 'zones should be defined according to their environmental problems, which may be regional'. For the UK delegate there was an obvious solution: four zones—England, Wales, Scotland, and Northern Ireland. All this was yet further evidence of the Commission's reluctance to formalize a precise agri-environmental Regulation, and for the Agriculture Council a clear signal of the Commission's flexibility in this regard.

Flexibility over financial matters was, however, an altogether more contentious issue. The Commission adopted a stubborn and inflexible position on funding of the agri-environmental proposal, despite some of the Council's key players ranged against it. With the support of the UK, Irish, and Mediterranean delegates, the Commission refused to budge on its position that the proposal as an 'accompanying measure' to CAP market reform should be funded from the Guarantee Fund, with 50 per cent of policy costs paid, and the remainder falling on the shoulders of national administrations. In terms of the qualified majority procedure 54 out of a total of 76 votes for the twelve member states would be required. The Commission could call on 41 votes in support of its financial proposition (UK, Italy, Spain, Ireland, Greece, and Portugal) with 35 against (Germany, France, Netherlands, Denmark, Belgium, and Luxembourg—all of whom were in favour of the measure being funded from the Guidance Fund of the EU's agricultural budget). To ensure that the Mediterranean group were kept 'on-side', the Commission agreed that, in the Union's poorest regions (Objective 1 Status), 75 per cent of the policy's cost would be met from the Guarantee Fund. The Spanish delegation sought 100 per cent funding for the policy, a request immediately turned down by the Commission under pressure from the financially austere UK delegation. The deadlock over funding was mirrored in the COREPER meeting, though the Commission official present repeated the agreed line. It fell to the Portuguese Presidency to broker an agreement between the two factions in the Council, knowing that the Commission was not prepared to agree to the Guidance Fund being used for this policy measure. The Franco-German alliance was perceived as the key to resolving the dispute, and a round of formal and informal discussions was held with Council delegates from both countries by the Council President. As was shown in Chapter 5, the German Farm Minister Ignaz Kiechle was able to persuade his French counterpart into accepting Commission intransigence over this issue, and therefore paved the away for its political settlement in the Agriculture Council.

7.7. Conclusions

In this chapter we have developed the MLG conceptualization through the treatment of the EU's Council of Ministers as a concordance system. Intrinsic to the concordance system is a shared compulsion among Council delegates to cooperate and respond to efforts to mediate between their policy preferences. National delegates are sensitive to the historically embedded values and norms associated with the operation of the Council, and equally respectful of the rules and procedures surrounding their participation in its decision-taking activities. The structure for decision-making in the Council facilitates this concordance, with lower-order Committee work enabling more important political decisions to be taken higher up the Council hierarchy. This process facilitates the brokerage of compromise in the concordance system of the Council.

While this chapter has emphasized the key role played by member states in explaining policy outcomes in the EU polity, we share the views of Wincott (1995), Garrett and Tsebelis (1996), and Pollack (1996), who argue that it is not just the preferences of member states that have to be factored in to these explanations. As Rosamond (2000: 144) claims: 'the preferences of [EU] institutions . . . [also] figure as an important variable influencing the style and substance of intergovernmental bargaining.' In the case of the agri-environmental Regulation, we have shown how the interactions between the preferences of the DG Agri and those of the member states were a major factor in explaining the precise configuration and content of the agri-environmental Regulation. The DG Agri was not a marginal player in the Council's activities, as intergovernmentalist interpretations would suggest (see Moravcsik 1998). Rather, it was a crucial actor for member states in their search to establish advantageous negotiating and secure their political preferences. Moreover, the DG Agri was instrumental in structuring the differences in choice between the member states in Council. As Rosamond (2000: 143) suggests, 'the exploitation of these differences between Member States provide[s] the Commission with a definite opportunity for entrepreneurial supranational activity' (see Chapter 3).

Explanations of EU policy-making do not end with discussions of the Council. Multi-scalar policy-making is distinguished by the links between supranational arenas and those operating at the national and subnational scales. The interfacing and intersection of these political scales have a profoundly significant role in the outcome of supranationally negotiated policy. While national delegates may offer concessions in the Council's concordance system, they may do so in the knowledge that the implementation of policy in national and subnational arenas may be deliberately obstructionist. This may enable the scale of concessions to be 'clawed back' or hitherto undisclosed preferences to be factored into EU policy implementation. Moreover, the subnational scale presents a range of possibilities for local elites to 'unstitch' EU Council agreements as different administrative structures, cultural histories, and socio-economic pathways sap the energy of supranational policy at the local level. We address these vital features of MLG in the next two chapters, using case studies of the implementation of the agri-environmental Regulation in Castilla la Mancha in Spain, and Languedoc-Roussillon in France.

8

Theorizing Policy Implementation in a Multi-Level Governance System

Previous chapters have identified the modalities of policy-making used by EU actors and institutions to configure the agri-environmental Regulation. Here, we outline a theoretical framework for analysing the Regulation's implementation in the EU–15. This framework is founded on our belief that an understanding of the activities of EU actors and institutions during policy-shaping and policy-setting is essential if one is to grasp how EC 2078/92 has been implemented in the different member states. In particular, the contradictory viewpoints expressed in Agriculture Council discussions on EC 2078/92—and the petitioning of EU institutions by territorial and sectoral interests over the Regulation's goals—made its content more ambiguous, and allowed conflicting interpretations of its aims to become established. Both characteristics have greatly influenced implementation patterns in the EU–15, creating a situation where deliberation among territorial constituencies and administrative elites over agri-environmental policy aims is the norm, rather than the exception. We argue that the result is a bargained, iterative form of EU agri-environmental policy-making that has determined the 'implementation outcomes' (Matland 1995) of EC 2078/92 across the EU.

Outwardly, it would appear that Agriculture Council delegates were the architects of EC 2078/92's parameters of operation. As argued in Chapter 3, the European Commission drafted its agri-environmental proposals around the beliefs and conceptions of the environment, and agriculture's place within it, in the EU of (then) twelve member states, while also striving to uphold the norms of the CAP (see Chapter 2). Moreover, bargains were struck between national delegations and compromises made by them over the Regulation's content to ease its passage through Council, thereby justifying this institution's reputation as a 'concordance system' (see Chapter 7). However, the European Commission also sought to use EC 2078/92 to expedite the difficult CAP reform negotiations; ease the chronic overproduction problems endemic in the CAP common market organizations; and standardize environmental norms in agriculture with Article 130R of the Single European Act (see Chapter 2). As Chapters 3 and 7 prove, therefore, both member state delegations *and* EU institutions exercised a powerful influence on EC 2078/92, and were adept at exploiting 'policy routeways' within MLG to bring about their favoured outcomes.

But our contention here is that *other* actors within the EU MLG also shaped the implementation parameters of the agri-environmental Regulation. This chapter's analysis develops the notion that, within an MLG system, there are complex webs of interrelation and high levels of interaction between elites involved in policy-making, with these relational modalities linking together activities across politico-geographic scales (subnational through to supranational). These elite activities, and the scalar regimes they work within, are therefore not so much distinct and nested one within the other as interleaved and interactive.[1] In effect, the evolving EU governance structure is 'permeable' to its constituent policy communities, situated at different politico-geographic scales. Hence Mendrinou's comment (1996: 6): 'European policy formation . . . involves transgovernmental and transnational negotiations . . . at various levels between EU institutions, national administrations and interest groups.' Potentially, this interleaved form of governance allows not only for resource exchange (for example, flows of knowledges, experiences, and capital), but also for a high degree of deliberation and articulation of policy issues among actor constituencies. Liefferink and Skou-Andersen (1998: 255), for example, describe 'a continuous interrelation and exchange between policy making processes at [supranational, national, and subnational] levels'.

Consequently, what emerges is a *bargained, iterative form of EU agri-environmental policy-making* (see also Grande 1996; Benz and Eberlein 1999). In the context of EC 2078/92, this was demonstrated by the need for supranational institutions, especially the DG Agri of the European Commission, to *legitimize* EC 2078/92 during its formulation stages to a much larger and more diverse policy community than would have been the case for a national legislative instrument. Not only did the Commission have to convince the then twelve Council delegations of the merits of the proposal. Other actors and decision-making forums, situated at different politico-geographic scales, also had to be won over. These included individual MEPs, environmental NGOs, and the Praesidium of *COPA*, representing a vociferous territorially based agricultural lobby that, at one stage, threatened to derail the 1992 CAP reforms altogether (see Chapters 4 and 5).

---

[1] The characteristics of the EU's 'interleaved' governance include: greater informality in the policy process than that typically found in national arenas; an heterarchical, rather than an hierarchical, relationship among policy actors, with high levels of interaction among them; and *active* attempts by supranational institutions to reconcile actor negotiating agendas where these conflict (see Puchala 1975; Mazey and Richardson 1993; Pedlar and van Schendelen 1994; Peterson 1995*b*; Grande 1996; Nugent 1999).

The deliberative nature of EU MLG policy-making also guaranteed a *much more protracted policy process* (COM (90) 366 → COM (91) 415 final → EC 2078/92 → member state programmes → STAR → policy programmes in territorial arenas . . .) than that which would have arisen had this measure been defined within a sovereign state. Inevitably, this increased the political compromises to be made over the intent of EC 2078/92, and resulted in textual modification and reinterpretation of its content. This compromise process was accelerated by the array of supranational, national, and local actors pushing for development of the Regulation at different times, in different decision-making arenas, and often with entirely dissimilar negotiating agendas (see Chapters 3, 4, 5, 6, and 7).

Another important consequence of MLG for policy-making on EC 2078/92 was its interdependence with the recent *politico-administrative restructuring of the nation state*. According to Rhodes (1997), this restructuring process has gathered pace since the mid-1980s in response to globalizing processes of socio-economic change, and has had profound consequences for statehood in Europe. These include the 'hollowing-out' of traditional nation state activities and responsibilities, involving the 'loss of [national politico-administrative] functions upwards to the European Union, downwards to special purpose bodies and outwards to agencies' (Rhodes 1997: 17). This has contributed to the evolution of *sector-specific multi-level policy networks* (Rhodes 1986, 1992), comprising highly interdependent supranational, national, and local policy actors among whom knowledge and resources are exchanged, thereby increasing connectivity between different geographic scales. As we show in Chapter 9, these evolving networks have played a crucial role in the 'bargained implementation' of EC 2078/92 in France and Spain.

The effect of this 'iterative' policy-making made the final text of the agri-environmental Regulation ambiguous in meaning; opaque in its policy goals; and virtually silent in terms of establishing the precise mechanisms for achieving these goals. We argue, therefore, that the main results for EC 2078/92 of multi-levelled policy-making were greater *policy ambiguity*, and an increased potential for *policy conflict*[2] among its target groups, arising from differing interpretations of its equivocal goals. These two characteristics were introduced during the early stages of the policy cycle, and *as a direct consequence of the Regulation's formulation within an MLG system*.

Taken together, these points suggest that a theoretical framework for analysing implementation of EC 2078/92 needs to be sensitive to at least three issues. First, it must be robust enough to inform analyses of agri-environmental policy in the diverse socio-cultural contexts of the EU–15, yet be sensitive to these differences. Secondly, the traditional distinction made by implementation theorists between 'policy formulation' and 'policy implementation' appears

---

[2] As Hooghe and Keating (1994: 372) comment of EU regional policy: 'As the policy developed, more actors were brought into the [policy-making] process. This broadened its potential support base *but at the cost of increased conflict over objectives and control*' (emphasis added).

tenuous when applied to this Regulation (a similar argument has been made for other items of EU legislation (see Rhodes 1997; Jordan 1999)). Chiefly, this arises because of the characteristics of 'bargained' policy-making we have described: the interleaved EU governance form, which encouraged active participation by a wide range of actors; the length of time over which 'bargained' policy-making was transacted; the range and degree of involvement of national decision-making forums in this process; and the importance accorded these national forums under Article 3 of the Regulation, which prescribed the development of 'zonal programmes' for implementing agri-environmental policies in member states (see Chapter 1). Formulation and implementation are also commingled because of the inherently 'evolutionary' approach of EU policy-making, which relies heavily on the consolidation and refinement of previously implemented measures in promulgating new instruments. EC 2078/92 provides the archetype of this evolutionary approach (see Chapter 2), and has itself been subsumed in the RDR as part of the Agenda 2000 reforms. In the context of EU agri-environmental policy-making, it is thus more appropriate to view the supposedly discrete categories of formulation and implementation as fused in a single continuum of interrelated processes.

Thirdly, the analytical framework must be sensitive to the multiple goals of the Regulation. The 'success' or 'failure' of particular national, regional, or local agri-environmental programmes is not easily demonstrable, as precise aims and objectives were not set down in EC 2078/92's legislative text,[3] much less stated explicitly in subsequent enabling legislation enacted by member states. The clearest indication given by the Agriculture Council of its intended purpose is in Article 1 of the Regulation, which cites the following highly ambiguous goals: '[to] accompany the changes introduced under the [1992 MacSharry] market organisation rules; [to] contribute to the achievement of the Community's policy objectives regarding agriculture and the environment; [and to] contribute to providing an appropriate income for farmers' (CEC 1992: Article 1). Over the last ten years, the great majority of member states' agri-environmental programmes and projects have adopted a similarly equivocal approach, often providing few definitive economic, environmental, or ecological targets for agricultural constituencies.[4] Even where more precise goals have been established, sensitive environmental land management will need to be continued for extended periods before any final assessment can be made of the degree of scheme 'success' or 'failure' (CEC 1998b: 62, 125). Moreover, maintaining land under this form of management for decades is

[3] The explanation for this lies in the multi-actor participation in the EU's concordance system (see Chapter 7), particularly the Council. In these forums, policy measures with precise rather than ambiguous goals, and with singular rather than multiple objectives, would not command sufficient support from delegates.

[4] Commenting on this point in its preliminary evaluation of EU agri-environmental schemes, the European Commission noted (CEC 1998b: 128): 'Objective setting is vital. Precise and measurable objectives are needed. There is considerable room for improvement in many [national] programmes on this point.'

likely to be fraught with administrative, financial, social, and technical diffi-culties (Whitby and Lowe 1994).

So, in the short term at least, it may be misplaced to devise a framework for assessing the relative 'success' or 'failure' of zonal programmes established under EC 2078/92 on the basis of environmental or other outcomes. Rather than trying in this way to appraise the type and quality of policy *outcome*, it is perhaps more profitable to examine the modalities of policy-making *processes* that have arisen around the agri-environmental Regulation in different mem-ber states, and to determine to what extent these processes are shaping differ-ent implementation patterns. EC 2078/92 has, in effect, etched out a new domain of EU multi-level policy-making. Its immediate impact is thus more likely to be felt as an symbolic instrument initiating social, policy, and actor-based learning and change in the EU–15 than as a policy measure achieving particular socio-economic and environmental goals. As Wallace (1984: 141–2) comments on other EU policies: ' "Success" often lies in the gradual and often painful learning process through which national practices and attitudes are marginally adjusted to take account of . . . [EU] influence . . .'.

In the light of these requirements, in the following section we analyse critically the extensive literature on policy implementation, with the aim of developing a robust theoretical framework for the examination of the multi-level policy-making processes in the EU–15 arising from EC 2078/92.

8.1. The Implementation Literature and EU Multi-Level Policy-Making

There is an extensive literature on policy implementation, specifying a range of methodologies and analytical approaches. Generally, these approaches are distinguished by the different emphases each places on actor and/or structure within the policy implementation process. Three 'schools' of implementation studies have been identified on this basis: 'top down', 'bottom up', and what we term here 'composite' schools. Until recently, relatively little work had engaged with the complexities of implementation within MLG systems (see e.g. Conzelmann 1995; Mendrinou 1996; Bache 1999; Benz and Eberlein 1999), although there are many studies of policy implementation in broadly analogous governance structures—for example, federal and quasi-federal states (e.g. at the federal state level of the USA (see Pressman and Wildavsky 1973); the national and autonomous community level in Spain (Aguilar-Fernández 1994)). Some of these studies conducted in federal states constitute the bedrock of theorizing in this subdiscipline (see e.g. Pressman and Wildavsky 1973; Mazmanian and Sabatier 1981, 1983). Briefly, the defining characteristics of the three main schools are as follows.

The 'top-down' school sees the role played by overarching policy structures (for example, administrators, implementing legislation, and implementing organizations) as paramount to explaining implementation 'success' or 'failure' (Gunn 1978; Bryner 1981; Browne and Wildavsky 1984). Typically, 'top-down' research has included translation of the goals, aims, and objectives of implementing legislation into tangible outcomes (McLanahan 1980); the activities of organizations and institutions responsible for the actioning of policy (Rawson 1981); and the control exercised by administrative elites over the implementation process (Van Meter and Van Horn 1975; Elmore 1985).

As the longest-established of the three schools of implementation studies, this approach has been extensively critiqued. The main criticisms include that by taking the implementing legislation as the starting point of analysis, the 'top-down' approach fails to consider the significance of actions taken earlier in the policy formulation process (Winter 1985, 1986). Secondly, that such analyses attempt to depoliticize the implementation process, by focusing upon bureaucratic procedures and processes (Berman 1978). Thirdly, that, by emphasizing the role of 'statute framers' in implementation, researchers ignore the role of key policy actors at the local level (Elmore 1978, 1985). Finally, while the 'top-down' model has been used in a number of seminal implementation studies in the USA, Wallace (1984: 131) comments of its appropriateness for the analysis of EU policies: 'Powers [within the EU MLG] are horizontally and unevenly dispersed amongst the participants and thus a "top-down" strategy of implementation is hardly an option . . . The rules of the international game are . . . [to] some extent . . . conditional, leaving individual [member states] in practice the opportunity to opt out of implementing agreements which are unpalatable, irksome or practically difficult.' Coupled with the importance this approach attaches to determining policy 'success' and 'failure', these critiques limit the use of a 'top-down' methodology and analytical approach to examine the multi-levelled processes underlying policy implementation of EC 2078/92.[5]

The 'bottom-up' school of implementation studies was developed in response to the perceived shortcomings of the 'top-down' approach. Its rationale is that a realistic appraisal of the policy implementation process can be derived only from analysis of the activities of locally based organizations directly responsible for policy delivery, and the actions of those sectoral/ societal groups targeted by policies (Hjern and Porter 1981; Hjern 1982). In response, critics of 'bottom-up' approaches note that, very often, local policy actors directly involved in policy delivery are bureaucrats or administrators with no democratic mandate. While, therefore, they are almost certainly better acquainted with local contextual environments than centralized administrative elites, often they do not have the delegated powers to make significant changes to local policy structures (Sabatier 1986). A related criticism of the

---

[5] Researchers using different theoretical perspectives on European integration (notably intergovernmentalism, discussed in Chapter 1) would no doubt object; nonetheless, 'Most scholars now agree that the EU is best described as a loosely integrated multi-level system of governance characterized by fragmentation and complexity' (Benz and Eberlein 1999: 331).

'bottom-up' school is that the approach attributes more autonomy to the local level over policy decisions than might actually exist—for example, over financial or other resources. From the perspective of examining critically implementation of EC 2078/92 within MLG, the 'bottom-up' approach, therefore, also appears restricted and inflexible.

Latterly a third suite of methodological/analytical approaches has arisen, which is less well defined and coherent than either of the more formalized 'top-down' and 'bottom-up' approaches. There are few shared characteristics among these 'composite' approaches, although arguably all have attempted to examine policy-making 'in the round' rather than to analyse formulation and implementation stages as static, mutually exclusive categories. Hence, for example, they seek to 'show the policy making and implementation process as continuous, multilevel, and multifunctional rather than discrete, sequential and differentiated' (Hyman *et al.* 1991: 311). Such a position is fully consonant with our informing statist concept of MLG, which applies this pluralist perspective to the distribution of powers and competencies among subnational, national, and supranational actors.

Partly, 'composite' approaches have arisen in response to growing interest in transnational implementation studies, including greater awareness of an 'implementation deficit' (Mayntz 1980) between policy aims and outcomes. Researchers in the subfield of European integration have given this phenomenon much attention (Siedentopf and Ziller 1988; Mendrinou 1996; Knill and Lenschow 1998; Jordan 1999). Another characteristic of some 'composite' approaches is that, in shaping policy, influence and informal competencies within society are accorded a similar degree of importance as the possession of formalized governmental powers. Once again, these capabilities are depicted as being more evenly dispersed across state and societal groups than either classical 'top-down' or 'bottom-up' conceptions acknowledge (Sabatier and Pelkey 1987; Sabatier 1988).

A wide range of methodological and analytical techniques have been used by 'composite' researchers, which perhaps explains their increasing use in the analysis of MLG policies. These include the study over extended time periods of 'advocacy coalitions' of policy actors involved in implementation, situated within policy networks and identified by their articulation of specific beliefs and attitudes towards particular policies (see Sabatier 1986, 1988, 1991, 1998; for a study of EU steel policy using this approach, see Dudley and Richardson 1999). In the field of European integration studies especially, greater emphasis has been placed on the concept of networks to explain and clarify the profoundly social processes underpinning policy implementation (see e.g. O'Toole 1997; Rhodes 1997). Different networking conceptions drawn from the disciplines of anthropology (Callon 1986), organizational studies (Hjern 1982; Goggin *et al.* 1990), and political science (Heclo 1978; Wilks and Wright 1987; Marsh and Rhodes 1992) have been used for this purpose.

Other 'composite' analytical approaches seek to integrate constituent elements of the 'top-down' and 'bottom-up' schools to create new explanatory theories (in the US context, see Alexander 1985; Hyman and Miller 1986). By synthesizing 'top-down' and 'bottom-up' approaches (or moving away from the dichotomy altogether), the 'composite' school has instilled a new dynamism in implementation studies, advancing debate from justifying the success of particular methodologies and the identification of more variables, to bringing greater organization and coherence to the existing corpus of implementation research (e.g. Winter 1990; Matland 1995).

While 'composite' approaches have not been without criticism, we contend that they permit a more nuanced analysis to be made of the peculiarities of EU policy-making. For example, as discussed above, the high connectivity among certain policy actors within the EU MLG means many are involved in both the formulation *and* the implementation stages of policy, blurring the distinction between these two traditional elements of the policy cycle. The emergent field of European integration has begun to grapple with the consequences of this merging of policy stage and process (for an early account, see Wallace 1984), and we build upon recent research findings later in the chapter.

The case of EC 2078/92 illustrates very well the blurring of 'pre-agreement' and 'post-agreement' policy-making stages. Formal ratification by the Agriculture Council obliged member states to draw up 'zonal programmes', which on completion were referred back to the European Commission for scrutiny by its STAR Committee. STAR itself comprises representatives from the member states. Indeed, some individuals working on EC 2078/92 as part of Council delegations found themselves reassigned to STAR as the national representative for their countries, so placing them in the position of overseeing the approval of national programmes they had themselves contributed to formulating. For EC 2078/92, 'formulators' effectively oversaw 'implementation'. Given this iterative policy process between politico-administrative scales, and the resulting high level of interconnectivity between national and EU elites, it is difficult to define precisely when 'formulation' of EC 2078/92 ceased, and when 'implementation' began (cf. Rhodes 1997: 141).

This feature lends support to the use of a 'composite' theoretical framework, which can overcome the rigid distinction between formulation and implementation by permitting a more holistic examination of the interconnections between all stages of EU policy-making. Logically, it also suggests that the most profitable way to develop this framework is to base it broadly around the same theoretical approaches employed to examine formulation—namely, new institutional approaches and policy networks, set within a concept of statehood based upon MLG (see Chapter 1).

New institutional approaches can provide powerful insights into what we describe here as the *formulation/implementation continuum* of EC 2078/92 across the EU–15. The use of this suite of theoretical approaches is supported by the negotiating stances of policy actors (including Council delegations) on

EC 2078/92, which were often far removed from the physical needs of agricultural environments in member states (see Chapters 6 and 7). As Chapter 7 demonstrates, in their discussions on EC 2078/92, national delegations were motivated largely by issues of administrative expediency, financial considerations, and how the Regulation might be implemented with the least possible disruption to institutions and elite structures in national and local settings. These 'institutions' not only included relevant national/regional organizations with responsibility for agricultural and/or environmental policies. Equally important was ensuring that widely accepted attitudes and cultural beliefs were respected. These included national and local conceptions of 'environment', local agricultural production histories, and domestic regulatory regimes. As the preceding chapters have shown, all weighed heavily with national administrations in their formulation of goals for EC 2078/92 (see Chapters 2, 3, 6, and 7).

However, the selection of new institutional approaches needs to be informed by a coherent theoretical framework, attuned both to the deliberative EU policy-making process and to the different socio-cultural contexts of member states. Importantly, certain 'composite' theories can inform the selection of different institutional approaches in precisely this way, being highly compatible with new institutional and policy network analyses. Informing new institutional and policy network analyses through 'composite' implementation theory potentially provides a robust means for the evaluation of EU agri-environmental policy-making. For these reasons, we consider one such 'composite' approach, that advanced by Robert Matland, in more detail.

8.2. Matland's Ambiguity–Conflict Matrix

Matland (1995: 146) notes that 'A literature [implementation studies] with three hundred critical variables doesn't need more variables: it needs *structure*' (emphasis in original). Hence he proposes an organizing framework to inform the selection of methodological and analytical approaches used in implementation studies, with the aim of making these studies more consistent internally, more analytically rigorous, and more sensitive to specific policy contexts. Matland's organizing framework is based upon close scrutiny of implementation, organizational, and public administration literatures to identify two 'factors described as being crucial to the implementation process [of all policies. These factors are] a policy's ambiguity and conflict level' (Matland 1995: 145). As Chapters 2, 3, 5, and 6 have shown, these are also definitive features of the agri-environmental Regulation. For this reason we contend that Matland's framework, the 'ambiguity–conflict matrix', deserves closer examination. Crucially it provides a plausible theoretical linkage between the concept of state (MLG) used in this book by *informing* this analytically (in particular by placing emphasis on the role of deliberative processes in shaping the post-agreement phases of EU policy-making), while *contextualizing* the use of new institutionalist and policy network approaches within this statist concept. We adduce six reasons in support of this contention.

First, the framework's themes of conflict and ambiguity are logical consequences of the bargained and deliberative policy-making enacted within the MLG system. These dynamic themes enable analysis of policy-making at different geographic scales (supranational, national, local) and at different stages of the policy-making process (policy-shaping, policy-setting, and post-agreement) to be related to one another thematically, and to be interlinked analytically. Secondly, ambiguity and conflict are also at the heart of new institutional and policy network analyses, offering a high degree of compatibility between MLG and these approaches. Thirdly, by identifying and specifying certain 'central principles' (Matland 1995: 160) within the ambiguity–conflict matrix, Matland obviates the need for researchers to 'follow hunches' or 'intuition' by providing them with an objective scientific focus for study. Fourthly, as these 'central principles' provide strong thematic linkages for policy-making analyses across the interleaved levels of the EU MLG, they also enable the contribution made by constitutive politico-geographic scales within this polity to be emphasized. Importantly this facilitates an holistic, rather than a stratified or reductionist, examination of MLG policy-making. Fifthly, Matland sees implementation as a catalyst for social and policy learning. By recognizing that implementation might lead to a range of outcomes *other* than those intended by statute-makers, Matland (1995) advances the rather moribund portrayal of implementation as a matter simply of achieving certain specified 'goals', and hence of policies 'succeeding' or 'failing'. Furthermore, the diversity of actor constituencies within MLG means that the opportunities for this sort of social and policy learning arising from implementation are multiplied many times. Sixthly, Matland's framework specifies four implementation outcomes, which are sufficiently robust to reflect the different political, institutional, and socio-cultural mores of the EU–15. For these reasons, we believe Matland's organizing matrix provides an appropriate, powerful means for informing a new institutionalist analysis of EU agri-environmental policy implementation.

Matland identifies two ways in which policies can be ambiguous: *ambiguity of goals* and *ambiguity of means*. Some implementation theorists believe *ambiguity of goals* can lead to policy 'failure', by causing misunderstanding and uncertainty over its objectives (see e.g. Altenstetter and Bjorkman 1976). In the context of the EU MLG, it is clear there are trade-offs during policy-shaping and policy-setting between making policy goals explicit and retaining some degree of ambiguity over precise objectives. Matland notes that the more explicit policy goals are made, the more 'existing actors bec[o]me aware of threats to their turf and act . . . to limit the scope and range of [the] proposed policy [in order] to maintain [their own] existing patterns of bureaucratic power' (Matland 1995: 158). By contrast, 'legislative compromises [during policy-shaping and policy-setting] depend on language sufficiently ambiguous that diverse actors [for example, Council delegations] can interpret the same act in different ways' (Matland 1995: 158).

We have already shown that, within the EU MLG, *goal ambiguity* is highly prized to facilitate the passage of proposals and draft legislation through the multi-tiered decision-making process (see Chapters 3 and 7). Lewis (1984: 210, 217), in writing about the policy process more generally, comments: 'political language . . . functions . . . to mobilize, motivate and build coalitions, and generality, ambiguity and symbolic content are essential for those tasks . . . the initial statement of innovatory policies is likely to require ambiguity and symbolism.' On account of the sheer numbers and diversity of policy actors involved, the EU MLG has come to rely heavily on the subtleties provided by ambiguous legislative texts (Jordan 1999). Certainly, as we have seen in Chapters 3 and 7, EC 2078/92 was characterized by the ambiguity of its goals, and the opacity of its objectives. This ambiguity was heightened by the notion of subsidiarity implicit in the Regulation's 'zonal programmes' (see Chapter 1), allowing member states to implement EC 2078/92 in line with the specific requirements of agricultural landscapes, but also, and arguably more importantly, to ensure minimal disruption of administrative traditions, embedded cultural beliefs, and rural elite structures.

According to Matland, *ambiguity of policy means* is manifested in many ways, not least as a result of goal ambiguity. Essentially, it occurs when clear-cut procedures and mechanisms for achieving policy goals are not set out within the catechism of a policy measure. This form of ambiguity is common to much EU legislation—for example, many EU Directives permit member states considerable latitude in the means for achieving particular policy goals. It is also a feature of EC Regulation 2078/92, where 'zonal programmes' are defined on the basis of national, regional, or local criteria, as deemed appropriate by member state administrations (CEC 1992; see also above, Chapter 1). Moreover, Matland (1995: 158) notes that 'Policy means are . . . ambiguous when there are uncertainties about what roles various organizations are to play in the implementation process', a situation pertaining in virtually all of the EU when EC 2078/92 was introduced.

Policy conflict over the agri-environmental Regulation would not appear likely, given its highly ambiguous nature, and its essentially facilitative purpose in securing agreement on the rest of the 1992 CAP reforms. One of the main purposes of setting ambiguous policy goals is, after all, to diffuse conflict among policy stakeholders. Certainly, *overt* conflict during the policy-shaping and policy-setting stages was confined largely to disagreement in the Council over north and south European interpretations of environmental issues (see Chapter 7). Nonetheless, Matland (1995: 156) comments that policy conflict often arises during the implementation phase, when 'more than one organization sees a policy as directly relevant to its interests and when the[se] organizations have incongruous views. Such differences can arise regarding either the professed goal of a policy or the programmatic activities that are planned to carry out a policy.'

Similarly, Lewis (1984: 211) reflects:

where ambiguities and discrepancies do cause problems of course is at the implementation stage. The implementation of the compromise policy has to satisfy all the conflicting [supranational, national, and subnational] interests, and they in turn are expected to fulfil the commitments they made in the process of bargaining which led to the statement of the policy . . . It seems almost inevitable that some of those concerned will end up . . . discontented.

Undoubtedly conflict among organizations involved in the implementation of EC 2078/92 took place in some EU member states, often arising from disunity and lack of coordination caused by their being situated at different geographic scales. This was particularly the case in certain Spanish and French regions, as we show in Chapter 9.

Matland uses the two variables of ambiguity and conflict to construct a matrix, identifying four cells representing different generic *implementation outcomes*. For each implementation outcome, the matrix also identifies what Matland (1995: 160) describes as 'the central principle'—that is 'the factor expected to have the greatest influence on the implementation outcome' (see Figure 8.1). Matland labels the four categories *administrative, experimental, political*, and *symbolic* implementation outcomes respectively. In the next section, we identify the characteristics attributed by Matland to these four policy categories, and the 'central principle' associated with each. We also suggest particular new institutional approaches that are most suited to their analysis. We then proceed to classify EC 2078/92 using the matrix.

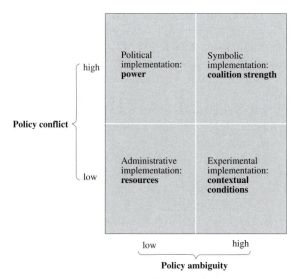

Figure 8.1. Matland's ambiguity-conflict matrix

8.3. 'Implementation Outcomes' and New Institutional Approaches

8.3.1. Administrative Implementation

Implementation outcomes classified under this heading have low levels of ambiguity and conflict. 'Goals are given and a technology (means) for solving the existing problem is known' (Matland 1995: 160). The most important consideration for implementing authorities and agencies is, therefore, to secure adequate policy resources. Indeed, 'outcomes are determined by resources . . . The paradigm invoked is Weberian bureaucrats[,] loyally carrying out their appointed duties' (Matland 1995: 160). Implicitly, this is almost a structuralist account of implementation, with actors perceiving policy objectives as legitimate, and beyond question. Problems that arise during the 'implementation continuum' are, therefore, confined largely to ensuring policy delivery mechanisms function correctly, and that resources are delivered expeditiously and in sufficient quantity. Matland insists that this is not to suggest that implementation of administrative policies is problem-free. Rather, problems tend to be technical in nature, or to arise as a result of failure of communication along what can be extended multi-level 'coordination chains' (Wright 1996: 149). Hence, in analysing the implementation of policies of this type, Matland's recommendation is for researchers to focus on resource constraint issues, using an approach akin to a 'top-down' methodology. From a new institutional perspective, the most appropriate explanatory framework would appear to be heavily structuralist—for example, 'reflectivist' institutionalism (Hix 1998).

8.3.2. Experimental Implementation

These policies are classified as having high policy ambiguity and low levels of policy conflict. Consequently, 'the central principle driving this type of implementation [is] contextual conditions . . . Policies where both goals and means are unclear naturally fall into the category of experimental implementation' (Matland 1995: 165–6). The outcomes of experimental implementation therefore come to depend very much on the micro-implementing environment, with local definitions of problems, solutions, and opportunities combining to create implementation outcomes that are very difficult to predict. Matland (1995: 167) notes that 'implementing policies of this type can be technology-forcing and can lead to the development of entirely new capabilities . . . On the other hand, ambiguous policies can breed limited accountability and can lead to the creation of mini-fiefdoms with leaders pursuing their own interests. These may have little, if any, connection to the public interest'. Matland concludes that, for examining the implementation of experimental policies, analysts should concentrate on local contextual conditions and a methodology analogous to a 'bottom-up', rather than a 'top-down', prescription. As the policies involved are almost always new, 'More important than a successful outcome is one that produces learning . . . Ambiguity should be seen as an opportunity to learn both new means and new goals' (Matland 1995: 167). Often, the precise aims and objectives of an experimental policy will rely less on the stated goals than on which regional and local level actors are involved in the implementation continuum in the 'early stages . . . at the microlevel[, what positions they took and] what resources they had at their disposal' (Matland 1995: 168). A synthesis of rational-choice and historical institutionalism, focused upon local contexts and actors, and informed by the activities of relevant actors at other scales, would appear to be the most suitable analytical approach for examining experimental implementation outcomes.

8.3.3. Political Implementation

Matland's third policy category, characterized by unambiguous goals and high levels of conflict, is political implementation. While policy goals are clearly defined, agreement among key actors over these goals—and how these goals should be achieved—becomes deeply problematic. Matland (1995: 163–4) notes that in such situations 'implementation outcomes are determined by power . . . successful implementation depends on either having sufficient power to force one's will on the other participants or having sufficient resources to be able to bargain an agreement on means. [Typically] coercive and remunerative [bargaining] mechanisms will predominate. However, implementing authorities may still face determined resistance from client groups who do not share their goals, even where bargaining and sanction mechanisms are comparatively well developed. Matland commends power analysis, and a methodology akin to the 'top-down' approach, for analysing political implementation. The description of political implementation emphasizes the actions of individuals working within particular implementation structures to maximize their own policy goals. This is most suggestive of a rational-choice institutional approach for analytical purposes.

8.3.4. Symbolic Implementation

Symbolic implementation outcomes arise when policy goals are highly ambiguous, resulting, perhaps surprisingly, in high levels of policy conflict. According to Matland, this occurs most frequently when 'policies . . . invoke highly salient symbols', including socio-cultural symbols, norms, or beliefs that hold deep resonances with particular groups of policy actors. Typically these symbols are deployed by policy formulators either to confirm new policy missions, or to reaffirm a commitment to old goals or principles. While policy goals may be unclear, Matland (1995: 169) notes that often 'the symbols [invoked] are sufficient to create significant opposition before any [implementation] plans are promulgated'. When symbolic implementation outcomes arise, it is local coalition strength that inevitably dictates the policy outcome. 'The policy course is determined by the coalition of actors at the local level . . . coalition strength at the local level [is] of central importance in determining . . . outcome[s]' (Matland 1995: 168).

Conflict occurs because 'differing perspectives will develop [among actors] as to how to translate the abstract [policy] goal into instrumental actions. The inherent ambiguity [of the policy] leads to a proliferation of interpretations. Competition ensues over the correct "vision". Actors see their interests tied to specific policy definitions, and therefore similar competing coalitions are likely to form at differing sites' (Matland 1995: 168). Moreover,

when faced with a vague referential goal and an ambiguous programme of action, actors with professional training are likely to step in quickly with proposals grounded in their professions. Professions with competing claims over an area and different standard programmes for attacking problems often form the core of competing coalitions . . . implementation battles are likely to be long and bitter. Policies aimed at redistributing power or goods are perhaps the most obvious examples of programmes that fall under this category. (Matland 1995: 169)

Matland's description of symbolic interpretation invokes local contextual factors (including the power of local interest/professional coalitions), and alludes to politicking at higher order politico-geographic scales (extra-local policy elites). This would suggest that a synthesis of rational-choice and historical institutionalist approaches be used by researchers to understand symbolic implementation outcomes, using a combination of 'top-down' and 'bottom-up' methodologies.

8.4. Classifying Agri-Environmental Policy Outcomes Using the Ambiguity–Conflict Matrix

Obviously, not all member states' experiences of implementing EC 2078/92 have been the same. Equally, not all regions and territories within the same state will have had identical, or even similar, implementation experiences. Classification of policy outcomes using the ambiguity–conflict matrix should instead proceed on a case-by-case basis. In the first instance, this should involve assessing the policy experience at the territorial level (for example, the interaction between farming groups, local elites, and environmental groups over the Regulation, as appropriate), thereafter tracing local elite involvement and engagement in regional, national, and supranational policy networks, to validate and provide a comparative context for this initial evaluation.

Given the differing political and cultural contexts of the EU MLG, it is highly likely that the 'post-agreement' stage of EC 2078/92 resulted in all four implementation outcomes. For example, even in member states with comparatively long experience of agri-environmental policies, a scheme with entirely

new objectives may have produced an 'experimental' implementation outcome. Conversely, a scheme with relatively straightforward objectives (for
example, to support farm incomes) in a member state with little or no previous
experience of these agri-environmental policies might be classified as an
'administrative' outcome.

Nonetheless, comparing 2078/92's characteristics, as set out in earlier chapters, to those ascribed by Matland to the different implementation categories
suggests that the 'aggregate' experience of this Regulation for most member
states falls into one of two outcomes: *experimental* or *symbolic* implementation. The Regulation is redistributive, and, for many member states, was a
wholly new development for their agricultural sectors, the intention being to
'confirm a new policy mission' (Matland 1995) for agriculture (that is, the environmental management of the farmed landscape). This novel policy goal
obliged both EU institutions and member states' administrators to set highly
ambiguous and equivocal policy aims (cf. Lewis 1984) (high ambiguity is a
characteristic of both *symbolic* and *experimental* categories). In some EU
localities, levels of conflict have been more marked than in others (classifying
these implementation outcomes as *symbolic*, according to Matland's matrix).
Elsewhere, local reactions to the Regulation have been far more favourable,
resulting in *experimental* implementation outcomes.

The disposition of domestic policy elites towards the Regulation is also an
important factor in explaining these two outcomes. As Wallace (1984: 137)
makes clear, the implementation of supranational policies intimately depends
on the activities, actions, and goodwill of national, state, and local authorities
and agencies. To be truly supportive of EU legislation, member states must
'agree [that the policy] carries the[ir] imprimatur and legitimacy' at national,
state, and local administrative levels. However, in virtually all of the EU–15,
the arm of government sponsoring EC 2078/92 was an agriculture department
or ministry, often deeply embued with a productivist agrarian ethic, and hence
providing only lukewarm endorsement for this innovative policy (see Chapters
2 and 6).

Without firmer backing, sectoral groups and local farming communities
have been able to use their existing power configurations to shape what were
invariably redistributive territorial programmes under the Regulation to suit
their own goals, as we show in Chapter 9. Furthermore, in some member
states, attempts by client groups to subvert the intent of the Regulation have
relied heavily on the deployment of socio-cultural beliefs and symbols relating
to agriculture and the natural environment, substantiating a *symbolic implementation* outcome for the Regulation. These issues are also investigated more
fully in the following chapter.

8.5. Bargained Implementation within the EU MLG: Methodological and Analytical Considerations

Matland's framework provides many useful insights into implementation within the EU's system of bargained deliberative policy-making. Importantly, this work also represents a major advance on earlier related conceptualizations, such as the 'bargaining' model of Barrett and Fudge (1981), by answering the methodological and analytical criticisms made by theorists of European policy implementation (Jordan 1995). First, the ambiguity–conflict approach provides a grounded theoretical basis for analysing the interplay between actors based at different politico-geographic scales, derived from a thorough evaluation of existing implementation, public administration, and organizational literatures (Matland 1995). Secondly, the ambiguity–conflict matrix identifies a variety of implementation outcomes that arise implicitly from deliberative multi-scalar policy processes, and that are sufficiently robust to encompass the diverse socio-cultural contexts of the EU–15. Each outcome has particular characteristics that can be used to elaborate new research hypotheses. Thirdly, by identifying 'central principles' for each implementation outcome, Matland offers a 'way in' to the complex multi-dimensional 'post-agreement' phase of the policy process (Grande 1996) by distinguishing the most profitable research focus—and the most important contingent variable—in each case. Fourthly, we have shown the compatibility of new institutional approaches and policy networks with Matland's theoretical framework, thereby providing a range of analytical tools with which to scrutinize the structure, substance, and dynamics of multi-level policy-making.

However, there remains the question of how an analysis using the ambiguity–conflict matrix and new institutional approaches should proceed. Specifically, how do the deliberative policy-making activities of actors at different politico-geographic scales interrelate, and how is this relationship to be conceptualized? The answer is intimately linked to the modalities of implementation within an MLG system, and has been the focus of much recent work in the field of European integration studies (Kooiman 1993; Wright 1996; Rhodes 1997; Kohler-Koch 1998; Borzel 1999; Wallace 1999).

For example, Borzel (1999: 576) notes that the 'different levels of [EU] government [are] increasingly dependent on each other's resources in European policy making. Europeanization does not strengthen or weaken but transforms the State by fostering the emergence of co-operation between the actors of different levels of government'. Increasingly, theorists in this field are examining how the roles, responsibilities, practices, and relationships between domestic formal and informal institutions are altered as a result of EU initiatives, showing especially how EU policies are utilized in 'the continuing struggle [between local interest coalitions] over resources and claims to authority' (Buller *et al.* 1993: 189). At the same time, however, these domestic institutions have themselves 'sought to shape the workings of the [European institutions]' (Buller *et al.* 1993: 186), including policies sanctioned by the Council of Ministers (for an example of this approach analysing UK national engagement with EU environmental policy, see Lowe and Ward 1999). This iterative process between multi-levelled policy-making and territorial preoccupations appears to suggest that, over time, the conflict surrounding policy aims and objectives foreseen by Matland may give way to compromise, cooperation, and a measure of interdependence among policy actors.

The bargained EU policy process therefore needs to be seen as a form of dialectical policy engagement across, between, and within politico-geographic scales, transacted through the medium of multi-level policy networks. One possible conceptualization of this relationship is to see EU policies not as fixed and static entities, but as 'regulatory templates' that evolve during the course of multi-level policy-making by configuring, and in turn being configured by, the territorial discourses encircling domestic formal and informal institutions. This conceptualization accords well with the evolutionary basis of much EU policy-making (see Chapter 2), and with the advocacy by EU policy practitioners of the 'guiding principles' of subsidiarity, partnership, and simplification. It also provides a structure within which the deliberative processes underpinning Matland's work on ambiguity and conflict in policy implementation can unfold. Crucially, it is fully compatible with the analytical rigour provided by new institutional approaches and policy networks, both of which provide Matland's theoretical framework with an insightful cutting edge. Chapter 9 develops this notion of a 'regulatory template' in the context of implementation of EC 2078/92 in southern France and central Spain.

8.6. Conclusions

We have outlined in this chapter a theoretical framework for analysing the implementation of the agri-environmental Regulation in the EU–15. This framework is founded on our belief that the activities of EU institutions and territorial actors during all stages of EC 2078/92's policy-making cycle—policy-shaping, policy-setting, and post-agreement—are highly interdependent, and thus profoundly difficult to disentangle in any meaningful sense. Logically, this also suggests that the most profitable way to develop a theoretical framework for implementation analysis is to base it around the same theoretical components used in earlier chapters to examine policy-shaping and policy-setting of EC 2078/92—namely, new institutional approaches and policy networks, informed and contextualized by a concept of statehood based upon MLG (see Chapter 1).

As a result of decision-making and decision-taking competencies being distributed and diffused throughout the EU MLG, we have argued that the 'post-agreement' stage of EU policy-making on EC 2078/92 has been characterized by a bargained, iterative quality. Consequently, the agri-environmental Regulation has particular features. These include: a blurring of its policy formulation and implementation processes; highly ambiguous policy goals and objectives; a difficulty in assessing policy 'success' or 'failure', because of the absence of clear-cut goals, and the extended time period needed to make such an assessment; and a tendency to contribute to an inherently 'evolutionary' supranational policy process, on account of the active participation in policy-making by a multiplicity of actors at a variety of politico-geographic scales.

In order to develop a theoretical framework that is sensitive to these features, we have refined and developed Matland's work on ambiguity and conflict. We have done so in three ways. First, we have demonstrated the compatibility and appropriateness of using new institutional approaches and policy networks to analyse the deliberative processes that are central to Matland's ambiguity–conflict matrix. Secondly, we have shown that by setting this matrix within the context of multi-level policy-making, the commonalities in deliberation between politico-administrative levels become clearer, so permitting a more nuanced understanding of the whole policy process. Thirdly, we have shown that, while conflict between actors may be an initial outcome of ambiguous policies, in the medium and long terms it might also be the precursor of enhanced cooperation and mutual dependence among them. We have conceptualized the medium for this dynamic policy relationship between the politico-administrative scales of the EU MLG as a 'regulatory template'. We have argued that initially conflict arises over 'regulatory templates', as they are configured by, and at the same time configure, domestic formal and informal institutions, and established policy communities and networks. However, over time, the conflict surrounding policy aims and objectives foreseen by Matland gives way to compromise, cooperation, and a measure of interdependence among policy actors operating at different politico-geographic scales. We assess the validity of this framework in Chapter 9.

The preceding analysis has been developed on the basis of modalities of policy-making within the EU agri-environmental domain. We would not wish to generalize these findings to other EU policy arenas, although we have no doubt that there are commonalities in the deliberative processes at work in all EU sectoral policy-making. It remains for scholars to establish precisely what these commonalities are.

9

Implementing the Agri-Environmental Regulation in Southern France and Central Spain

Our argument in Chapter 8 was that the deliberative processes driving formulation of the agri-environmental Regulation were also implicated in shaping its 'implementation outcomes' in the EU–15. In this chapter, we examine this proposition by analysing local implementation outcomes in two member states, France and Spain. We do so by using the nuanced conceptualization of Matland's ambiguity–conflict framework (Matland 1995), outlined in the last chapter, to inform new institutional analyses of multi-level agri-environment policy-making in both states.

The chapter contends that policy ambiguity enshrined in this Regulation at the policy-shaping and policy-setting stages also characterized crucial phases of the 'formulation/implementation continuum' in France and Spain. This argument is developed through detailed case studies in the region of Languedoc-Roussillon (southern France) and the autonomous community of Castilla la Mancha (south-central Spain). Reference is also made to previously restricted documentation from relevant EU Agriculture Council meetings. Crucially, bargaining, negotiation, and compromise among locally based actors over the Regulation, mediated through particular sets of power relations, characterized the formulation/implementation continuum in both study areas, just as it had done during policy-shaping and policy-setting at the supranational level. In turn, we show how this has made specific agri-environmental project objectives in Castilla la Mancha and Languedoc-Roussillon more malleable to the interests of local power coalitions, in effect leaving implementation outcomes heavily dependent on local contexts.

In neither the French nor the Spanish cases examined here have these ambiguities been responsible for anything as simplistic as 'policy failure'. Rather, as we show, they have increased the possibility for conflict among territorial coalitions over the meaning and purpose of agri-environmental projects set up under the Regulation, in the short term at least reducing programme efficiency and effectiveness by exacerbating historic struggles among local elite and sectoral groupings. Our analysis concurs broadly with Wallace's observation (1984: 131) of policies emerging from the EU MLG: 'there is far less chance of coherence of policy at the formulation phase and consequently more chance of divergent and contradictory patterns of implementation . . . The time lags between the initial definition of the problem and eventual policy output [i.e. policy-shaping and policy-setting → post-agreement] are often such that implementation takes place in an environment significantly different from that originally envisaged.'

In examining the formulation/implementation continuum of EC 2078/92 in Spain and France, we focus upon Matland's 'central principle' of *symbolic implementation*: the nature and manifestation of coalition strength at different politico-geographic scales. We focus in this chapter on the *symbolic implementation* outcome for two reasons. First, in both study areas, the reactions of prominent agricultural coalitions to agri-environmental policies was initially hostile, partly because of a deeply embedded productivist philosophy (especially in Languedoc-Roussillon), partly because of fears that these policies would create a set of beneficiaries other than agricultural cartels, but chiefly because of the inherent ambiguity of EU agri-environmental goals. This cluster of interrelated concerns matches perfectly Matland's observation (1995: 168) on symbolic policy outcomes: 'Policies that invoke highly salient symbols often produce high levels of conflict even when the policy is vague.' Secondly, conflict was also apparent among administrative elites of both states over the aims, goals, and objectives of the agri-environmental Regulation.

The theoretical approach we have adopted therefore utilizes rational-choice and historical institutionalism, and synthesizes 'top-down' and 'bottom-up' methodologies to reflect the fundamental importance of, and interconnections between, different politico-geographic scales within the EU's MLG system. Once again, this reflects Matland's recommendation (1995: 170): '[The] ambiguity [of symbolic policies] makes it difficult for . . . macro-implementors to monitor [policy] activities, and it is much more difficult to structure actions at the local level. Nevertheless, centrally located actors [i.e. supranational/national policy elites] do constitute an important influence [on these policies] through provision of resources and incentives and through focusing attention on an issue area.'

Our decision to conduct detailed case studies of multi-level agri-environmental policy making in southern France and central Spain is based on theoretical and contextual considerations. In the mid-1990s, these states had radically different levels of experience of agri-environmentalism (the French state implemented some of the first EU agri-environmental policies in 1987, while Spain had no previous experience of this policy prior to 1993). Secondly, they share some cultural preoccupations regarding the centrality of agriculture to the patterning of rural life, and have a high density and embeddedness of informal institutions that lend themselves well to new institutional analysis.

Thirdly, neither state had been particularly influential during the initial stages of policy-shaping and policy-setting on EC 2078/92 (see Chapter 7), making an examination of their territorial decision-making during the post-agreement phase especially worthy of study.[1] Fourthly, interesting contrasts exist in terms of domestic politico-administrative structure. Despite devolving powers to the regions in the 1980s, France retains a highly centralized state structure, while Spain is quasi-federal in character. As a founding member of the EU, France might be expected to have considerable experience, indeed mastery, of the modalities of multi-level agricultural policy-making. By contrast, the often antagonistic relations between different tiers of Spanish government might serve to impede the development of cooperative multi-level policy-making.

The selection of the specific study areas within France and Spain was made on the basis of local factors. Languedoc-Roussillon boasts highly developed territorial viticultural policy communities, still steeped in the logic of agricultural productivism. Such sectoral policy communities are far more localized in Spain, and have only recently evolved in parts of Castilla la Mancha. More typical to this Spanish region are mutable and transitory agricultural policy networks, forming around specific issues and dissolving once these issues are resolved. Both study areas also exhibit a strong sense of territorial identity, distinctive territorial economies, and, in the French case, social solidarity based around a rich heritage of local political, religious, and linguistic affiliations.

For both states, we follow the negotiated agri-environmental policy process through all its stages: policy-shaping, policy-setting, and post-agreement. In doing so, our intention is not only to test the validity of the theoretical framework set out in Chapter 8. We also seek to demonstrate the commonalities in deliberative processes between the supposedly discrete categories of 'formulation' and 'implementation' in multi-level agri-environmental policy-making. We show how constructive synergies between the multiple layers of governance have now begun to emerge. Policy ambiguity may have provoked initial conflict among local coalitions in EU territories, but, on the basis of the case studies presented in this chapter, increasingly this is giving way to compromise and growing compatibility between them. As Matland (1995: 168–9) notes of symbolic policies: 'The high level of conflict is important, because it structures the way resolutions are developed . . . disagreements are resolved through coercion or bargaining.' In addition, the case studies offer a detailed insight into local and regional involvement in MLG policy-making, an aspect that researchers have hitherto neglected (cf. Jeffrey 2000).

---

[1] For example, Ionescu (1988: 208) comments: 'Member States which negotiate vigorously before a decision is made . . . apply the decision more strictly than the Member States whose delegates have been more conciliatory and more accommodating in the preceding negotiations.'

9.1. Activities of the French and Spanish Delegates in the Agriculture Council, 1991–1992

The complexities of EU policy-shaping and policy-setting are critical in explaining the origins of the agri-environmental Regulation's ambiguities, and its potential for provoking deliberation and conflict. As we have seen, disagreement among Council delegations was relatively muted (see Chapter 7), but this was testament to that institution's effectiveness as a 'concordance system' rather than to a shared vision among delegates for EC 2078/92. In fact, the divisions between member states, which are often the precursors to opposition and conflict, were never far from the surface of their discussions on the Regulation. We analyse these differences in this section from the viewpoints of the French and Spanish delegations, and, using a historical institutional approach, expose their socio-cultural foundations.

The Spanish and French negotiating positions in Council discussions on EC 2078/92 had little in common with north European environmental goals. Neither delegation saw these considerations as a national priority (indeed, the Spanish viewed EC 2078/92 as a distraction from, and hindrance to, the modernization and intensification of traditional agriculture). This position reflected a mutual feeling among southern member states, and in southern French regions such as the Languedoc, that 'the environment' was inseparable from the social and economic vitality of rural communities, a notion that remained largely unrecognized in the texts of the Regulation drafted by the Commission. Hence, these two states' negotiating positions were informed by the needs of their most important rural constituencies, certain socio-cultural beliefs, and relevant political priorities. Wherever possible, these delegations sought to oppose the raising of environmental standards in domestic agriculture through the Regulation, bringing them into conflict with the 'knowledgeable advocates'—states with growing experience of the first generation of European agri-environmental policies, and a history of environmental activism, including Denmark, the Netherlands, and the UK (see Chapter 6). The following extracts from previously restricted Council documents demonstrate how this 'interest-led' approach of France and Spain brought both delegations into conflict with the north European 'environmental agenda' (Baldock and Lowe 1996: 9).

9.1.1. The French Position on EC 2078/92

The French delegation viewed the agri-environmental Regulation mainly as a mechanism for expediting market surpluses in the CAP, and for assisting the adjustment of national agricultural structures. Only secondly did it regard EC 2078/92 as an instrument with the explicit goal of addressing 'environmental management' of farmland (Le Clerc 1993; Boisson and Buller 1996). This perception arose largely from the Commission's promotion of EC 2078/92 to the French as an 'accompanying measure' to the main body of the MacSharry reforms, which would not ratchet up environmental obligations beyond that imposed by existing national agri-environmental schemes (see Chapter 2). As important was to ensure that these schemes remain largely unchanged under the new Regulation, and would continue to be fully eligible for the high levels of EU cofinancing available under it.

While the Commission's approach assuaged French fears and led to a more favourable assessment of the Regulation by this delegation, it also downplayed its environmental significance. Indirectly, the Commission's approach confirmed strongly held socio-cultural norms. Attitudes towards the agri-environmental Regulation were thus refracted through the prism of (largely southern) French fears of *désertification*, and the culturally embedded productivist export-oriented conception of agriculture common to northern regions, pithily summarized by Giscard D'Estaing in the phrase *petrol vert*. Both concepts conflicted with embedded beliefs in northern member states—for example, notions of 'stewardship' in the UK (see Chapter 6).

These cultural norms are evident in the French delegation's interventions in Council discussions. Minutes from the Council's ASG meeting of 25 November 1991 note the French 'stating that the . . . [agri-environment] proposal . . . needs to ensure a coherence . . . with respect to the market organization reforms, particularly for arable and for livestock rearing' (CoEC 1991*b*), and their tabling on 3 December of a proposal calling for the Regulation's scope to be widened to finance 'increasing the grazed area [of EU agricultural holdings,] with the aim of reducing pollution arising from excessive livestock stocking rates' (CoEC 1991*c*). These interventions point to the French determination that environmental regulation should not impinge on the activities of the nation's thriving export-oriented agricultural sector.

Disregarding the indifference of other delegates to their proposal of 3 December, the French amplified this demand at the final ASG meeting on 16 January 1992. The Council secretariat commented somewhat exasperatedly: 'France raised the issue of . . . expansion of a farm with a view to reducing environmental deterioration [through overstocking] although delegates noted such efforts may result in an increase in the number of animals kept'—that is, in the intensification of livestock production (CoEC 1992). In short, the French sought to capitalize on EC 2078/92's multiple objectives, by using the Regulation to improve the viability of arable and livestock farming through restructuring agricultural production, rather than to promote active environmental management of farmland. Such an approach also supported the French assertion that 'preference for payments [should] be made through the Guidance section since the [agri-environmental] measure . . . [is] of a structural nature' (AGRIFIN 1991).[2]

---

[2] Council Committee on Agricultural Finance (AGRIFIN).

9.1.2. The Spanish Position on EC 2078/92

By contrast, the Spanish delegation wanted the Regulation to strengthen agriculture's position within local rural economies, and to widen EC 2078/92's terms of reference to include rural occupational groupings other than farmers. Judging by Council working documents, it was these two considerations, rather than lobbying for new measures to reflect Hispanic agri-environmental concerns, that were paramount for this delegation, although some anxieties were expressed in ASG discussions over the depletion of natural resources, particularly soil erosion.

The importance attached by the Spanish delegation to strengthening rural communities explains its declaration, made at the first meeting of the ASG, that 'the objectives of [EC 2078/92] should be clearly defined, in particular putting emphasis on its rural structural aspects' (CoEC 1991*d*). This delegation's attempts to broaden the exclusive agricultural focus of the Regulation to encompass other rural interests became clearer in subsequent ASG meetings. For example, at the meeting of 25 November 1991, the Council Secretariat noted 'Spain states that attention should be given to the . . . more global aspects of . . . forestry, and the agri-environmental measures need to . . . take . . . account of . . . marginal farming areas' (CoEC 1991*b*).

The Spanish position crystallized around this broadly based rural development imperative. The last meeting of the ASG on 16 January 1992 saw the delegation insisting that 'people other than farmers should have equal access to [training] courses [funded under] Art. 5(c) [of EC 2078/92]' (CoEC 1992), and that grants be offered to farmers for forestry management. In a direct reference to the need for 'modulation' of financial support offered under the Regulation to favour smaller farms prevalent in southern Europe, and away from larger primarily north European holdings, the Spanish delegation also commented that 'it is necessary to specify in the Regulation's text the maximum amount payable to each farm' (CoEC 1992). In contrast to the French position on financing for EC 2078/92, the Spanish maintained that the Regulation should be financed from the *FEOGA* Guarantee Fund, partly reflecting the country's status as a net beneficiary of CAP spending.

This brief institutionalist examination of the Spanish and French positions in Council reveals the degree to which they differed from those of north European states. Major differences were evident, but open conflict did not emerge because the French and Spanish positions were not entirely compatible with each other, much less with those of other Council delegations. Consequently, a Council regime espousing a distinctive Mediterranean viewpoint did not emerge, leaving both states unable to exert more than slight influence on the final text of the Regulation. Inevitably though, to diffuse potential conflict among delegations, textual compromises had to be made by the Commission and the Portuguese Presidency. The Regulation's inherent ambiguities were directly related to these facilitative efforts.

Rational-choice institutionalism provides other insights into why the French and Spanish contributions were muted. First, southern member state delegations, including Spain's, had little previous experience of agri-environmental policy and little interest in the goals championed by this new policy area, preventing a meaningful exchange of views with the Council's 'knowledgeable advocates'. Secondly, and arguably more importantly, both delegations recognized the opportunities afforded policy-makers within an MLG system. Formulation of the Regulation, however defined, was only the starting point of policy-making on EC 2078/92. Both delegations were fully aware that the policy-shaping and policy-setting stages were essentially opening shots in the iterative bargained MLG policy-making process (Peters 1994; Richardson 1996*a*, *b*). Coupled with the lack of a regime advocating a coherent Mediterranean viewpoint, and the Regulation's distributive character, these points explain why conflict over EC 2078/92 was largely suppressed during discussions in the ASG. Both the French and Spanish delegations knew their national agendas would be better advanced during the implementation continuum—those stages of the MLG policy-making process acted out in territorial arenas. Hence Wallace's comment (1984: 131) that: 'The rules of the international game . . . leav[e member states] . . . the opportunity to opt out of implementing agreements which are unpalatable, irksome or practically difficult.'

9.2. The Modalities of Multi-Level Governance in EU Territories

The EU's evolving system of governance is intimately linked with recent political/administrative restructuring in its constituent member states. In both France and Spain, there have been waves of political and administrative decentralization since the early 1970s, and similar processes of statist transformation have been discerned in many other EU member states since the mid-1980s (Keating 1998; Le Galès and Lequesne 1998). We contend that these transformations have assisted in the creation of modalities of policy transfer between the interleaved levels of EU governance (see also Wright 1996; Wallace 1999; Jeffrey 2000). Statist transformation has also contributed to the establishment and consolidation of multi-level policy networks. These networks, we argue, have acted as the principal medium for the bargained, negotiated joint decision-making characteristic of EU agri-environmental policy. Together with the consequences flowing from ongoing statist processes of devolution and decentralization, these networks provide the substance of MLG in many EU territories (cf. with Wallace's (1999: 30) notion of 'transmission systems').

Multi-level agri-environmental policy networks have woven together interest coalitions across the EU MLG, and have arisen from 'loose coupling'

(Weick 1985) of their deliberative processes. 'Loose coupling' occurs when issues of common interest emerge between coalitions and other actors situated at different politico-geographic scales, such that 'pooled' deliberation of issues offers mutual advantages to all parties. This may happen during any or all stages of the MLG policy-making process—that is, policy-shaping, policy-setting, and post-agreement phases. Inevitably, such policy-making, involving a multiplicity of actors at different scales, favours a more ambiguous policy outcome than that dictated by traditional 'command-and-control' politico-administrative hierarchies (Jordan 1999).

During the latter stages of policy-making on Regulation 2078/92, two mechanisms institutionalized these nascent multi-level agri-environmental policy networks. These were debates among member state representatives over national agri-environmental programmes within the European Commission's STAR Committee, leading to their formal approval or rejection; and what we describe as the 'bargained implementation' of formally approved 'zonal programmes' across the EU.

The zonal programme structure was formulated by the European Commission with the express purpose of establishing a triadic relationship between the DG Agri, national administrations, and territorial coalitions (cf. Rhodes 1997), giving genuine expression to 'multi-level governance' in territories. 'Loose coupling' in this triadic relationship has provided a number of mutual benefits for different scalar partners. For the Commission, it has offered the chance to develop closer working relations with territorial actors across the EU–15. National administrations have benefited from access to EU co-financing for agri-environment policy, and have sought to exercise greater control from the centre by improving vertical coordination with local actors. Territorial coalitions have had the opportunity to shape agri-environmental policy to suit local contexts, and potentially at least to establish direct linkages with the supranational level (more questionable is whether these linkages actually 'bypass' the political channels of the national state (Jeffrey 2000)). Furthermore, the Commission intended the zonal structure to increase mutual reliance among scalar actors. Hence 'different levels of government become increasingly dependent on each others' resources in European policy making' (Borzel 1999: 576). 'Loose coupling' has, therefore, provided a structural linkage between geographic scales for the bargained agri-environmental policy form characteristic of the EU MLG. It has also provided a context for subsequent stages of the policy-making process.

However, implementation has also been mediated by a range of formal and less formal institutions, particular to member state and to locality. Chief among these are domestic politico-administrative structures. Major consequences of 'hollowing out' include the redefinition of the responsibilities of the central state, increased reliance on private-sector involvement in 'traditional' areas of public-sector responsibility, and renewed calls from local and regional administrations for greater devolved powers from the state. Overall, the result has been institutional fragmentation, and an overlapping of organizational responsibilities, increasing the potential for policy conflict among key actors. Crucially, these disjunctures have actually provided greater impetus for developing joint decision-making initiatives between geographic scales. This impetus has been further enhanced by the inherent ambiguities of EC 2078/92, prompting deliberation among scalar actors over implementation strategies in all EU member states.

Hence we argue that the transposition of EC 2078/92 to France and Spain has provoked a type of 'dialectical governance'. In the first place, it has initiated a reappraisal of, and change in, national, regional, and local institutional and organizational forms. Inevitably, these changes have occasioned conflict within and between territorial elites, conflict made more profound by the Regulation's ambiguous goals and mechanisms. At the same time, however, territorial constituencies and informal institutions in both states have configured the Regulation's implementation, not only questioning its aims, goals, and objectives, but often also recasting the deliberative assumptions underpinning it.

In effect, the outcome of the policy-shaping and policy-setting process at EU level—in this case, an EC Regulation—has provided a 'regulatory template' around which nationally and regionally specific implementation decisions have been negotiated and struck in both states (see Chapter 8). The French and Spanish central authorities have sought to stamp their mark on these templates—for example, by specifying the objectives of 'zonal programmes', controlling the disbursal of finances, and sanctioning the approval of schemes. However, perhaps inevitably, the territorial parameters for this negotiated form of policy-making have not proved so easy to pin down. As we show, implementation has unfolded through the involvement of a wide spectrum of policy actors, situated at different spatial scales, subjecting agri-environmental 'regulatory templates' to reinterpretation, revision, and amendment. This deliberative response has been accentuated because of the essentially ambiguous character of the Regulation. Hence in the following case studies we emphasize the creative interplay between the EU regulatory form and local territorial identity. Our contention is that this interplay constitutes the essence of MLG as it applies to agri-environmental policy-making in these two member states.

9.3. The French National Policy Context

Since 1970, three major politico-administrative reforms have been undertaken. Greater powers were devolved to the country's *départements* in 1970, while in 1982 the 22 *régions* gained political representation and the ability to raise their own finances for the first time. The 1990s witnessed further devolution of powers, notably to the French mayoralities, and to *départements* and other local authorities in the area of public finances (Guyomarch *et al.* 1998).

Nonetheless the state remains a potent influence in territorial administration. *Régions,* for example, are heavily dependent on financial transfers from the centre to enact territorial policies, which have proved critically important to the implementation of French agri-environment programmes. As a comparatively new politico-administrative unit, the *région* also faces stiff competition from long-established *départements* in exercising its administrative competencies, some of which overlap with this lower tier of government. In southern France especially, relations between the *région* and the *département* have also been made more problematic, as *départements* here are often bastions for deeply entrenched rural regimes, whose fortunes are closely intertwined with local political elite structures (Verlaque 1987; Jones and Clark 2000). As we show later, this is certainly the case in the Languedoc *département* of L'Hérault.

A further complication in centre–local political relations is that certain national ministries have territorial representation. The *Ministère de l'Agriculture et de la Forêt (MAF)*, for example, has direct representation at regional (the *Direction Régionale de l'Agriculture et de la Forêt (DRAF)*) and departmental levels (the *Direction Départementale de l'Agriculture et de la Forêt (DDAF)*), although, in practice, many of their officials appear to have stronger loyalties to territory than to state.

What emerges is a pattern of overlapping administrative responsibilities and conflicting centre/local obligations and duties, a situation that in certain *régions* has stoked intense debate over possible implementation strategies for Regulation 2078/92. The *MAF*'s interpretation of the Regulation involved the designation of two 'horizontal programmes' (that is, programmes available to all French farmers). These are the *prime à l'herbe* (grassland premium), offering payments to livestock farmers to keep animal 'stocking densities' at or below certain thresholds, and the *plan de développement durable* (sustainable development plan) to encourage the adoption by farmers of more environmentally sustainable agricultural practices over their whole farmed area. Entry conditions for the *prime* are comparatively undemanding, ensuring the eligibility of very many livestock holdings. It therefore fulfils the French delegation's aim articulated in the Agriculture Council to assist domestic livestock producers under the Regulation. In 1998, approximately 5 million hectares were enrolled in the *prime à l'herbe* (*Agra Europe* 1999), accounting for almost three-quarters of the total national area in agri-environmental contracts.

However, recognizing the strength of agricultural feeling in the territories, and the embedded political power of the *départements*, the *MAF* also placed great emphasis on the development of more locally appropriate schemes, through 'zonal programmes'. In conjunction with the *Ministère de l'Environnement*, the *MAF* formulated a horizontal framework of six zonal programme objectives. These objectives were: (1) the conversion from conventional to organic agriculture; (2) the reduction of livestock 'stocking densities'; (3) the protection of water bodies from pollution; (4) the conservation of flora and fauna; (5) the conservation of traditional livestock breeds; and (6) the provision of environmental training for farmers. The *MAF* controlled regional budgets for the agri-environmental Regulation (setting budget lines for both zonal and local programmes), and assigned monies to each *région* on the basis of its total farm population.

In turn, the 'regulatory template' of EC 2078/92 obliged the wholesale reorganization of procedures and protocols for regional and local agricultural structures policy. The resulting territorial policy process is highly complex, but basically is as follows. At the regional level, *Comités Régionals Agriculture-Environnementals* (*CRAE*s) were established to supervise the allocation of funds for zonal and local schemes, and to appraise schemes for approval. Each *CRAE* is chaired by the regional *préfect*, with limited powers to switch funds between local and zonal budget headings. *CRAE*s bring together regional and local scalar elites: the *DRAF* and *DDAF*s, personnel from the regional sections of the national environment ministry, the *Direction Régionale de l'Environnement* (*DIREN*), and farming and environmental interests. Formulation and management of zonal and local schemes became the responsibility of a parallel set of new committees, the *Comités de Pilotage de l'Opération* (*CPO*s). Typically, one *CPO* was established to oversee each zonal or local scheme. *CPO* membership is drawn from *DDAF*s, the *DIREN*, and farming and environmental bodies, although departmental *préfets*, who chair *CPO*s, have some discretion to appoint persons they deem appropriate.

Since 1992, the creative tensions between the EU 'regulatory template' and the 'identities' of different French territories have become clear. Some *régions* and *départements* have shown considerable ingenuity in developing locally appropriate schemes. However, the new formulation process instituted under EC 2078/92 strongly favours the adoption at the local level of one or other of the six zonal objectives. This is because prior approval for them was granted by STAR, enabling local programmes duplicating these objectives to receive 'fast-track' authorization (usually simply by referral to the relevant *CRAE*). By contrast, scheme proposals with radically dissimilar objectives have had to go through complex multi-scalar decision-making, involving consideration by *DDAF* staff, the relevant *CPO*, the relevant *CRAE*, the *MAF*, and possibly STAR.

Hence, while some effort was made by Paris to encourage local participation in agri-environmental policy, the state sought to retain control of the all-important levers of scheme approval and financing. The intention, presumably, was to make truly local agri-environmental policy-making subject to rigorous national supervision. Despite (or possibly because of) this, the emerging politics of the agri-environmental sector, in southern France at least, has been characterized by the mobilization of local power structures and non-formal institutions to configure policy to suit territorial preoccupations. Often, this configuration has been driven by the development of local rural coalitions with their own distinctive agendas, as the following case study demonstrates.

9.4. Case Study: Agri-Environmental Policy in Languedoc's Lower Aude Valley

For over 150 years, the economic development of the southern French *région* of Languedoc-Roussillon has been ineluctably linked to viticulture, and the production and marketing of wine (see Figure 9.1). By the mid-twentieth century, Languedoc had established a formidable reputation for the production of cheap *vin de table* that was virtually unmatched in the rest of France. A sectoral regime began to emerge at this time, based around *vignerons* (vine-growers) and the local policy elites who represented and sponsored their interests, which subsequently wielded considerable influence in the region. More recently, this regime has been obliged to retrench in the face of a profound EU-wide viticultural crisis, and attempts by both the state and the EU to redirect the regional economy away from wine production (Jones and Clark 2000).

One example of this strategy was the introduction in the mid-1990s of agri-environmental policy into the region. Languedoc's viticultural regime has invoked potent symbolic concepts in its attempt to confirm its established power position within this new policy arena. Touzard (1995: 318) notes these efforts have been rooted in 'common symbolic references designed to inexorably associate sector with territory (for example . . . defence of southern viticulture, the cultural linguistic differentiation encapsulated in *occitan* [the southern French dialect]) and by the identification of external enemies: Italian wine producers . . . Brussels administrators, the state'. The regime has also capitalized on the region's own reflexive image as France's premier production space for cheap table wines. This image is founded upon work routines of *vignerons*; the phytosanitary requirements of vines; and the cultivation specificities that have traditionally fashioned and fostered a particular relationship between *vigneron* and vine. Hence the comment of a leading Languedoc wine policy official: 'the vine is the real embodiment of this region, and its cultivation shapes the management of rural space [here]' (*CRAF*-Languedoc source, July 1997). Institutionally, this regional self-image is bound up with the existence and functioning of a wine cooperative system and the nature of its activities in grape collection, processing, and wine commercialization.

Viticulture's dominance of the regional economy has had inevitable political ramifications. At one level, it has tended to direct the economic choices of viticultural elites in their response to external regulatory pressures. More profoundly, it has enabled the viticultural regime to insinuate all strata of the regional and local political process. As Verlaque (1987:48) argues, 'for decades, the vine has dominated the Languedoc, taken over the rural economy, served as a justification for social struggle, acted as the basis of expression of the cultural patrimony, and permeated all aspects of regional political life'. This use of locally specified concepts of 'environment', coupled with

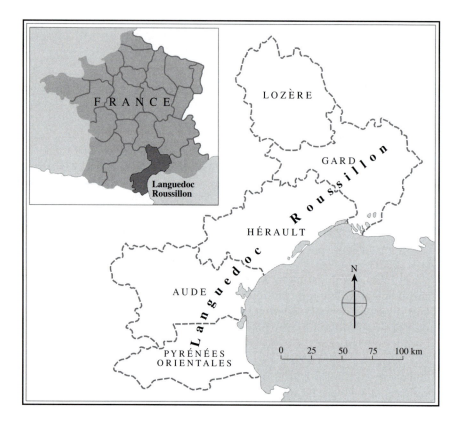

Figure 9.1. France and the Languedoc-Roussillon

access to territorial bases of political power, has enabled the viticultural regime to define its interests within local agri-environmental policy projects.

However, just as the regime has sought to configure the 'regulatory template' of this policy, so too has this template acted as a catalyst for recasting local notions of 'environment', and revitalizing local deliberation over the goals, meanings, and purposes of viticulture. In the process, new territorial coalitions have come to the fore. As discussed above, the state's implementation of the Regulation has also put in place an entirely new suite of institutional and administrative procedures, which threatens to undercut the informal political channels underpinning the viticultural regime's power base. Agri-environment policy in this region, therefore, provides an apposite example of a 'symbolic implementation outcome' (Matland 1995).

9.4.1. The Basses Plaines d'Aude Scheme (1): Local Coalition Influences on the EU Regulatory Template

This agri-environmental scheme offers financial incentives to *vignerons* in the Lower Aude valley to maintain one of the Languedoc's most valued viticultural landscapes. It emerged following heated and vociferous exchanges between the local viticultural regime, and what might broadly be described as a territorial coalition, championing environmental interests.

Historically, vineyards along the lowest reaches of the Aude river have depended on an intricate network of dykes and channels to provide fresh water, with the excess drained out to sea. The downturn in viticultural markets and the introduction of the EC's *prime d'arrachage* (grubbing-up) measure encouraged the gradual abandonment of these less productive vineyards, many of which were subject to severe and prolonged winter flooding. Over time, these abandoned vineyards became infiltrated by brackish estuarine water, leading to their colonization by salt-tolerant plants and grass species, some of high nature conservation value. Grubbed-up vineyards also provided ideal feeding ranges for the rare Lesser Grey Shrike (Fr.: *pie-grièche à poitrine rose*; L.: *Lanius minor*).

Wine cooperatives of the Basse Aude regarded the introduction of the agri-environmental Regulation as an ideal opportunity to finance the reinstatement of traditional viticultural management of lands in the river delta, by repairing and restoring the old dyke and channel system. However, local environmental groups argued that the reinstatement of drainage would irreparably damage the now flourishing salt-tolerant ecosystems, and destroy the Shrike's feeding ranges (according to staff in L'Hérault's *DDAF*, the delta provides habitat for about 50 per cent of the total French population of the species). Antagonism between *vignerons* and environmentalists escalated throughout the 1990s (in 1991, for example, an official complaint was lodged by environmental groups with the European Commission's Environment Directorate against the French government). By the mid-1990s relations had deteriorated so much that L'Hérault's *préfet départemental* felt unable to enforce management restrictions protecting trees used as roosts by the Lesser Grey Shrike, for fear of inciting the *vignerons* further. In the face of seeming intransigence from farm groups, conservationists branded *vignerons* as 'environmental vandals'.

Matland's theoretical framework provides a number of valuable insights into the evolution of this agri-environmental project. At its heart were different symbolic conceptions of 'environment' around which two local coalitions gathered, and through which coalition members constructed and legitimized diametrically opposed sets of human roles and responsibilities towards 'nature'. As Matland (1995: 169) notes:

when faced with a vague referential goal and an ambiguous programme of action [agri-environmentalism], actors with professional training are likely to step in quickly with proposals grounded in their professions. Professions with competing claims over an area and different standard programmes for attacking problems often form the core of competing coalitions . . . symbolic implementation battles are likely to be long and bitter.

Among *vignerons* and their supporters, reinstating a traditional viticultural landscape was seen as a logical step, reaffirming the commitment and dedication shown by previous generations in the Basses Plaines by bringing *friches* back into productive use. For this coalition (the local viticultural regime), 'environment' was intrinsically bound up with the quotidian round of viticultural activities, centred on human management of the natural resource base. The emergent environmental coalition saw things differently. For its members, '*protégeant l'environnement*' meant returning the Basses Plaines to a pristine state, unencumbered by human intervention. Not only did this rule out reintroducing viticultural management. It also required the minimization of disturbance of the delta's natural patterns of drainage, in order to protect the saline habitats and species reliant upon brackish water that had colonized abandoned vineyards.

Matland notes that the implementation of symbolic policies depends fundamentally on local coalition strength. As the local arm of the sponsoring ministry for viticulture, L'Hérault's *DDAF* staff have traditionally had a vested interest in supporting the *département*'s vine-growers, thereby consolidating the viticultural regime's economic strength by providing it with political influence. Even today, the DDAF-L'Hérault remains embued with a sense of 'viticultural destiny' for the *département*, with the rationale for local agri-environmental projects cast in these terms:

It's pretty obvious [why] the Lesser Grey Shrike [scheme started]. It was an emergency situation. [The scheme] was needed to rebut the accusations made [by the conservationists] that farmers were environmental vandals; the farmers wanted to show that, quite to the contrary, they had reorganized the management of land by themselves. The agri-environmental scheme [has] built on their reorganization, and rounded off some of its rough edges.   (*DDAF*-L'Hérault source, July 1997)

However, the *DDAF* has statutory environmental responsibilities as well. In this guise, staff recognized that, while the ambiguous 'regulatory template' of the Regulation could fuel the long-running dispute between the two conflicting symbolic interpretations of the environment, its inherent flexibility might also enable a deliberative compromise to be struck between the two coalitions. As a *fonctionnaire* in the Regional Agricultural Ministry commented: 'I think one of the strengths of this Regulation is that it brings many conflicting interests together around the same table' (*CRAF*-Languedoc source, July 1997). Ministry officials in Paris also share this opinion: 'one of the big plusses of the agri-environmental measure was establishing a social dialogue on the problems of territorial management, which hitherto hadn't existed . . . one of the most important outcomes was breaking the ice that prevented dialogue between very different [local] groups with contradictory interests—*vignerons,* . . . and the environmentalists' (*MAF* source, July 1997). *DDAF* staff therefore sought a locally appropriate agri-environmental pilot project that would fuse together mutually compatible elements of the two environmental interpretations.

Such a project emerged in 1992, from the enterprising leader of a *cave* (a wine cooperative) comprising seven *communes* (the smallest administrative districts in the French state) around the village of Maurassan. *DDAF* staff recognized it might give tangible expression to a deliberative compromise between *vignerons* and environmentalists. The pilot project sought actively to support the Lesser Grey Shrike population through sensitive land management aimed at extending the species' feeding ranges, while causing minimal disturbance to the high natural value saline-tolerant ecosystems. Farmers would also plant trees in field corners and along boundaries to provide roosts for the Shrike. In return for observing these environmental safeguards, farmers sought a premium for the wines produced from these vineyards (the *Cru pie-grièche* (The Shrike vintage), see Guihéneuf and Prat 1999).

The comparative success of the pilot scheme enabled the *DDAF* to win over other *vignerons*, but resistance among the majority was not so easily overcome. Partly, this can be attributed to land tenure issues (some of the delta land is *bien de village* (common land), which presented legal obstacles), but chiefly it was the regime's rooted opposition to the conception of environment advanced by conservationists that threatened the scheme's introduction. This necessitated many meetings in 1994 to thrash out differences. Undoubtedly, in these debates *vignerons* benefited from the support of local political elites:

The [Maurassan co-op] President . . . thought quite rightly that at the same time as one sells wine, one must sell *terroir*, or the landscape. His goal was to conserve his viticultural territory. This [Lesser Grey Shrike] project was devised to this end, but there were 'ayatollahs' of the environment, as I like to call them, who in their typically excessive behaviour . . . put this project in jeopardy . . . something that started as a very small, relatively low-key project is now characterized by outrageous positions. (*DDAF*-L'Hérault source, July 1997)

Despite these early setbacks, by the mid-1990s the scheme was relatively well received by the local farming community. In 1994, it was approved under EC 2078/92 as a five-year 'pluriannual programme' with annual funding of FF600,000, and an eligible (delimited) area of 1,500 hectares, extending over parts of L'Hérault and its neighbouring *département* of Aude (see Figure 9.1). Approximately 400 hectares were enrolled by the end of 1997, split roughly equally between the two *départements*, with forty farms participating.

9.4.2. The Basses Plaines d'Aude Scheme (2): The Impact of the EU Regulatory Template on the Local Institutional Mosaic

While local formal institutional structures and historical ties within Languedoc have configured EC 2078/92's implementation, so too has the agri-environmental 'template' recast patterns of governance at the *départemental* and regional level. An entirely new institutional-administrative structure has been brought into being in Languedoc to deliver agri-environmental policy, which threatens to undercut the political bases of established local coalitions, such as Aude's viticultural regime, by reconfiguring local political networks. This process has been assisted by the ambiguity of the Regulation:

We worried about the Regulation's diffuse nature, because it made things difficult for us to follow through and set up. There were deadlines to meet and, of course, there are always problems when you start something entirely new. The real problem was that [new] procedures [under the Regulation] were being defined little by little, instead of having them ready to frame everything. Most of the old [administrative] structure had been swept away, and the new procedures were often found not to work, so it's not always been easy to mobilize [popular] support. As [the Regulation] goes in all directions, evaluation has proved especially problematic, and while it was relatively easy to establish a starting point for this, it's become less so over time because [the evaluative procedure for the Regulation] was not clearly established at the outset . . . The *DDAF*s are already overwhelmed with the new administrative responsibilities. (*CRAE*-Languedoc source, July 1997)

This reorganization has resulted in a wealth of new responsibilities and duties for existing agencies, some of which overlap, creating new administrative turfs to defend. Entirely new structures, such as *CRAE*-Languedoc, have also been introduced. The range of agencies involved in processing farmer applications for the Basses Plaines d'Aude scheme conveys the byzantine complexity of the new administrative arrangements (although complexity was apparent under the pre-existing policy structure). A farmer who wants to participate fills out an application and submits it to the *Association Départementale pour l'Aménagement des Structures des Exploitations Agricoles* (*ADASEA*—the *DDAF*'s representation at the farm level). The *ADASEA* checks the application for completeness, and ensures it falls within the terms of the scheme. If so, the application is dispatched to the *DDAF*. The *DDAF* checks over the technical details of the application, and submits it to the relevant *CPO*. The *CPO*'s task is to identify any problems of interpretation, and to prioritize certain applications over others for funding—for example, on environmental grounds, or whether the applicant's land abuts land already enrolled into the agri-environmental scheme. The *CPO* sends on the application to the *departémental* Agricultural Guidance Committee (*Comité Départemental d'Orientation de l'Agriculture* (*CDOA*)), chaired by the *préfet*, which gives its opinion. Assuming this is positive, the farmer is informed by the *DDAF* that the application has been successful, told what *prime* will be offered, and asked when he/she proposes to join the scheme. Once the *DDAF* has received this information, it sends the completed papers to the *Centre National pour l'Aménagement des Structures des Exploitations Agricoles* (*CNASEA*), which is responsible for all financial matters connected with the Lesser Grey Shrike scheme.

The *DDAF* runs day-to-day scheme management, but its brief is also by no means straightforward: 'At the *départemental* level, the *DDAF* enforces policies from the *Ministère de l'Agriculture* and the *Ministère de l'Environnement*. We have two bosses. So we try to steer a middle course, [although] having this dual responsibility isn't always easy' (*DDAF*-L'Hérault source, July 1997). In summary, this Regulation appears to have had some effect on existing elite structures in the Basses Plaines, by catalysing the development of an environmental consciousness that is opposed to traditional productivist viticulture; and by carving out new politico-institutional structures, and new administrative routines. However, only time will show how significant and deep-rooted such changes might be to existing symmetries of governance. Among elites, informal channels of political influence still clearly operate, and there remains a fierce pride in the territorial identity and independence of the area. As the Director of *DDAF*-L'Hérault commented in interview: 'In the *Midi*, we don't like to follow rules established by others. We have our own way of doing things. The peculiarity of the Languedoc programme is its reliance on local operations, with terms and conditions established locally. There are no similar measures established by the Government elsewhere on French territory' (*DDAF* L'Hérault source, Aug. 1998).

9.5. The Spanish National Policy Context

The Spanish implementation of EC 2078/92 has tended towards symbolic policy outcomes because of the state's embedded socio-cultural traditions, and the consequences of sweeping regulatory reforms instituted following the collapse of the Republic in 1979. Before these reforms, the Spanish state had been highly centralized with local, but little regional representation (the exception being the *provincias*, analogous to the French *département*). The main feature of the 1979 reforms was the creation of seventeen regions, the *Comunidades Autonomas* or autonomous communities, which radically recast the system of Spanish political administration and gave national political life a quasi-federal flavour. More recently, national and regional governments of all political hues have adopted neoliberal economic policies, centred on privatization of public-sector services and deregulation. This process has created new forms of 'horizontal governance' (Peters 1998*b*), including non-governmental agencies and public bodies, which have begun to offset the vertical divisions between national and regional government.

Within their jurisdiction, the autonomous communities have extensive powers over agriculture and environmental policy—for example, permitting the formulation of environmental statutes governing agricultural land management, and the 'modulation' of EC arable area payments to suit regional agricultural sectors. Nonetheless, the state retains responsibility for framework legislation on environmental protection and management. It also has direct responsibility for the country's ten national parks, the twenty-five Spanish wetlands recognized under the international Ramsar convention, and the 139 areas of high natural value guaranteed under EU nature conservation law. Undoubtedly there are strong rivalries between the national and regional levels (Borzel 1999). For example, national government retains competence for all inter-governmental negotiations with the EU, which is a source of conflict with many of the autonomous communities.

Regional governments (*Juntas*) have sought to overcome this obstruction by establishing permanent diplomatic missions in Brussels, allowing productive linkages to be built with specific DGs of the European Commission and other EU institutional actors, and effectively opening new 'policy routeways' within the EU MLG for the autonomous communities. The *Junta de Castilla la Mancha* was particularly effective in this respect at the supranational level. Its *Programa de Compensación de las Rentas Agrarias* (*PCR*—the 'Agricultural Income Compensation Scheme'), designed to compensate farmers for reducing their use of irrigation water, was the first zonal programme approved by STAR, with the largest Spanish zonal budget (ptas. 16.2 billion for the 1993–7 period), and one of the highest in the EU–15. This supports Genieys's claim (1998: 179) that 'the autonomous community is strengthened by [its] dynamic relations [with] the European Community institutions . . . this form of State [has] become . . . a privileged place of interaction where networks are institutionalised according to differentiated sectoral logics.'

In response to EC 2078/92's regulatory template, the national agriculture ministry, the *Ministerio de Agricultura Pesca y Alimentacion* (*MAPA*), drafted framework legislation for four 'horizontal' measures. These were: (1) the maintenance of fallow in extensive arable systems; (2) training for farmers in environmentally sustainable forms of agricultural management (reflecting one of the main Spanish preoccupations in Council discussions on EC 2078/92 (see Section 9.1.2)); (3) the rearing of traditional endangered livestock breeds; and (4) measures to encourage the adoption of organic farming. The *MAPA* also drafted framework legislation enabling 'zonal programmes' to be established at the discretion of *Juntas* in areas deemed to be of 'high environmental value'. These included endangered habitats and species, wetlands of high conservation value, as well as areas of environmental sensitivity—for example, landscapes at risk from soil erosion, aquifers in danger of over-exploitation, and extensively farmed landscapes.

As in France, this legal delimitation of agri-environmental objectives by the national government had two aims. First, it conferred enabling powers on the autonomous communities to operate legitimately in this policy. Arguably as important, however, it sought to establish the parameters for these operations (at one level understandable, in that Spain had no experience of agri-environmental policy prior to EC 2078/92). Nonetheless, the existing division of legislative competencies for the natural environment between state and region meant responsibility for agri-environmental policy overlapped between these two politico-administrative levels. This increased the potential for 'bargained implementation' between geographic scales. Moreover, a glut of schemes and zonal programmes was submitted by the autonomous communities to the *MAPA* for approval, covering geographical areas of high environmental value, requiring lengthy negotiations between Madrid and the *Juntas*.

Implementation of EC 2078/92 was considerably delayed, as some *Juntas* could not reach agreement with the national government, or were unable to enact enabling legislation promptly. Over the last decade, regional responses to the Regulation have also been severely hindered by financial shortages, lack of experience of agri-environmental policies, and limited staff resources (Segura 1996). While the fact that all the options under EC 2078/92 were adopted by the autonomous communities has been taken by some (rightly) to indicate a lack of coordination between the *MAPA* and the regional agriculture ministries (Wilson *et al.* 1999), it is also indicative of the exploitation by *Juntas* of channels of advice and guidance at the supranational level, in particular the Environment Directorate of the EC.

These overlapping legal/administrative responsibilities, and the way in which territorial groups have responded, are well demonstrated by the *PCR* zonal programme in the Castilla la Mancha region of central Spain (see Figure 9.2). This case study demonstrates how an emerging agri-environmental policy coalition has questioned the scope, aims, and purpose of the *PCR*, and how entrenched agricultural interests have utilized power configurations and socio-cultural norms and symbols to respond to this development.

9.6. Case Study: Agri-Environmental Policy in Mancha Occidental and Campo de Montiel, Castilla la Mancha

Historically, Castilla la Mancha's arid climate dictated a pattern of dryland arable farming, with small-scale irrigated agriculture mostly confined to river valleys and a few towns and villages. This changed in the mid-1970s, with the introduction of new irrigation techniques that enabled the region's farmers to intensify production, through greater water abstraction from aquifers. Intensification became more widespread following Spanish accession to the then EC in 1986. Under Objective 1 of the EEC Structural Funds, generous subsidies were offered to Spain's farmers to overcome 'natural handicaps'—in Mancha's case, its intense aridity. These moneys, disbursed by the regional government (*Junta de Castilla la Mancha*), financed the sinking of deeper boreholes. Premiums for irrigated crops under the CAP further encouraged the conversion of dryland arable systems. A massive expansion in the area of

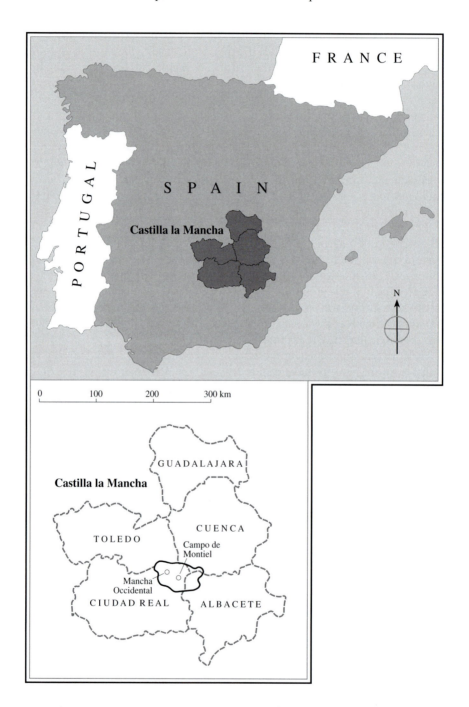

Figure 9.2. Spain and Castilla la Mancha

irrigated agriculture followed, with water-demanding crops being grown on a scale unprecedented in the region's history.

This explosion in irrigated agriculture was concentrated on the two largest aquifers in the region, Mancha Occidental (Aquifer 23) and Campo de Montiel (Aquifer 24) (see Figure 9.3). These aquifers boast Spain's most valuable wetland habitats after the Cota Doñana National Park—Las Tablas de Daimiel National Park, and the Lagunas de Ruidera Natural Park. However, during the first half of the 1990s, the size and environmental diversity of both wetlands declined rapidly, as a result of extreme drought. This ecological impoverishment also coincided with the mounting demands made on both aquifers by agricultural users. Between 1981 and 1987, the water table of Aquifer 23 fell by 2 metres a year, and by a similar amount during 1994–5. In response, in

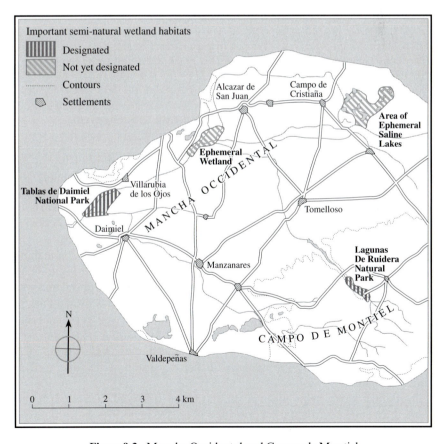

Figure 9.3. Mancha Occidental and Campo de Montiel

1993 under the agri-environmental Regulation, Castilla la Mancha's *Junta* introduced the *PCR*, to encourage farmers to become less reliant on irrigation.

The *PCR* provides a strong example of the deliberative brokered policy-making characteristic of the EU, chiefly because its focus—water management—is replete with powerful and often conflicting symbolic associations for Castilla la Mancha's territorial constituencies. These constituencies have approached the *PCR* from their own idiosyncratic perspectives, clouding scheme goals and adding to the ambiguity inherent in the underlying EU legislation. An aggravating factor is that little scientific evidence has been adduced to defend the claims made by these constituencies, either in support of, or in opposition to, the scheme. The *PCR*'s fundamentally deliberative quality is demonstrated by the recent remarks of a local environmental campaigner:

> in theory [the *PCR* is] supposed to have as its main [aim rectifying] the environmental damage of the locality. But the main problem with this is that there's no way of judging very well whether the scheme's had any environmental benefits. We don't have any unambiguous data on the recovery of the aquifers . . . up until now all the calculations of how much water has been abstracted from the aquifer has been derived from satellite imagery and from ground surveys. But it's crazy to make calculations on this basis. If you go there in summer, farmers are just irrigating their crops at three o'clock in the afternoon. The calculations don't tell you how much water farmers are really using. (SEO source, Aug. 1997)

9.6.1. The *PCR* (1): Local Coalition Influences on the EU Regulatory Template

As in L'Hérault, the implementation of EC 2078/92 in La Mancha can be understood only in its proper politico-institutional context. Traditionally, the Manchegan wetlands have held a symbolic importance for both the local agricultural lobby and national ecological groups. For many years they were considered hazardous to health, and attempts were made to drain and convert them for farming. The most far-reaching of these projects in the 1960s sought to drain some 25,000 hectares of wetland, by dredging and channelling stretches of the Guadiana river close to the town of Daimiel (see Figure 9.3). This sparked protests between local farmers and environmentalists, and was instrumental in the Tablas de Daimiel being recognized as a National Park in 1973. Following this designation, its management transferred to the national organization *Instituto Nacional para la Conservacion de la Naturaleza* (*ICONA*). Almost at once *ICONA* was at loggerheads with the *Junta* and local agricultural unions, as it opposed any further expansion of irrigated agriculture in Mancha.

Matland's work helps unravel the nature of this conflict over different agricultural and environmental priorities. From the mid-1970s onwards, agricultural intensification in Castilla la Mancha has been the focus of conflicting symbolic interpretations of the environment, mobilized respectively by farmers and, initially, extra-local ecological interests. These conflicting environmental discourses have centred on water resource management issues.

For Mancha's farmers and members of the *Junta's* agricultural policy elite, water was critical to the modernization project targeted at the regional agricultural sector. Since the 1970s, this loosely knit 'productivist' coalition has successfully argued that new irrigation technologies merely allow agricultural modernization to proceed at a faster pace, assisting the rural development effort by enabling local and regional economies to develop valuable agricultural export markets. This position is strengthened by a strong sense of independence among Manchegan farmers. Hence comments made by a prominent agricultural leader in Campo de Montiel: 'Our mentality is: "It's my farm, my borehole, I'll do what I want. If I've got the money, I'll make it deeper, I'll irrigate as much as I want." Farmers here are very stubborn. And still are, I might add . . . they'll still tell you "Why shouldn't we use the water while it's still here?" ' (*ASAJA* source, Aug. 1997). This coalition's response to the impoverishment of Mancha's wild life-rich wetlands—a direct consequence of irrigation—is well summarized by leading agricultural unionist José Sanroma: 'farmers[' livelihoods] are more important than ducks' (cited in Viladomiu and Rosell 1996).

Opposing this position was an ecological coalition, which portrayed the growth of irrigated agriculture in the region as a textbook example of the negative environmental consequences of productivist farming. Until the late 1980s, this coalition was not particularly well defined at the local level, relying primarily on extra-local representation. However, during the 1990s, the coalition began to mobilize new environmental discourses to brand La Mancha's irrigated agriculture as 'unsustainable', and, on this basis, attracted the attention of those (mostly small-scale traditional) farmers who had never been particularly well represented by productivism. Coalition members emphasized that existing water demands exceeded natural rates of replenishment for both aquifers, so that, whereas traditional dryland agriculture and local environmental concerns once peacefully co-existed, they no longer could. A senior official in the *Sociedad Espanola de Onitologia* (*SEO*; the Spanish Ornithological Society) explained: 'Farmers want to irrigate at any price—I think this is so they can improve the area payments they claim [from dryland to irrigated arable area payments] . . . They want water at any price, it's one of the things you need to change with farmers and it's a message that must be given by the *Junta*. Otherwise they just say "Oh, it's environmentalists saying 'no to development' " ' (SEO source, July 1997).

As in Languedoc, this coalition's argument has also capitalized on the reflexive 'image' of the traditional Manchegan landscape, contrasting its small-scale vineyards and dryland cereals with the modern prairie landscape of intensively cultivated maize, swept out by huge pivot irrigators. Environmentalists claim that, throughout the 1980s and 1990s, the *Junta* was unwilling to confront the problems arising from the massive expansion in irrigation, still less to address issues of ecological management of the wetlands. Such steps as were taken by the *Junta* (for example, the authorization in 1987 of transferral of waters from other river basins to maintain the Tablas de Daimiel) were dismissed by them as artificial, piecemeal, and reactive (Naredo and Gascó 1992).

This conflict between local interest coalitions has been exacerbated by other formalized regional institutions. Arguably the most important of these has been the change in juridical status of groundwater. Water policy is the responsibility of the Federal Ministry of Public Works, Transport, and the Environment (*Ministerio de Obras Públicas, Transportas y Medio Ambiente* (*MOPTMA*)), through its regional representation, the *Confederación Hidrográphicas*. In 1987 the local Hydrographic Confederation (*Confederacíon Hidrográphica del Guadiana* (*CHG*)) announced that Aquifer 23 was overexploited, requiring an annually determined 'extraction regime' to be imposed under the terms of the *Ley del Agua* (Water Law) (1985). Similar restrictions were imposed on Aquifer 24 by the *CHG* in April 1988.

This law made underground waters a public good for the first time. Henceforth, it became obligatory for farmers to make a formal application to the Hydrographic Confederation to sink any new borehole for irrigation purposes, with Irrigators' Associations (IAs) (*Comunidades de Regantes*) established to ensure the law was enforced. The law also required a register of 'authorized' water-users to be drawn up, although its compilation has been very problematic (for example, checking the position and ownership of almost 60,000 boreholes in Campo de Montiel/Mancha Occidental). All boreholes sunk since 1985 and not ratified in this way are liable to be sealed up by the *CHG* or its representatives, with farmers facing stiff financial penalties.

However, knowing the intractable difficulties of enforcement, many farmers turned a blind eye to this legislation. This was not helped by the fact that no compensation was offered to them for the change in the juridical basis of water ownership (private→public good). Reflecting on this, a leader of one of the most prominent and powerful Irrigators' Associations commented:

When the new law came in, what the Government should have said was 'we will compensate you. The water [now] belongs to the State, it is ours. We'll give you concessions. You will just pay for what you consume . . .' But that wasn't done. What they said was 'We'll respect your rights'. But these rights were conceded under the 1985 Law . . . of course this water's [now] public [property], but the fact is they didn't buy back the rights we had.   (interview, July 1997)

Henceforth, groundwater could be abstracted only by 'legalized' owners, who, under the terms of the extraction regime, received an annual quota for water based on their farmed area.

EC 2078/92 was implemented against this backdrop of increasing social tensions and growing acrimony between local interest coalitions. When the Regulation was formally ratified by the EU Council of Ministers, plans for a *PCR* scheme were already quite far advanced. These were developed by the

Junta and the *MAPA*, with some assistance from the *MOPTMA*. The regional and national administrations agreed to share the state element of cofinancing, while the EU provided the majority of finance (national and regional exchequers each providing 12.5 per cent of funds; Castilla la Mancha's status as an Objective 1 area ensured the rest came from the EU). STAR approved the *PCR* on 29 March 1993.

In essence, the *PCR* offers payment to farmers who reduce the volume of water they use for irrigation over a five-year period, with three levels available: a 'zero option' (i.e. farmers forgoing all rights to irrigate); a 70 per cent reduction in their existing use of irrigated water; and a 50 per cent reduction. A basic condition of entry is that all participants must have legal entitlement to water use for irrigation purposes, and must reduce their use of agrochemicals. The scheme's main objectives are twofold: the maintenance of a viable regional agricultural sector, through provision of income compensation; and the conservation of natural resources (aquiferous waters). Payments are made on the basis of a farm's area, and there is no ceiling on the amount each holding can receive. This fuelled criticisms that the scheme disproportionately favours larger farms. While the scheme is voluntary, the *CHG*'s extraction regime already imposed a quota on water use anyway. In effect, the *PCR* compensated farmers for fulfilling their legal obligations under the existing *Ley del Agua*.

These aspects have been the focus for bitter criticism by the *PCR*'s critics, notably members of the environmental coalition, such as the *SEO*. Originally, the *SEO*'s involvement in the *PCR* focused exclusively on the welfare of rare bird species in the Daimiel wetlands, but in the early 1990s the Society began to elaborate a more holistic position around the sustainability agenda, leading to the formation of a more inclusive rural coalition that now comprises small farmers, local community representatives, academics, and other ecological groups. The *SEO* has been pivotal in cementing this coalition together, as an official of the Agriculture and Environment Ministry, the *Consejeria de Agricultura y Medio Ambiente* (*CAMA*) explained: 'they are very important when it comes to pushing for change—especially in Daimiel, because the *SEO* is a member of the National Parks Board, the forum for discussing these things. Local ecological groups have played a part, but they have not been as active as *SEO*, who have always brought a lot of pressure to bear on us' (*CAMA* source, July 1997). This coalition has argued forcibly for the *PCR* to address environmental and social issues in the round, rather than simply targeting aquifer depletion and farmer compensation.

Initial results of the *PCR* were mixed to say the least, and strengthened the new rural coalition's position at the expense of the productivist claque of farmers. For example, despite high levels of farmer participation, between March 1994 and May 1995 the water table level of Aquifer 24 fell by 2.5–3 metres, twice that of previous years. The *CHG* concluded: 'despite the efforts of the [irrigating] farmers, their associations and the public authorities, the aquifer's condition continues to decline. Current rainfall figures are abnormally low, hence cancelling [out these] efforts . . .' (*CHG* 1995). Heavy rains in winter–spring 1995–6 changed the situation, increasing the flooded area of the Tablas de Daimiel. However, this merely confirmed the long-held suspicions of the *SEO* and others that the environmental claims made for the *PCR* by the *Junta's Consejeria de Agricultura* had been bogus all along.

By playing upon the region's traditional self-image, building upon the growing public environmental consciousness, and exploiting the growing divisions between small and large farmers, the rural coalition wrongfooted its productivist opponents. Skilful use by the *SEO* of the media to portray 'the dying Manchegan wetlands' enabled the *PCR* to be criticized for failing to achieve targets it was not expressly designed for. The rural coalition also benefited from the *SEO*'s extra-local political contacts—for example, its close relationship with *ICONA*, and its liaison with DG Env (one of the *SEO*'s Directors was seconded for a year to this Directorate-General, advising on ornithological matters). This form of 'loose coupling' between politico-administrative scales proved highly successful in advancing the ecological cause.

By contrast, the productivist coalition did not developed such linkages, relying instead upon the politics of local protest. For example, an active social movement (the *Asociación de Titulares de Aguas Privadas del Acuífero de Campo de Montiel* (The Association of Owners of Private Waters in the Campo de Montiel Aquifer)), comprising large intensive farms and spearheaded by local representatives from the farm union the *Asociación Agraria-Jovenes Agricultores* (*ASAJA*)), contested the enforcement of the *Ley del Agua*. Ironically high rates of abstraction by these larger farms (often exceeding their legal entitlement under the *CHG*'s extraction regime) denied small farms their legal entitlement to surface and ground water. Perhaps surprisingly given its previous enthusiastic support for intensive farming, the *Junta* has been relatively disinterested in supporting the productivist coalition. However, there is still a sizeable contingent of farmers calling for waters to be diverted to the Tablas, ostensibly to recharge Aquifer 23, but, according to the *SEO*: 'they want the water to irrigate, they want the water to go into the Aquifer just to pump it out again, that's for sure' (*SEO* source, July 1997).

9.6.2. The *PCR* (2): The Impact of the EU Regulatory Template on the Local Institutional Mosaic

While territorial coalitions and institutions have recast EC 2078/92, the 'regulatory template' also had a profound impact on the politico-administrative matrix of Castilla la Mancha. This measure ushered in an array of new organizational and intra-organizational responsibilities, and there were substantial problems of inter-organizational coordination arising from what is a wholly new policy area for this *Junta*.

Partly this arose because of difficulties in coordinating the activities of scalar policy elites. In late 1997, a change in the national government had considerable repercussions for the management and operation of the *PCR*, with a *CAMA* administrator complaining: 'At present we're [national government and *Junta*] not working very closely, because of political differences. Madrid is conservative and the *Junta* is socialist . . . in fact, funds for the *PCR* could be frozen, everything could be stopped' (SEO source, Aug. 1997)

Scheme administration is the overall responsibility of the *Junta*. The *CAMA* signed agreements with each of the IAs, granting them responsibilities and discretionary powers over day-to-day scheme management. Applications to join the *PCR* are handled by the *Junta's* representation at the level of the *provincia*, although IAs play an important role as the intermediary between scheme participants and the *Junta*. Final approval for each application is made by *CAMA*. At the same time, the *CHG* has responsibility for setting the extraction regime annually, which has a critical impact on one of the basic goals of the PCR.

Crucial elements of the management of water policy in Mancha are thus discharged by different arms of federal and regional government, creating parallel sets of policy networks at regional and local levels that seldom interact, a fact that has demonstrably contributed to the *PCR*'s problematic implementation. This has been further exacerbated as different environmental and agrarian goals are administered by a host of agencies, situated at different geographic scales (for example, *MAPA*, *MOPTMA* and *ICONA* at national scale; *CAMA* and *CHG* at the level of the autonomous community).

IAs, set up under the *Ley del Agua* and comprising farmers, have emerged as the pivotal institutional form at the local level for mediating and coordinating these often conflicting objectives. In a sense, these Associations have become the organizational nexus for this strand of Spanish agri-environmental policy. Crucially, any farmer participating in the *PCR* must be a member of an IA. No other interest is represented in these Associations, and, as they are also responsible for the enforcement and monitoring of water restrictions under the *CHG*'s extraction regime, this enabled the rural coalition to claim with some justification that the *PCR* was a 'self-regulated' policy. The effectiveness of IAs in enforcing the *PCR*'s restrictions varies. The Chairman of the Alcazar IA in Aquifer 23 commented: 'We have proved how effectively we're administering the Compensation scheme. We're doing it impeccably. No one gets through the net' (interview, Aug. 1997). However an ex-Director of the *CHG* had altogether different experiences of IAs:

Proof of how irrigators do not defend legitimate water users is that, between 1987 and 1997, our staff reported 4,000 illegal actions and 1,597 infractions, whereas the IAs reported 23 cases in total. When we talk to the IAs about sealing boreholes, they tell us straight that they aren't going to cooperate, and that [if we persist] we will find ourselves up against a union prepared to paralyse the region.   (interview, Aug. 1997)

Importantly IAs also act as forums for representation of farmer opinion, and for the articulation of activities based upon these opinions. Surprisingly these opinions can vary greatly, even where Associations cover adjacent areas. Clearly though the *PCR* is having some effect on farmer attitudes and opinions, as an IA Deputy near Tomelloso (see Figure 9.3) explained: 'I can tell you that the first few years, I don't know if you'll believe this, but when I told farmers they had to reduce consumption, they said they'd be waiting for me in the fields with a shotgun. Waiting with a gun, they said. And now they're monitoring themselves. That's a big step' (interview, Aug. 1997). Another IA leader in Manzanares (see Figure 9.3) noted: 'We're changing farmers' mentalities. It's no longer a matter of resources, we have to think of our children and the future . . . it's been hard to do, but we're making headway' (interview, July 1997). These comments substantiate the important role that Matland (1995) accords symbolic policies in triggering policy learning among local coalitions.

To some extent, the 'regulatory template' provided by EC 2078/92 seems to have inhibited the widespread acceptance of productivism among the region's farmers. Indeed it could be argued that the introduction of EC 2078/92 exposed splits in the productivist coalition. Smaller traditional dryland farmers in Campo de Montiel have been placed at odds with the aims of larger, more intensive holdings, as they benefited less from the *PCR*, and invariably found larger producers were circumventing the quota system by declaring large land parcels as separate 'farms' with different 'owners'. Unquestionably, the *PCR*'s implementation has prompted small farmers to look to alternative discourses, including 'sustainable agriculture', around which to reorientate their activities. Some in Campo de Montiel have joined La Mancha's emergent rural coalition in supporting a 'zero option'—namely, the complete prohibition of irrigation on that aquifer. Growing disunity in the productivist coalition has been materially assisted by the relatively weak historical ties between the *CAMA* and the region's farmers, and the recent addition of environmental responsibilities to the *Consejeria's* administrative brief.

During the late 1990s, the progressive rural coalition commissioned a group of independent experts to examine the situation in Mancha Occidental, and thereby mediate between the conflicting coalitions. This exercise was comparatively successful, and has been complemented by the activities of other local actors. An umbrella group representing the interests of many of the IAs has produced a strategy document that, significantly, acknowledged the environmental objectives of the *PCR*, and that made constructive suggestions for its amendment. The *CAMA*, too, has brought forward new proposals for redirecting agriculture in the region towards more sustainable practices. Gradually, conflict between local coalitions appears to be giving way to a new climate of compromise and cooperation.

9.7. Conclusions

In this chapter, we have developed our argument that a bargained, negotiated form of multi-level decision-making characterizes the EU's emergent agri-environmental policy sector, by examining the ongoing policy processes in two territorial arenas, Languedoc-Roussillon in France and Castilla la Mancha in Spain. Using Matland's notion of 'implementation outcomes', we have shown how in both cases local coalitions and reflexive images of region and locality are critically important to this iterative negotiated policy process. EC 2078/92 appears to have reawakened rather than transcended popular sentiments in both territories, and revitalized local notions of territorial identities, while placing them under renewed pressure. Both case studies provide examples of dynamic territorial coalitions that, to some extent, have destabilized their productivist counterparts by exploiting the heterarchical nature of MLG. Extra-local contacts such as, in the French case, the European Commission's Environment Directorate, DG Env, and, in the case of Castilla la Mancha, national conservation bodies (*ICONA*) and national pressure groups (*SEO*), have been utilized in this process. Territorial coalitions have also capitalized on the weaknesses of interorganizational rivalries (for example, in Spain, *MOPTMA* and *MAPA*). Evidently, coalitions in both southern France and central Spain are actively contributing to the elaboration of EU MLG, and, indeed, are recasting existing governance forms through, for example, the creation of multi-level agri-environmental policy networks, and the establishment of new economic development trajectories for localities (for example, *Cru pie-grièche*). In short, both case examples provide evidence of active MLG, rather than simply multi-level participation (Bache 1999).

The two case studies also support our contention that supranational legislation can be conceived as a 'regulatory template' that is refined, reappraised, and recast by local coalitions, in accordance with locally specific informal institutions and territorial 'rules of the game' (Rhodes 1997). These 'regulatory templates' are debated and negotiated at regional and local levels, prompting formal (creation of new agencies, institutional procedures, and so on) and non-formal institutional change (the genesis of agri-environmental networks, new concepts of environmental responsibility within agriculture, and the transformation of old agricultural policy communities). In both case studies, local coalitions have not only questioned nationally and regionally determined implementation strategies in the form of 'zonal programmes' established under EC 2078/92. They have also sought to determine whether the Regulation's goals and aims can be made consonant with their own locality's historical-institutional endowments. In the process, different tiers of government have become embroiled in new deliberative processes, and hence have become increasingly dependent on each other's resources (principally knowledges, finances, and experiences). Consequently, conflict during the initial phases of implementation has been replaced by compromise and cooperation in later stages.

On the basis of the detailed case studies, two criticisms might be levelled at local, regional, and national authorities in the case study areas. First, that local and regional administrations did not prosecute the agri-environmental Regulation with sufficient rigour; secondly, that national administrations did not provide enough assistance to local administrative elites and policy partici-pants in what, for both areas, was a new policy area. However, such outcomes should not be considered surprising given the Regulation's ambiguous goals and objectives, its imprecision in terms of mechanisms for fulfilling these aims, and the considerable degree of subsidiarity vested in EC 2078/92. In any event, the implementation 'outcomes' in Languedoc and Castilla la Mancha must be harnessed. Potentially, EC 2078/92 has provided both regions with an institu-tionalized framework for negotiation and long-term cooperation between competing local coalitions, and for social learning by them. At the same time, far greater emphasis should also be given by policy practitioners to organiza-tional learning, not just in France and Spain but across the EU–15, particu-larly in states with no previous experience of this policy. In short, results from EU-wide implementation must also be used to 'resteer' (Richardson 1996*b*), refine, improve, and, where necessary, redirect agri-environmental policy. There have been some encouraging developments already, with introduction in 1996 of the Implementation Regulation (CEC 1996), setting out mecha-nisms and procedures for monitoring zonal programmes (see Chapter 6), and in 1999 the consolidation of EC 2078/92 in the RDR (CEC 1999*a*) (see Chapters 1 and 2). The RDR addresses directly southern member states' envi-ronmental concerns, by taking a more holistic approach towards the needs of European rural economies.

Both case studies have shown there is a high level of inter- and intra-regional involvement in, and mobilization over, local agri-environmental policies, resulting in substantial change in existing patterns of territorial governance. What is less clear is the precise influence of 'the local' on national and supra-national policy-making, although we have attempted to conceptualize this influence through the notion of a 'regulatory template', both configuring and being configured by territorial institutional forms. Indeed, the political 'weight' of regions within the EU MLG would appear to depend on these local institutional endowments—the political economic importance of each; the political skills and expertise of local elites; their capacity to capture and to manipulate territorial identities, and local 'self-image'; the assertiveness and flexibility of collective social movements; and the ability of local leaders to coordinate and mobilize these movements in such a way as to catalyse change at other scales within the EU polity. These characteristics appear to provide new modalities for pushing local political agendas at other politico-geographic scales, including the supranational. Overall, our findings tend to confirm Jeffrey's assertion (2000: 2) that 'subnational mobilization has served primarily to undermine the capacity of central State institutions to maintain a monopoly competence over European [Union] policy'.

An inter-governmentalist perspective of the findings presented here might conclude, quite legitimately, that both states have retained control over the essential levers of power in the agri-environmental arena—namely, finance and programme approval. However, drawing on the UK, French, and Spanish examples in this book, such a perspective cannot account for vital drivers of change determining the modalities of agricultural policy-making at supranational, national, and subnational levels. In particular, it appears that none of these states can any longer dictate which actor(s) participate in the agricultural policy-making process, a vital ingredient of the old 'command-and-control' style of sectoral management. Similarly, an inter-governmental perspective also considerably underplays the role of EU institutions in structuring new forms of territorial accountability, in particular the agricultural and environmental Directorates of the European Commission. As we have demonstrated in this book, both DGs have played a major role in orchestrating multi-level agri-environmental policy networks, comprising actors operating at a variety of politico-geographic scales. By contrast, an MLG perspective accounts well for the broad contours of development in EU agri-environmental policy over the last decade. Not least, the new forms of territorial governance that have emerged around agri-environmental policy in many EU states, involving many more actors in multi-scalar policy-making than hitherto, are a logical corollary of MLG. In the short term, this is likely to increase conflict over policy objectives, resulting in policy instability and unpredictability. In the longer term, however, judging by the Spanish experience, these novel forms of political engagement may well provide new modalities for the delivery of policy outcomes that are more effective and equitable for *all* territorial groupings, and not just for specific clienteles.

10

Conclusions

The preceding chapters have offered a historically grounded examination of multi-scalar policy-making, recognized as a defining feature of EU governance. We have sought to develop new synergies between political science and geography, by conceptualizing the EU using the political-science notion of MLG, while at the same time building upon and elaborating this notion's geographical resonances—namely, ideas of scale, space, place, and territorial identity. To this end, we have used two analytical approaches: new institutionalism (now heralded by geographers as 'a [theoretical] movement which seems certain to grow in importance [in the discipline] over the coming years' (Martin 2000: 4) and policy networks. These complementary approaches have enabled us to make explicit the scalar connections between the activity 'spaces' of EU MLG implicated in agri-environmental policy (the institutional arenas of the European Commission, the EP, the Council of Ministers, and national administrations), and the territorial 'places' of constituent member states (illustrated here with reference to France, Spain, and the UK). New institutionalism and policy networks have also been instrumental in our identification of a range of formal and informal modalities of policy-making at work within the EU polity, which have mediated the 'environmentalization' (Buttel 1993) of the CAP.

Our analysis enables conclusions to be drawn in three main areas. First, on the likely development of EU agri-environmental policy; secondly, on the nature and functioning of the EU polity; and, thirdly, by drawing together these two themes, on the implications for future geographical research on EU public policies. We examine these issues in turn below.

All the modalities analysed in this volume are recognized in the EU as legitimate forms of agri-environmental policy procedure and practice. As such, they also provide us with important insights into the future trajectory of this fledgling public policy. In the first place, all the modalities emerge from relational processes—that is, socialization, deliberation, and negotiation of the 'regulatory template' provided by EC 2078/92. It is highly likely, therefore, that EU agri-environmentalism will continue to develop in this discursive, relatively unpredictable way. Indeed, if the longitudinal analysis presented here is anything to go by, the intrinsic modalities of the agri-environmental domain point towards this policy continuing to evolve organically, but in future responding more to local territorial imperatives, rather than following some pathway carefully orchestrated at the national or, indeed, the supranational level (see Chapters 8 and 9). It remains to be seen whether in time these local territorial imperatives come to rival globalizing influences such as existing EU commitments under the GATT, and future obligations under the WTO, as significant drivers of EU agri-environmental policy development.

We adduce three reasons for the increased importance of the territorial dimension in the development of agri-environmental policy. First, as the case studies show (Chapters 6 and 9), there is now a pressing need for a greater differentiation of decision-making and decision-taking responsibilities in this policy at the territorial scale. If anything, this is likely to grow more pronounced in the future, particularly with the impending eastward enlargement of the EU. Undoubtedly, clearer differentiation of these responsibilities, and their more equitable distribution between national, regional, and local levels, would improve the efficiency and effectiveness of agri-environmentalal policy (cf. Benz and Eberlein 1999 on regional policy). Moreover, if designed appropriately, such changes could satisfy the demands of territorial constituencies for greater involvement in policy at regional and local scales. National administrations will need to weigh up whether ceding powers to subnational administrations in this way is preferable to granting the European Commission additional powers to carry out functions such as the monitoring and the supervision of policy on their behalf (Richardson 1996*b*; Jordan 1999). In either case, such changes are likely to undercut the centralizing powers of the nation state, requiring improved coordination between government departments sponsoring agri-environmental policies, local agencies providing policy delivery functions, and territorial groups, if disruption and destabilization among actors are to be minimized.

The territorial dimension is also likely to grow more significant in developmental terms as local coalitions become more involved in day-to-day policy operations. This has both positive and negative aspects. For example, one lesson to emerge from the first decade of EU agri-environmental implementation is that, while ambiguity was a useful quantity in building strategic alliances during policy-shaping and policy-setting on EC 2078/92, it has had considerable disadvantages at the post-agreement stage. As we have seen, in some situations the Regulation's inherent ambiguities have exacerbated historic tensions and rivalries at the local level that, in turn, have raised the potential for policy conflict, impeding the effectiveness of programmes. The case studies in Chapter 9 have demonstrated that some locally based coalitions are in a powerful position to manipulate this conflict to their own ends, and with it to control the trajectory of local agri-environmental programmes. Thirdly, it is already apparent that local agri-environmental projects and programmes are instituting new forms of governance in EU rural areas—for example, new markets (for example, *Cru pie-grièche*), new policy networks, and the reformulation of existing local elite structures (e.g. Castilla la Mancha's progressive rural coalition). Indeed, in the long term, alongside more potent agents of restructuring, this policy may become implicated in promoting new elite structures across many EU rural regions. By itself, therefore, an MLG perspective on EU agri-environmentalism provides valuable insights into this policy's future development.

However, as we noted in Chapter 1, our main objective in writing this book was to provide a more informed perspective on the nature and functioning of the EU polity than that offered by recent macro-level analyses of EU policy sectors. Specifically, we have sought to develop a more analytically rigorous understanding of MLG, by scrutinizing the modalities associated with EU agri-environmental policy. As mentioned in Chapter 1, our choice of the CAP as a focus for study, and within that sector of agri-environmental policy as a case example, was carefully considered. The CAP represents the EU's longest-established common public policy. The modalities associated with this sector may, therefore, provide insights into those likely to emerge in the future in other arenas of EU multi-scalar policy-making. At the same time, they should offer a valuable preliminary understanding of the way in which the evolving EU polity operates, in particular by showing how the political actions of elites in EU policy arenas find their eventual expression in territorial outcomes. Increasingly, geographers are recognizing the importance of shedding light on these interrelationships, and of analysing the growing interdependence between the different scalar elites within the EU polity. For example, Swyngedouw (2000: 21) notes that:

A new configuration of articulated economic spaces and scales of governance is rapidly emerging [in the global economy]. Spatial economic analysis and policy that ignores the subtleties of power relations, [and] the new institutional configurations and the shifting power geometries associated with this . . . will invariably fail to account for or influence . . . socio-economic development trajectories.

In short, the policy modalities examined here represent the putative mechanisms by and through which different scalar regimes in the EU polity are being brought together and coordinated. Modalities are thus contributing both a means and a rationale for the emergence of interdependencies between scalar policy elites within the EU, making them eminently worthy of geographers' attention.

Moreover, modalities also provide a unique insight into

the subnational scale . . . together with . . . supranational formations. These have become the pivotal domains for launching pro-active development strategies. The often non-democratic and little transparent organization and decision making procedures and mechanisms at these scales of governance turn them into . . . explicit . . . playing-fields that permit [the] shaping [of] territorial trajectories in the image of dominant or hegemonic elite coalitions. These new elite-based and led institutions and networks have become key forms of governance and have—at least to some extent—replaced the State as rule-making, policy formulating and implementing . . . powers that influence and shape a broadening range of socio-economic aspects.   (Swyngedouw 2000: 19)

Hence, as Swyngedouw implies and as we have shown, not only do policy modalities represent important conduits in the EU for coordinating and transacting the legitimate business of agri-environment policy-making. They also provide policy elites with a repertoire of licit procedures and mechanisms in multi-scalar policy-making with which to advance their *own* ambitions and agendas within the EU polity. For example, specific procedures have been used by policy elites to co-opt 'environmentalization' to reinforce their own political and/or power positions; to secure 'side-payments' from other actors during the early stages of the agri-environmental policy-making process, or to gain derogations from certain agri-environmental policy conditions; to undermine or conversely to buttress dominant agrarian ideologies; to recast local territorial identities, and notions of 'the environment', in order to further the political projects of elite constituencies within rural regimes (see Jones and Clark 2000); and to further specific organizational ambitions through the creation of multi-level agri-environmental policy networks, comprising highly interdependent supranational, national, and local policy actors, among whom knowledge and other resources are exchanged, thereby increasing connectivity between different geographic scales. This insight into the multi-scalar politics behind EU policy-making provides a second compelling reason for a geographically informed analysis of EU policy modalities.

The modalities analysed here have been tremendously varied. Some are formalized, others less formal. Some emerge from the architecture of the CAP itself. Others spring from the intra- and interrelationships within and between EU institutions. Yet others are micro-level (individual actor) based. Variety is also evident in the interrelationships between EU modalities. In some cases, they have combined to advance mutual organizational interests (agenda-interlocking, Chapter 4), while elsewhere they have thwarted the actions of actors, or provided a means of tactical obstruction (counter-lobbying strategies, Chapter 5). The effect of these modalities on the CAP's 'environmentalization' has been similarly mixed. Occasionally, the interplay between modalities has furthered environmentalization's cause—for example, through the operation of multi-level policy networks (Chapters 8 and 9). Other modalities, however, have unquestionably retarded this complex process (for example, the mobilization by the UK's MAFF of socio-cultural traditions to shape national agri-environmental policies, Chapter 6).

In effect, modalities have defined, delimited, and etched out the parameters of operation of the agri-environmental domain, by providing the terms of engagement within which the EU's relevant political, policy, and administrative elites work. At the same time, however, the activities of these elites have subtly changed these terms of engagement. So EU modalities would appear to be a nascent structural form in the supranational polity, with greater cohesiveness and 'stickiness' than, say, the day-to-day routinized activities of actors within policy networks, but without having the longevity, universality, or sense of permanence of less formal institutions. On the basis of evidence provided here, they can also provide mechanisms for transforming 'low politics'—that is, the great majority of policy-making activity transacted within the EU polity—into the 'high' political issues of the moment.

Modalities, therefore, provide a critical structuring element in EU policy-making. In earlier chapters, we demonstrated this structuring effect on agri-environmental policy in three principal ways. First, we showed how agri-environmentalism has been perceived as a challenge to existing EU agricultural elite interests, obliging them to respond and, in some instances, to capitalize on this new EU policy domain for their own purposes (see Chapters 2, 4, 5, and 6). Secondly, we demonstrated how mutual dependencies between these elite interests at subnational, national, and supranational scales have gradually developed around and through this new policy domain (see Chapters 6, 8, and 9). Lastly, we examined how certain elites have utilized the discursive concept of agri-environmentalism to create allegiances to the emergent multi-level polity, through the perception of a need for an 'EU level solution' to agri-environmental issues (Chapters 2, 3, and 7). This important structuring effect of modalities makes it vital for political geographers to be sensitive to those emerging in different EU policy domains, to examine how they operate, and, in particular, to analyse how these procedures and strategies capitalize on, and meld together, scale, space, place, and territorial identity within the EU polity.

A number of key issues emerge from this exploration of the modalities of EU policy-making: for example, why have these modalities emerged, and not others? There are both sectoral and geographical explanations. In the first place, the particular resource base of the EU agricultural policy community, and the flows of these resources among its policy elites, have favoured the creation of certain modalities. Three such flows can be distinguished: knowledge-based resources, for example, domestic agricultural preoccupations, policy-relevant administrative skills, and expertise as it relates to the intricacies of the CAP (giving rise, for example, to modalities based around shared norms and values). The flow of material resources also provides an important explanation—such as finance and capital flows—and inter-organizational relations within the policy superstructure defined by the CAP (providing a range of modalities including inter-organizational coordination strategies—for example, agenda-interlocking). There is also the politico-geographic resource offered by territorial identities being made and remade within multi-level agri-environmental policy networks, which has ensured that some modalities have greater prominence than others.

Secondly, what are the wider implications for political geographical studies of the EU flowing from this study? There appear to us to be at least five major consequences for future work. As a first step, researchers will need to map out the scalar extent and 'reach' of multi-level policy networks (the identity of their constituent actors, the precise activities and functions of these actors as they relate to particular sectoral areas, and the relative importance of these networks at different politico-geographic scales of operation). Most importantly, there is the requirement to identify the 'nodes' within these networks that serve to link different politico-geographic scales. These 'nodes' may be particular key individuals (possibly having membership of a number of elite constituencies at different scales: often, but not necessarily, European Commission administrators); key decision-making forums (such as STAR (see Chapters 8 and 9) that bring together subnational, national, and supranational policy elites); organizations/organizational filières that rely on the active participation of scalar elites as part of their daily business (such as *COPA* and its constituent national membership), or a combination of these possibilities.

We have also demonstrated that policy-making modalities often have profoundly politico-geographic origins. They both rely upon and reshape national, regional, and local territorial customs, traditions, and identities. As the political scientist Charlie Jeffrey (2000: 20) notes: 'the existing architecture of [the nation State] is being chipped away into a new, diverse and dynamic pattern of multi-level governance by a profusion of larger or smaller waves of sub-national mobilization and policy influence', a process that geographers are uniquely placed to examine. Future political geographical studies of the EU will have much of value to say about this interrelationship. Paradoxically, as the autonomy of politico-geographic scales begins to melt away, territorial identity and sense of place appear to be reasserting their importance.

Thirdly, and closely related to this last point, we have demonstrated the discursive and deliberative nature of EU policy-making. Crucial to this policy-making process are local territorial signifiers and identities, and less formal institutions, which inform, shape, and dictate national policy outcomes. There is considerable potential here for political geographers to investigate how these discursive processes work in practice, how they are mobilized and how they interrelate between different geographic scales, and how in turn they contribute to the creation of the 'horizontal' participative polity of the EU.

Fourthly, there is great scope for political geographers to quantify the nature and extent of 'flows' of policy resources (knowledge, material resources, and the repackaging and refashioning of territorial identities) between the different scales of the EU polity. Clearly, these scalar flows will vary in their volume and their intensity, depending on sectoral and territorial factors. Fifthly and finally, while we have stressed the growing interdependencies between territorial groupings and elites at these different scales, we have also sought to draw attention to the competitive relationship that still exists between them. As we have seen, heterarchical forms of governance, such as EU MLG, are as strongly associated with particular geometries of power as more hierarchically structured regimes. Assessing which social constituency or institution or territory benefits, and which loses out, is as important as ever, and depends, crucially, on the interaction between particular modalities of governance.

GLOSSARY

Agriculture Council main forum at the supranational level for decision-taking on the Common Agricultural Policy. As with other EU Councils, the Agriculture Council consists of national delegations from each member state and representatives from the European Commission (in this case the DG Agri (q.v.)), and is chaired by the national delegation holding the EU Presidency.

agri-environmental policy a policy strand of the CAP (q.v.) with three main objectives—to complement CAP market policy reforms; to raise farm incomes; and to encourage the uptake by farmers of more environmentally sensitive agricultural practices and less intensive farming techniques.

agri-environmental regulation Regulation EC 2078/92. One of three Council Regulations accompanying the MacSharry reforms (q.v.) to the CAP. The main EU policy instrument for achieving agri-environmental policy (q.v.) objectives, by offering financial incentives to farmers to deintensify their production methods, and to adopt environmentally sensitive farming practices. The Regulation was obligatory for member states to implement, although participation by farmers was voluntary. Now subsumed within the Rural Development Regulation (q.v.).

arable area payments payments introduced under the 1992 CAP reforms, and made to EU farmers as partial compensation for reduction in the historic levels of price support offered under the policy.

Commissioner EU official with overall responsibility for the activities of a Directorate-General (q.v.). Typically, Commissioners are drawn from among the political elites of member states in such a way as to ensure that all states are represented within the 'College' of twenty-four Commissioners.

Common Agricultural Policy (CAP) EU public policy regulating the production, processing, marketing, and trade in agricultural commodities in and between EU member states, and between the EU and third countries. Introduced in 1962, the CAP remains one of the EU's most far-reaching and ambitious policies.

Common Market Organizations principal mechanisms of the CAP for managing market supply and demand for each of the 'commodities'—principally livestock, and arable crops—regulated under the policy. Each CMO comprises a body of market Regulations (q.v.) governing issues such as price stabilization, intervention purchase, and product differentiation. CMOs intervene at virtually every stage of the EU food chain, including production, marketing, export and processing of commodities, etc.

Common Rural Development Policy one of the most significant developments in the CAP's forty year history, announced in 1999 in the preamble to the Rural Development Regulation (q.v.), and heralded by the European Commission as the policy's 'second pillar'. According to the Agriculture Council (1999*a*: 80) the CRDP seeks to 'contribute to the achievement of the [rural development objectives] as laid down in Article 33(1) of the Treaty [of Rome]'.

concordance system an international system wherein actors find it possible consistently to harmonize their interests, compromise their differences, and reap mutual rewards from their interactions.

core principles basic ideological assumptions and tenets of a public policy that, in certain circumstances, can dictate its evolution. Identified by Giandomenico Majone (1989).

Directive EU legislative measure that is obligatory on all member states to implement, although the precise means of implementation is left at the discretion of national administrations; cf. Regulation.

Directorate-General (DG) an organizational division of the European Commission, with responsibility for developing and managing policy in a specific sectoral area, or areas. Roughly equivalent to a government department or ministry. In 2000–1 there were twenty-four Directorates-General within the European Commission.

DG Agri Directorate-General (q.v.) of the European Commission with responsibility for the EU's agricultural policy, the CAP (q.v.), and latterly the Common Rural Development Policy (q.v.). Formerly DG VI.

DG Env Directorate-General (q.v.) of the European Commission with responsibility for EU environmental policy. Formerly DG XI.

environmentalization a multifaceted process described by the rural sociologist Frederick Buttel (1993: 12) as 'the trend towards environmental considerations being increasingly brought to bear in political and economic decisions'—for example, through decision-making and decision-taking in public policies.

European Commission EU institution charged with managing the corpus of existing supranational policies, and developing new policies for the Council of Ministers in order to further European integration among the EU's member states. In 2000 the EC comprised twenty-four Directorates-General, each lead by a Commissioner (q.v.).

European Parliament directly elected Parliament of the European Union with, depending on the policy sector, varying degrees of power in EU governance. In 2000 there were 626 Members of the European Parliament drawn from the fifteen member states of the EU.

FEOGA (*Fond Européen d'Orientation et de Garantie Agricole*) French acronym for the European Agricultural Guidance and Guarantee Fund, the EU Structural Fund financing the CAP. Comprises two agricultural budgetary Funds, the Guidance (q.v.) and Guarantee (q.v) funds.

GATT (General Agreement on Tariffs and Trade) global institution established after the Second World War to promote greater trade liberalization among trading nations, in sectoral areas including agriculture, through the abolition of quotas, tariffs, and other duties on international trade. Wound up in 1992 and replaced by the World Trade Organization (q.v.).

Guarantee Fund budgetary fund of the Common Agricultural Policy that, until 1992, was used exclusively to finance the policy's Common Market Organizations (q.v.). Now also finances most elements of the Union's Common Rural Development Policy (q.v.).

Guidance Fund budgetary fund of the Common Agricultural Policy that finances part of its structures policy (q.v.).

institution a formalized or non-formalized set of procedures, norms, or routines that influences decision-making and decision-taking. 'Formalized' institutions include organizations with defined goals aims and objectives—for example, the agriculture ministries in EU member states, or the institutions of the EU (including the Council of Ministers, European Commission (q.v.), and European Parliament (q.v.)). 'Non-formal' or 'less formal' institutions might include social conventions, socio-cultural beliefs, or political ideologies.

inter-governmentalism an approach to integration that treats states, and national governments in particular, as the primary actors in the integration process.

MacSharry reforms a package of reforms drawn up by the then Agriculture Commissioner Ray MacSharry and approved by the EU Agriculture Council (q.v.) in May 1992. The MacSharry reforms instituted the first effective reductions in levels of price support in the CAP's history. Despite being hailed as far-reaching in its scope, this package of measures focused on the arable and beef sectors, and left much of the policy untouched.

modalities the strategies and methods of procedure in EU policy-making that are selected by policy and organizational elites to advance their own interests and influence, given the constraints imposed by specific institutional contexts.

modulation the concept of varying the amount of subsidy or payment offered to farmers in relation to the particular characteristics of their farm holdings or businesses—for example, farm size; environmental characteristics; or farm enterprise type.

multi-level governance a conceptualization that depicts the EU as having dispersed rather than concentrated authority, and with political action occurring at and between various levels of governance.

multi-level policy networks sector-specific networks, comprising highly interdependent supranational, national, and local policy actors, among whom knowledge and other resources are exchanged, thereby increasing connectivity between different geographic scales.

new institutionalism a broad movement in contemporary political science that seeks to reinstate and refine the study of institutions as key variables in political life.

Regulation EU legislative measure that is obligatory for member states to implement in the manner set down in the legislation.

Rural Development Regulation the centrepiece legislative measure of the 1999 CAP reforms, comprising a range of new and existing EU instruments on rural development, agricultural structures (q.v.), and the agricultural environment, including the agri-environmental regulation (q.v.).

Stresa conference conference organized in 1958 by the then European Commissioner for Agriculture, Sicco Mansholt, with the aim of developing the Articles on agriculture, contained in the Treaty of Rome (q.v.), into a workable EU public policy. The conference resulted in the overall design and core principles (q.v.) of the CAP.

STAR (*Comité des Structures Agricoles*) a management committee of the DG Agri, responsible for overseeing the implementation and operation of all EU agricultural structures policy, including agri-environmental policy.

structures policy a branch of policy within the CAP, targeting the characteristics of agriculture common to all member states—for example, farm size, land consolidation, land type and quality, and age structure of the agricultural population—with the aim of improving productivity. As with the Common Market Organizations (q.v.), structures policy is highly subsidized. Now largely consolidated within the Rural Development Regulation (q.v.).

Treaty of Rome founding treaty of the European Union, signed in 1957 between the member states of the then EU–6.

World Trade Organization (WTO) successor body to the GATT, and instituted under its auspices. WTO is a global institution regulating international trade, with the aim of ensuring trade flows are made in a regular, predictable, and unimpeded fashion. The WTO also has responsibility for ensuring the enforcement of existing domestic and international agreements promoting trade liberalization, negotiated under GATT.

REFERENCES

Adshead, M. (1996). 'Beyond Clientelism: Agricultural Networks in Ireland and the European Union'. *West European Politics*, 19: 583–608.

Agra Europe (1985). *A New Perspective for the CAP? The Commission's Policy Options*. Agra Briefing 8. Tunbridge Wells: Agra Europe (London) Ltd.

——(1999). *Agriculture and the Environment: Development of European Union Agri-Environment Policy*. Agra Europe Special Report No. 110. Tunbridge Wells: Agra Europe (London) Ltd.

AGRIFIN (1991). Council Committee on Agricultural Finance, 'Report From the AGRIFIN Group to COREPER on the Evaluation of the Financial Impact of the Accompanying Measures'. Document 9618/91. Brussels: Council of the European Communities.

Aguilar-Fernández, S. (1994). 'Convergence in Environmental Policy? The Resilience of National Institutional Designs in Spain and Germany'. *Journal of Public Policy*, 14/1: 39–56.

Alexander, E. R. (1985). 'From Idea to Action: Notes for a Contingency Theory of the Policy Implementation Process'. *Administration and Society*, 16/4: 403–26.

Allington, N., and O'Shaughnessy, N. (1987). 'Growing Insanity: the Effects of the Common Agricultural Policy'. *Enlightenment*, PPl–4. London: Adam Smith Institute (Research) Ltd.

Altenstetter, C., and Bjorkman, J. W. (1976). 'The Rediscovery of Federalism: The Impact of Federal Child Health Programs on Connecticut State Health Policy Formation and Service Delivery', in C. Jones and R. Thomas (eds.), *Public Policy Making in the Federal System*. Beverley Hills, CA: Sage, 217–37.

Andersen, S. S., and Eliassen, K. A. (1995). 'EU Lobbying: the New Research Agenda'. *European Journal of Political Research*, 27: 427–41.

Armstrong, K., and Bulmer, S. (1998). *The Governance of the Single European Market*. Manchester: Manchester University Press.

Arp, H. (1992). 'The European Parliament in European Community Environmental Policy'. European University Institute Working Paper 92/13. Florence: European University Institute.

Aspinwall, M. D., and Schneider, G. (1998). 'Same Menu, Separate Tables: The Institutionalist Turn in Political Science and the Study of European Integration'. Paper presented to Joint Sessions of the European Consortium for Political Research, University of Warwick, Mar.

Averyt, W. (1975). 'Eurogroups, Clientela, and the European Community'. *International Organization*, 29: 948–72.

Bache, I. (1999). 'The Extended Gatekeeper: Central Government and the Implementation of EC Regional Policy in the UK'. *Journal of European Public Policy*, 6/1: 28–45.

Baldock, D. M. (1985). *Wetland Drainage in Europe: The Effects of Agricultural Policy in Four EEC Countries*. London: Institute for International Environment and Development/Institute for European Environmental Policy.

——(1992). 'The Polluter Pays Principle and its Relevance to the European Community's Common Agricultural Policy'. *Sociologia Ruralis*, 32/1: 49–65.

——and Lowe, P. D. (1996). 'The Development of European Agri-Environmental Policy', in M.C. Whitby (ed.), *The European Experience of Policies for the Agricultural Environment*. Wallingford: CAB International, 8–25.

Barrett, S., and Fudge, C. (1981). *Policy and Action: Essays on the Implementation of Public Policy*. London: Methuen.

Benson, J. K. (1975). 'The Interorganizational Network as a Political Economy'. *Administrative Science Quarterly*, 20/1: 229–49.

——(1980). 'A Framework for Policy Analysis', in D. L. Rogers and D. A. Whetten (eds.), *Interorganizational Coordination: Theory, Research, and Implementation*. Ames, IA: Iowa State University Press, 137–76.

Benz, A., and Eberlein, B. (1999). 'The Europeanization of Regional Policies: Patterns of Multi-Level Governance'. *Journal of European Public Policy*, 6/2: 329–48.

Berman, P. (1978). 'The Study of Macro- and Micro-Implementation'. *Public Policy*, 26/2: 157–84.

Boehmer-Christiansen, S. (1994). 'Politics and Environmental Management'. *Journal of Environmental Planning and Management*, 37/1: 69–85.

Boisson, J.-M., and Buller, H. (1996). 'France', in M. C. Whitby (ed.), *The European Experience of Policies for the Agricultural Environment*. Wallingford: CAB International, 105–30.

Borzel, T. A. (1999). 'Towards Convergence in Europe? Institutional Adaptation to Europeanization in Germany and Spain'. *Journal of Common Market Studies*, 37/4: 573–96.

Bowler, S., and Farrell D. M. (1995). 'The Organizing of the European Parliament: Committees, Specialization and Co-ordination'. *British Journal of Political Science*, 25: 219–43.

Brinkhorst, L. (1991). 'Subsidiarity and European Environmental Policy'. Paper presented at the Jacques Delors Colloquium on Subsidiarity, organized by the European Institute of Public Administration, Maastricht, 22 Mar. Reproduced in *Subsidiarity—The Challenge of Change*. Maastricht: EIPA, 89–100.

Browne, A., and Wildavsky, A. (1984). 'Implementation as Mutual Adaptation', in J. L. Pressman and A. Wildavsky (eds.), *Implementation*. Berkeley and Los Angeles: University of California Press, 206–31.

Bryner, G. (1981). 'Congress, Courts and Agencies: Equal Employment and the Limits of Policy Implementation'. *Political Science Quarterly*, 96/3: 411–30.

Buckwell, A. E. (1997). 'Agenda 2000 and the Countryside'. *ECOS*, 18/2: 13–14.

Buller, H. (1992). 'Agricultural Change and the Environment in Western Europe', in K. Hoggart (ed.), *Agricultural Change, Environment and Economy*. London: Mansell, 68–88.

——Lowe, P. D., and Flynn, A. (1993). 'National Responses to the Europeanization of Environmental Policy: A Selective Review of Comparative Literature', in J. D. Liefferink, P. D. Lowe, and A. P. J. Mol (eds.), *European Integration and Environmental Policy*. London: Belhaven Press, 175–95.

Bulmer, S. J. (1994). 'The Governance of the European Union: A New Institutionalist Approach'. *Journal of Public Policy*, 13/4: 351–80.

Buttel, F. (1993). 'Environmentalization and Greening: Origins, Processes and Implications', in S. Harper (ed.), *The Greening of Rural Policy: International Perspectives*. London: Belhaven Press, 12–26.

Buttel, F. (1997). 'Social Institutions and Environmental Change', in M. Redclift, and G. Woodgate (eds.), *The International Handbook of Environmental Sociology*. London: Edward Elgar, 40–54.

—— (1998). 'Some Observations on States, World Orders, and the Politics of Sustainability'. *Organization and Environment*, 11: 261–86.

Callon, M. (1986). 'Some Elements of a Sociology of Translation: Domestication of the Scallops and the Fishermen of St Brieuc Bay', in J. Law (ed.), *Power, Action and Belief*. London: Routledge & Kegan Paul, 196–233.

CEC (1968), Commission for the European Communities (1968). *Memorandum on the Reform of Agriculture in the European Economic Community*. COM (68) 1000. Brussels: CEC.

——(1973). *Proposal for a Directive on Agriculture in Mountain Areas and in Certain Other Poorer Farming Areas*. COM (73) 202 final. Brussels: CEC.

——(1975*a*). 'Directive Number 75/268/EEC of 28 April 1975 on Mountain and Hill Farming and Farming in Certain Less Favoured Areas'. *Official Journal*, L128: 1–20.

——(1975*b*). *Stocktaking of the Common Agricultural Policy*. COM (75) 100. Brussels: CEC.

——(1985*a*). *Perspectives for the Common Agricultural Policy*. COM (85) 333 final. Brussels: CEC.

——(1985*b*). 'Council Regulation EEC No. 797/85 of 12 March 1985 on Improving the Efficiency of Agricultural Structures'. *Official Journal*, L93: 1–18.

——(1986). 'Propositions complémentaires dans le domaine socio-structurel visant l'adaptation de l'agriculture à la nouvelle situation des marchés et le maintien de l'espace rural'. Press release, Apr. Brussels: CEC.

——(1987*a*). 'Environment and the CAP'. *Green Europe*, Mar. Brussels: CEC.

——(1987*b*). 'Council Regulation EEC Number 1760/87 of 15 June 1987 . . . as Regards Agricultural Structures, the Adjustment of Agriculture to the New Market Situation and the Preservation of the Countryside'. *Official Journal*, L167: 1–14.

——(1987*c*). *Review of Action Taken to Control the Agricultural Markets and Outlook for the Common Agricultural Policy*. COM (87) 410. Brussels: CEC.

——(1988). *Environment and Agriculture*. COM (88) 338 final. Brussels: CEC.

——(1990*a*). 'Agriculture and the Environment'. Press release, 25 July. Brussels: CEC.

——(1990*b*). 'Commission Proposal for a Council Regulation (EEC) on the Introduction and the Maintenance of Agricultural Production Methods Compatible with the Requirements of the Protection of the Environment and the Maintenance of the Countryside'. COM (90) 366. *Official Journal*, C267: 11–14.

——(1991*a*). 'The Development and Future of the CAP. Proposals of the Commission'. *Green Europe*, Feb.: 1–40.

——(1991*b*). 'Commission Proposal for a Council Regulation (EEC) on the Introduction and Maintenance of Agricultural Production Methods Compatible with the Requirements of the Protection of the Environment and the Maintenance of the Countryside'. COM (91) 415. Brussels: CEC.

——(1991*c*). 'Commission Proposal for a Council Regulation (EEC) on Agricultural Production Methods Compatible with the Requirements of the Protection of the Environment and the Maintenance of the Countryside'. COM (91) 415 final. *Official Journal*, C300: 7–11.

——(1991*d*). 'Proposition pour une Règlement du Conseil concernant l'introduction et le maintien des méthodes de production agricole compatibles avec les exigencies de la production de l'environnement ainsi que l'entretien de l'espace naturel'. Revision 4 4. Mar. Unpublished; copies available from authors.

——(1992). 'Council Regulation EEC Number 2078/92 of 30 June 1992 on Agricultural Production Methods Compatible with the Requirements of the Protection of the Environment and the Maintenance of the Countryside'. *Official Journal*, L215: 85–90.

——(1996). 'Commission Regulation EC Number 746/96 of 24 April 1996 Laying Down Detailed Rules for the Application of Council Regulation (EEC) No. 2078/92 on Agricultural Production Methods Compatible with the Requirements of the Protection of the Environment and the Maintenance of the Countryside'. *Official Journal*, L102: 19–27.

——(1998a). *Agenda 2000. The European Commission's Legislative Proposals.* COM (98) 158 final. *Official Journal*, C170: 93 ff.

——(1998b). *State of Application of Regulation (EEC) Number 2078/92: Evaluation of Agri-Environment Programmes.* DG Agri Working Document. VI/7655/98. Brussels: CEC.

——(1999a). 'Council Regulation (EC) Number 1257/99 of 17 May 1999 on Support for Rural Development from the European Agricultural Guidance and Guarantee Fund (EAGGF) and Amending and Repealing Certain Regulations'. *Official Journal*, L160: 80–102.

——(1999b). 'The New Rural Development Policy. Elements of the Political Agreement of the Agriculture Council, 22 February–11 March 1999'. DG Agri press notice. 11 Mar. Brussels: CEC.

CHG (1995), *Confederacion Hidrográphica del Guadiana. Informe Sobre la Situación Hidrológica del Acúifero de la Mancha Occidental.* Ciudad Real: CHG.

Christiansen, T. (1996). 'A Maturing Bureaucracy? The Role of the Commission in the Policy Process', in J. J. Richardson, (ed.), *European Union: Power and Policy Making.* London: Routledge, 77–95.

Cini, M. (1996). *The European Commission: Leadership, Organization and Culture in the EU Administration.* Manchester: Manchester University Press.

Clark, A. (1993). *Diaries.* London: Weidenfeld & Nicolson.

Clark, J. R. A., and Jones, A. (1998). 'Agricultural Elites, Agrarian Beliefs and their Impact on the Evolution of EU Agri-Environment Policies: An Examination of the British Experience, 1981–1992'. *Environment and Planning A*, 30: 2227–43.

————(1999). 'From Policy Insider to Policy Outcast? *COPA*, European Union Policy Making, and the EU's Agri-Environment Regulation'. *Environment and Planning C*, 17: 637–53.

————Potter, C. A., and Lobley, M. (1997). 'Conceptualizing the Evolution of the European Union's Agri-Environment Policy: A Discourse Approach'. *Environment and Planning A*, 29: 1869–85.

Cloke, P., and MacLaughlin, B. (1989). 'Politics of the Alternative Land Use and Rural Economy (ALURE) Proposals in the UK: Crossroads or Blind Alley?' *Land Use Policy,* July: 235–50.

Club de Bruxelles (1995). *Proceedings of the Conference 'Agriculture and Environment in Europe'.* Brussels: Club de Bruxelles.

Clunies-Ross, T., and Cox, G. (1994). 'Challenging the Productivist Paradigm: Organic Farming and the Politics of Agricultural Change', in P. D. Lowe, T. K. Marsden, and S. Whatmore, (eds.), *Regulating Agriculture.* London: David Fulton, 53–74.

CoEC (1991*a*), Council of the European Communities. 'Note de Transmission: From the Dutch Delegation to the Agriculture Structures Group Concerning the Accompanying Measures to the CAP Reform'. Agriculture Council Working Document 8922/91. Brussels: CEC.

——(1991*b*). 'Rapport Interimaire: From the Agriculture Structures Group to the Special Committee on Agriculture Concerning the Accompanying Measures of the CAP Reforms'. Agriculture Council Working Document 9566/91. Brussels: CEC.

——(1991*c*). 'Rapport complémentaire: From the Agriculture Structures Group to the Special Committee on Agriculture Concerning the Accompanying Measures of the CAP Reforms'. Agriculture Council Working Document 9945/91. Brussels: CEC.

——(1991*d*). 'Aide-Memoire: For the Agriculture Structures Group Concerning the Accompanying Measures of the CAP Reforms'. Agriculture Council Working Document 9463/91. Brussels: CEC.

—— (1991*e*). 'From the Special committee on Agriculture Concerning the Accompanying Measures of the CAP Reforms'. Agricultural Council Working Document 10061/91 6 Dec. Brussels: CEC.

——(1992*a*). 'Aide-Memoire on COM (91) 415 Final for the attention of the President of the Agriculture Structures Group'. 16 Jan. Brussels: CEC.

——(1992*b*). 'Document de la Présidence'. 2 Mar. Brussels: CEC.

Conrad, J. (1991). *Options and Restrictions of Environmental Policy in Agriculture*. Baden Baden: Nomos.

Conzelmann, T. (1995). 'Networking and the Politics of EU Regional Policy: Lessons from North Rhine Westphalia, Nord Pas de Calais and North West England'. *Regional and Federal Studies*, 5/2: 134–72.

Coombes, D. (1970). *Politics and Bureaucracy in the European Community: A Portrait of the Commission of the EEC.* Hemel Hempstead: Allen & Unwin.

COPA (1992), *Comité des Organisations Professionnelles Agricoles.* '*COPA* Observations on the Commission Proposals on Agricultural Production Methods Compatible with the Requirements of the Protection of the Environment and the Maintenance of the Countryside'. Pr (92) 11. 9 Apr. 1992. Brussels: *COPA.*

——(2000). 'Committee of Agricultural Organizations in the European Union'. Brussels: *COPA.*

Coss, S. (1997). 'Farm Lobby Seeks Unity'. *European Voice*, 27 Feb.–5 Mar.: 20.

Cox, G., and Lowe, P. D. (1983). 'A Battle not the War: The Politics of the Wildlife and Countryside Act', in A. Gilg (ed.), *Countryside Planning Yearbook 4.* Norwich: Geo Books, 48–76.

————and Winter, M. (1985). 'Land Use Conflict after the Wildlife and Countryside Act 1981: the Role of the Farming and Wildlife Advisory Group'. *Journal of Rural Studies*, 1/2: 173–83.

————and Winter, M. (1988). 'Private Rights and Public Responsibilities: The Prospects for Agricultural and Environmental Controls'. *Journal of Rural Studies*, 4/4: 323–38.

CPL (1991), *Centrale Paysanne Luxembourgoise.* 'Reflexions de la Centrale Paysanne Luxembourgeoise sur la Réforme de la PAC'. 6 May. Luxembourg: *CPL.*

Cram, L. (1993). 'Calling the Tune without Paying the Piper? Social Policy Regulation: The Role of the Commission in European Social Policy'. *Policy and Politics*, 21: 135–46.

——(1996). 'The European Commission as a Multi-Organization: Social Policy and IT Policy in the EU'. *Journal of Public Policy*, 3: 195–217.

——(1997). *Policy Making in the EU: Conceptual Lenses and the Integration Process.* London: Routledge.

Davidson, J. (1978). 'Practical Conservation and Land Use Management: The Case of Modern Agriculture', in J. G. Hawes (ed.), *Conservation and Agriculture.* London: Gerald Duckworth and Company, 95–100.

DBV (1991), *Deutscher Bauernverband.* 'Prise de position du Praesidium du Deutscher Bauernverband du 26 fevrier relative aux dernières propositions de la Commission sur la Réforme de la Politique Agricole Commune'. *DBV* position paper. 26 Feb. Bonn: *DBV.*

De Bassompierre, G. (1988). *Changing the Guard in Brussels: An Insider's View of the EC Presidency.* New York: Praeger.

DETR (1998), Department of Transport, Environment, and the Regions. *Building Partnerships for Prosperity.* Cm. 3814. London: The Stationery Office.

DoE/MAFF (1995), Department of the Environment/Ministry of Agriculture, Fisheries, and Food. *Rural England.* Cm. 3016. London: The Stationery Office.

Dudley, G., and Richardson, J. J. (1999). 'Competing Advocacy Coalitions and the Process of "Frame Reflection": A Longitudinal Analysis of EU Steel Policy'. *Journal of European Public Policy*, 6/2: 225–48.

Edwards, G. (1996). 'National Sovereignty versus Integration', in J. J. Richardson (ed.), *European Union: Power and Policy Making.* London: Routledge, 127–47.

Elmore, R. F. (1978). 'Organizational Models of Social Programme Implementation'. *Public Policy*, 26/2: 185–226.

——(1985). 'Forward and Backward Mapping', in K. Hanf and T. Toonen (eds.), *Policy Implementation in Federal and Unitary Systems.* Dordrecht: Martinus Nijhoff, 33–70.

EP (1986), European Parliament. *Report on Behalf of the Committee on the Environment, Public Health and Consumer Protection of Agriculture and the Environment.* Rapporteur F. Roelants du Vivier. PE 101.184/fin. Brussels: EP.

——(1991). 'Debates of the European Parliament 1990–1991 Session: Report of Proceedings on 11 March 1991'. *Official Journal*, 3–402.

——(1992). 'Debates of the European Parliament 1991–1992 Session: Report of Proceedings for 10–13 March 1992'. *Official Journal*, 3–416.

Epstein, P. J. (1997). 'Beyond Policy Community: French Agriculture and the GATT'. *Journal of European Public Policy,* 4/3: 355–72.

Eriksen, E. D., and Fossum, J. (2000) (eds.). *Democracy in the European Union.* London: Routledge.

Fearne, A. (1991). 'The CAP Decision Making Process', in C. Ritson and D. Harvey (eds.), *The Common Agricultural Policy and the World Economy: Essays in Honour of John Ashton.* Wallingford: CAB International.

FNSEA (1991), *Fédération Nationale des Syndicats d'Exploitants Agricoles.* 'Communiqué du 22 avril 1991'. 22 Apr. Paris: FNSEA.

Friedrich, P. (1989). 'Language, Ideology and Political Economy'. *American Anthropologist*, 91/2: 295–312.

Gardner, B. (1987). 'The Common Agricultural Policy: The Political Obstacle to Reform'. *Political Quarterly*, 58: 167–79.

Garrett, C., and Tsebelis, C. (1996). 'An Institutional Critique of Intergovernmentalism'. *International Organization*, 50: 269–99.

Gay, F., and Wagret, P. (1986). *L'Économie d'Italie.* Paris: Presses Universitaires de France.

Genieys, W. (1998). 'Autonomous Communities and the State in Spain', in P. Le Gàles, and C. Lequesne (eds.), *Regions in Europe.* London: Routledge, 166–80.

Goggin, M. L., Bowman, A., Lester, J. P., and O'Toole, L. J. (1990). *Implementation Theory and Practice: Toward a Third Generation.* Glenview, IL: Little, Brown.

Graham, G. (1991). 'Reform Plan Goes Against the Grain'. *Financial Times,* 28 Feb.: 32.

Grande, E. (1996). 'The State and Interest Groups in a Framework of Multi-Level Decision-Making: The Case of the European Union'. *Journal of European Public Policy*, 3/3: 318–38.

Grant, W. (1993*a*). 'Pressure Groups and the European Community", in S. Mazey and J. J. Richardson (eds.), *Lobbying in the European Community.* Oxford: Oxford University Press, 27–46.

——(1993*b*). 'Transnational Companies and Environmental Policy Making: The Trend of Globalization', in J. D. Liefferink, P. D. Lowe, and A. P. J. Mol (eds.), *European Integration and Environmental Policy.* London: Belhaven Press, 59–74.

——(1995). 'The Limits of Common Agricultural Policy Reform and the Option of Denationalization'. *Journal of European Public Policy*, 2/1: 1–18.

——(1997). *The Common Agricultural Policy.* Basingstoke: Macmillan.

Gray, O. W. (1989). 'Pressure Groups and their Influence on Agricultural Policy and its Reform in the European Community'. Unpublished Ph.D. thesis. Bath: University of Bath Department of Social and Policy Sciences.

Grove-White, R. (1987). 'Putting on the Pressure'. *The Countryman*, Summer, 92/2: 22–8.

Guihéneuf, P.-Y., and Prat, F. (1999). 'Les Mesures agri-environnementales en Languedoc-Roussillon'. *Revue de l'Économie Mériodionale*, 47/186: 19–30.

Gunn, L. (1978). 'Why is Implementation so Difficult?' *Management Services in Government*, 33: 169–76.

Guyomarch, A., Machin, H., and Ritchie, E. (1998). *France in the European Union.* London: Macmillan.

Hagedorn, K. (1985). 'CAP Reform and Agricultural Economics: A Dialogue of the Deaf?', in J. Pelkmans (ed.), *Can the CAP be Reformed?* Paris: Institut Européen d'Administration Publique, 13–51.

Hajer, M. (1995). *The Politics of Environmental Discourse.* Oxford: Oxford University Press.

Hall, P. A. (1986). *Governing the Economy: The Politics of State Intervention in Britain and France.* New York: Oxford University Press.

——(1993). 'Policy Paradigms, Social Learning, and the State: The Case of Economic Policymaking in Britain'. *Comparative Politics*, 25: 275–96.

Harris, S., and Swinbank, A. (1997). 'The Common Agricultural Policy and the Food Industry', in C. Ritson and D. R. Harvey (eds.), *The Common Agricultural Policy.* 2nd edn. Wallingford: CAB International, 265–85.

Hayes-Renshaw, F., and Wallace, H. (1997). *The Council of Ministers.* Basingstoke: Macmillan.

Healey, P., and Shaw, T. (1995). 'Changing Meanings of Environment in the British Planning System'. *Transactions of the Institute of British Geographers*, NS 19: 425–38.

Heclo, H. (1978). 'Issue Networks and the Executive Establishment', in A. King (ed.), *The New American Political System*. Washington: AEI.

Heritier, A. (1996). 'The Accommodation of Diversity in European Policy Making and its Outcomes: Regulatory Policy as a Patchwork'. *Journal of European Public Policy*, 3: 149–67.

——(1999). *Policy Making and Diversity in Europe: Escape from Deadlock*. Cambridge: Cambridge University Press.

Hix, S. (1994). 'The Study of the European Community: The Challenge to Comparative Politics'. *West European Politics*, 17/1: 1–30.

——(1998). 'The Study of the European Union II: The "New Governance" Agenda and its Rival'. *Journal of European Public Policy*, 5/1: 38–65.

——(1999). *The Political System of the European Union*. Basingstoke: Macmillan.

Hjern, B. (1982). 'Implementation Research: The Link Gone Missing'. *Journal of Public Policy*, 2/3: 301–08.

——and Porter, D. (1981). 'Implementation Structures: A New Unit of Administrative Analysis'. *Organization Studies*, 2: 211–227.

HoC (1999), House of Commons. *British Farming and the Reform of the Common Agricultural Policy*. House of Commons Library. Research Paper 99/77. London: The Stationery Office.

HoC [House of Commons] Agriculture Select Committee (1997). *Environmentally Sensitive Areas and other Schemes under the Agri-Environment Regulation*. Second Report, i. 1996–1997 Session. HC 45-I. London: The Stationery Office.

——(1998). *CAP Reform: Agenda 2000*. Second Report, i. 1997–1998 Session. HC 311-I. London: The Stationery Office.

——(1999). *CAP Reform: Rural Development*. Second Report, i. 1998–1999 Session. HC 61-I. London: The Stationery Office.

Hoggart, K., Buller, H., and Black, R. (1995). *Rural Europe. Identity and Change*. London: Arnold.

Holland, M. (1994). *European Integration: From Community to Union*. London: Pinter.

Hooghe, L. (1999). 'Images of Europe: Orientations to European Integration among Senior Officials of the Commission'. *British Journal of Political Science*, 29/2: 345–67.

——and Keating, M. (1994). 'The Politics of European Union Regional Policy'. *Journal of European Public Policy*, 367–93.

Hubschmid, C., and Moser P. (1997). 'The Cooperation Procedure in the EU: Why was the European Parliament Influential in the Decision on Car Emission Standards?' *Journal of Common Market Studies,* 35: 225–42.

Hull, R. (1993). 'Lobbying Brussels: A View from Within', in S. Mazey and J. J. Richardson (eds.), *Lobbying in the European Community*. Oxford: Oxford University Press, 82–92.

Hurrell, A., and Menon A. (1996). 'Politics like any Other? Comparative Politics, International Relations and the Study of the EU'. *West European Politics*, 19/2: 386–402.

Hyman, D., and Miller, J. A. (1986). *Community Systems and Human Services: An Ecological Approach to Policy, Planning and Management*. Dubuque, IA: Kendall-Hunt.

——Wadsworth, M., and Alexander, D. P. (1991). 'Values, Policy Making and Implementation: The Roots of Bias in Utility Regulatory and Energy Mediation Policy'. *Administration and Society*, 23/3: 310–32.

IFA (1991), Irish Farmers' Association. 'Proposed IFA Submission to COPA on Long-Term CAP Reform'. 19 Mar. Dublin: IFA.

Ionescu, G. (1988). 'The Application of Law and the Community Perspective', in H. Siedentopf and J. Ziller (eds.), *Making European Policies Work*. i. *Comparative Synthesis*. London: Sage, 202–8.

Jachtenfuchs, M. (1997). 'Conceptualizing European Governance', in K. E. Jorgensen (ed.), *Reflective Approaches to European Governance*. Basingstoke: Macmillan, 39–50.

Jacobs, F., and Corbett, R. (1994). *The European Parliament*. Harlow: Longman.

Jeffrey, C. (2000). 'Sub-National Mobilization and European Integration: Does it Make any Difference?' *Journal of Common Market Studies*, 38/1: 1–23.

Jessop, B. (1995*a*). 'Post-Fordism and the State', in A. Amin (ed.), *Post-Fordism*. Oxford: Blackwell, 251–79.

——(1995*b*). 'The Regulation Approach, Governance, and Post-Fordism'. *Economy and Society*, 3/24.

Jones, A. (1994*a*). *The European Union: A Guide through the Maze*. London: Kogan Page.

——(1994*b*). *The New Germany. A Human Geography*. Chichester: John Wiley.

——and Clark, J. R. A (1997). 'New Directions in Rural Policy: A German Perspective'. *Built Environment* 23/3: 229–35.

————(1998). 'The Agri-Environment Regulation EC 2078/92: The Role of the European Commission in Policy Shaping and Setting'. *Environment and Planning C*, 16: 51–68.

————(1999). 'The European Parliament and EU Agri-Environment Policy Making'. *Environment and Planning C*, 17: 127–44.

————(2000). 'Of Vines and Policy Vignettes: Sectoral Evolution and Institutional Thickness in the Languedoc'. *Transactions of the Institute of British Geographers* N.s. 25: 333–357.

Jordan, A. (1995). 'Implementation Failure or Policy Making? How do we Theorise the Implementation of European Environmental Legislation?' CSERGE Working Paper. GEC 19–18. Norwich: University of East Anglia.

——(1999). 'The Implementation of EU Environmental Policy: A Policy Problem without a Political Solution?' *Environment and Planning C*, 17: 69–90.

Jordan, G., Maloney, W. A., and McLaughlin, A. (1994). 'Characterizing Agricultural Policy Making'. *Public Administration,* 72 (Winter), 505–26.

Judge, D. (1992). 'Predestined to Save the Earth: The Environment Committee of the European Parliament'. *Environmental Politics*, 1/4: 186–212.

——Earnshaw, D., and Cowan, N. (1994). 'Ripples or Waves: The European Parliament in the European Community Policy Process'. *Journal of European Public Policy*, 1: 27–51.

Kassim, H. (1994). 'Policy Networks, Networks and European Union Policy Making: A Sceptical View'. *West European Politics*, 17/4: 15–27.

Keating, M. (1998). *The New Regionalism in Western Europe*. Cheltenham: Edward Elgar.

Keeler, J. T. S. (1996). 'Agricultural Power in the European Community: Explaining the Fate of CAP and GATT Negotiations'. *Comparative Politics*, 28: 127–49.

Kerremans, B. (1996). 'Do Institutions Make a Difference: Non-Institutionalism, Neo-Institutionalism, and the Logic of Common Decision-Making in the European Union'. *Governance,* 9: 215–40.

Kingdon, J. W. (1984). *Agendas, Alternatives, and Public Policies.* Boston: Little, Brown.

Kirchner, E., and Williams, K. (1983). 'The Legal, Political and Institutional Implications of the Isoglucose Judgements 1980'. *Journal of Common Market Studies*, 22: 173–90.

Knill, C., and Lenschow, A. (1998). 'Coping with Europe: The Impact of British and German Administrations on the Implementation of EU Environmental Policy'. *Journal of European Public Policy*, 5/4: 595–614.

Kohler-Koch, B. (1998). *Interaktiv Politik in Europa. Regionen im Netzwerk der Integration.* Opladen: Leske & Budrich.

Kooiman, J. (1993) (ed.). *Modern Governance: New Government-Society Interactions.* London: Sage.

Kreppel, A. (1999). 'What Affects the EP's Legislative Influence?' *Journal of Common Market Studies*, 37/3: 521–38.

Laffan, B. (1997). 'From Policy Entrepreneur to Policy Manager: The Challenge Facing the European Commission', *Journal of European Public Policy*, 4/3: 422–38.

——O'Donnell, R., and Smith, M. (2000). *Europe's Experimental Union: Rethinking Integration.* London: Routledge.

Le Clerc, S. (1993). *Politique agricole commune et environnement.* Rennes: Éditions Apogée.

Le Galès, P., and Lequesne, C. (1998). *Regions in Europe.* London: Routledge.

Lenschow, A. (1998). 'The World Trade Dimension of "Greening" the EC's Common Agricultural Policy'. European University Institute Working Paper No. 98/7. Florence: European University Institute.

Leroy, P., and van Tattenhove, J. (forthcoming). 'New Policy Arrangements In Environmental Politics: The Relevance of Political and Ecological Modernization', in G. Spaargaren, A. P. J. Mol, and F. Buttel (eds.), *Environmental Sociology and Global Modernity.* London: Sage.

Lewis, D. (1984). 'Conclusion. Improving Implementation', in D. Lewis and H. Wallace (eds.), *Policies into Practice: National and International Case Studies in Implementation.* London: Heinemann, 203–26.

Liefferink, D., and Skou-Andersen, M. (1998). 'Strategies of the Green Member States in EU Environmental Policy Making'. *Journal of European Public Policy*, 5/2: 254–70.

Lodge, J. (1993) (ed.). *The EC and the Challenge of the Future.* London: Pinter.

Louloudis, L., Martinos, N., and Panagiotou, A. (1989). 'Patterns of Agrarian Change in East Central Greece: The Case of Anthili community'. *Sociologia Ruralis*, 29/2: 49–85.

Louwes, S. (1985). 'Squeezing Structural Agricultural Policy: From the Mansholt Plan to a Mini-Policy', in J. Pelkmans (ed.), *Can the CAP be Reformed?* Paris: Institut Européen d'Administration Publique, 93–105.

Lowe, P. D., and Bodiguel, M. (1990) (eds.). *Rural Studies in Britain and France.* London: Belhaven.

——and Ward, N. (1998). *A Second Pillar for the CAP? The European Rural Development Regulation and its Implications for the UK.* Newcastle: Centre for Rural Economy.

——and Ward, S. (1999). *British Environmental Policy and Europe: Politics and Policy in Transition.* London: Routledge.

Lowe, P. D. and Whitby, M. C. (1997). 'The CAP and the European Environment', in D. R. Harvey and C. Ritson (eds.), *The Common Agricultural Policy*. 2nd edn. Wallingford: CAB International.

—— Cox, G., MacEwan, M., O'Riordan, T., and Winter, M. (1986). *Countryside Conflicts: The Politics of Farming, Forestry and Conservation*. Aldershot: Gower & Maurice Temple Smith.

Lowenthal, D. (1991). 'British National Identity and the English Landscape'. *Rural History*, 2/2: 205–30.

Lowndes, V. (1996). 'Varieties of New Institutionalism: A Critical Appraisal'. *Public Administration*, 74 (Summer), 181–97.

LUPA (1991), L'Union des Petits Agriculteurs. 'LUPA face à la Réforme de la PAC'. 6 May. Madrid: LUPA.

McLanahan, S. (1980). 'Organizational Issues in U.S. Health Policy Implementation: Participation, Discretion, and Accountability'. *Journal of Applied Behavioural Science*, 16/3: 354–69.

Mabey, R. (1987). 'Promised Land?' *Country Living*. June. 31: 22–7.

MAFF (1988), Ministry of Agriculture, Fisheries, and Food. 'Three Reasons why Agriculture is Important to City Dwellers'. MAFF News Release No. 200/88. 28 May. London: MAFF.

——(1989a). Ministerial Speech to Oxford Farmers' Conference. MAFF News Release unnumbered. 4 Jan. London: MAFF.

——(1989b). 'Environmental Protection should be Science Based'. MAFF News Release No. 167/89. 18 Apr. London: MAFF.

——(1990a). 'Conservation and Farming can Work together'. MAFF News Release No. 279/90. 2 Aug. London: MAFF.

——(1990b). 'Positive Stewardship of the Countryside'. MAFF News Release No. 377/90. 28 Nov. London: MAFF.

——(1992a). 'Environment now at the Centre of the CAP'. Press Release No. 216/92. 3 July. London: MAFF.

——(1992b). 'Environmental Protection is not an Add-on Extra—Minister'. MAFF News Release No. 290/92. 7 Sept. London: MAFF.

——(1993). *Agriculture and England's Environment*. London: MAFF.

——(1996). *Memorandum of Evidence Submitted by MAFF to the House of Commons Agriculture Select Committee Inquiry 'Environmentally Sensitive Areas and Other Schemes under the Agri-Environment Regulation'*. London: MAFF.

——(2000). *The English Rural Development Plan. Executive Summary*. London: MAFF.

Maitland, A. (1998). 'Shrewd Farmers see the way the Wind is Blowing'. *Financial Times* 17 March: 2.

Majone, G. (1989). *Evidence, Argument and Persuasion in the Policy Process*. New Haven CT: Yale University Press.

——(1991). 'Public Policy Beyond the Headlines'. European University Institute Working Paper SPS 91/9. Florence: European University Institute.

——(1992a). 'Ideas, Interests and Policy Change'. European University Institute Working Paper SPS 92/21. Florence: European University Institute.

——(1992b). 'Market Integration and Regulation: Europe after 1992'. *Metroeconomica*, 43: 131–56.

——(1995). 'The Development of Social Regulation in the European Community:

Policy Externalities, Transaction Costs, and Motivational Factors'. European University Institute Working Paper 95/2. Florence: European University Institute.

——(1996*a*). 'Public Policy: Ideas, Interests, and Institutions', in R. E. Goodin, H.-D. Klingemann (eds.), *A New Handbook of Political Science*. Oxford: Oxford University Press, 61–79.

——(1996*b*). *Regulating Europe*. London: Routledge.

March, J. G., and Olsen, J. P. (1984). 'The New Institutionalism: Organizational Factors in Political Life', *American Political Science Review*, 78: 738–49.

————(1989). *Rediscovering Institutions*. New York: Free Press.

Marks, G. (1996). 'Decision-Making in Cohesion Policy: Describing and Explaining the Variation', in L. Hooghe (ed.), *Cohesion Policy and European Integration: Building Multi-Level Governance*. Oxford: Oxford University Press, 342–88.

——Hooghe, L., and Blank, K. (1996). 'European Integration since the 1980s: State-Centric versus Multi-Level Governance'. *Journal of Common Market Studies,* 34/3: 341–78.

Marquand, D. (1997). *The New Reckoning. Capitalism, States and Citizens.* Cambridge: Polity Press.

Marsden, T. (1993). *Constructing the Countryside*. London: University College London Press.

Marsh, D., and Rhodes, R. A. W. (1992) (eds.), *Policy Networks in British Government*. Oxford: Clarendon Press.

Martin, R. (2000). 'Institutional Approaches in Economic Geography', in T. Barnes and E. Sheppard (eds.), *A Companion to Economic Geography*. Oxford: Blackwell, 1–28.

Matland, R. E. (1995). 'Synthesizing the Implementation Literature: The Ambiguity-Conflict Model of Policy Implementation'. *Journal of Public Administration Research and Theory*, 5/2: 145–75.

Mayntz, R. (1980). *Implementation Politischer Programme: Empirische Forschungs-berichte*. Konigstein: Verlagruppe Athenaum, Hain, Scriptor, Hanstein.

Mazey, S., and Richardson, J. J. (1993*a*) (eds.), *Lobbying in the European Community*. Oxford: Oxford University Press.

————(1993*b*). 'Introduction: Transference of Power, Decision Rules, and Rules of the Game', in S. Mazey and J. J. Richardson, (eds.), *Lobbying in the European Community*. Oxford: Oxford University Press, 3–26.

————(1993*c*). 'Policy Coordination in Brussels: Environmental and Regional Policy'. *Regional Politics and Policy,* 4/1: 22–43.

————(1994). 'The Commission and the Lobby', in G. Edwards and D. Spence (eds.), *The European Commission*. Harlow: Longman, 169–87.

Mazmanian, D., and Sabatier, P. A. (1981). *Effective Policy Implementation*. Lexington, MS: Lexington Books.

————(1983). *Implementation and Public Policy*. Glenview, IL: Scott, Foresman.

Mendrinou, M. (1996). 'Non-Compliance and the European Commission's Role in Integration'. *Journal of European Public Policy*, 3/1: 1–22.

Metcalfe, L. (1996). 'Building Capacities for Integration: The Future Role of the European Commission'. *EIPASCOPE*, 2: 2–8.

Meyer, C. (1999). 'Political Legitimacy and the Invisibility of Politics: Exploring the EU's Communication Deficit'. *Journal of Common Market Studies*, 37/4: 617–39.

Mingay, G. E. (1981). *The Victorian Countryside* (2 vols.). London: Routledge & Kegan Paul.

MoI (1945), Ministry of Information. *Land at War. The Official Story of British Farming 1939–1944*. London: HMSO.

Moravcsik, A. (1993). 'Preferences and Power in the European Community'. *Journal of Common Market Studies,* 31: 473–524.

——(1998). *The Choice for Europe: Social Purpose and State Power from Messina to Maastricht*. London: UCL Press.

Morgan, R., and Bray, C. (1986) (eds.). *Partners and Rivals in Western Europe: Britain, France and Germany*. London: Gower.

Moser, P. (1996). 'The European Parliament as a Conditional Agenda Setter: What are the Conditions? A Critique of Tsebelis (1994)'. *American Political Science Review*, 90: 834–8.

Naredo, J. M., and Gascó, J. M. (1992). 'Enjuiciamiento Económico de la Géstion de los Humedales: El Caso de Las Tablas de Daimiel'. *Estudios Regionales*, 26: 215–27.

NFU (1991), National Farmers' Union. 'Considerations on the Reform of the CAP'. 27 Mar. London: NFU.

Nguyen-Dan, G., Schneider,V., and Werle, R. (1993). 'Corporate Actor Networks in European Policy Making: Harmonizing Telecommunications Policy'. DP 93/4. Department of Political Science, Max Planck Institut, Koln.

Noirfalise, A. (1988). *Paysages: L'Europe de la Diversité*. EUR 11452 FR. Brussels: Commission of the European Communities.

North, D. C. (1990). *Institutions, Institutional Change, and Economic Performance*. Cambridge: Cambridge University Press.

Nugent, N. (1999). *The Government and Politics of the European Community*. 3rd edn. Basingstoke: Macmillan.

Obradovic, D. (1995). 'Prospects for Corporatist Decision-Making in the European Union: The Social Policy Agreement'. *Journal of European Public Policy*, 3: 261–83.

O'Riordan, T. (1985). 'Halvergate: The Politics of Policy Change', in A Gilg (ed.), *Countryside Planning Yearbook 1985*. Norwich: Geo Books, 101–6.

Ostrom, E. (1990). *Governing the Commons: The Evolution of Institutions of Collective Action*. Cambridge: Cambridge University Press.

O'Toole, L. J. (1997). 'Networking Requirements, Institutional Capacity, and Implementation Gaps in Transitional Regimes: The Case of Acidification Policy in Hungary'. *Journal of European Public Policy*, 4/1: 1–17.

Paseges-Gesase (1991). 'Paseges-Gesase Joint Position on CAP Reform'. 25 Apr. Athens: Paseges-Gesase.

Patterson, L. A. (1997). 'Agricultural Policy Reform in the European Community: A Three-Level Game Analysis'. *International Organization*, 51/1: 135–56.

Pedlar, R. H., and van Schendelen, M. P. C. M. (1994) (eds.). *Lobbying in the European Union. Companies, Trade Associations and Issue Groups*. Aldershot: Dartmouth.

Peters, B. G. (1994). 'Agenda-Setting in the European Community'. *Journal of European Public Policy*, 1: 9–26.

——(1998a). *Comparative Politics: Theory and Methods*. Basingstoke: Macmillan.

——(1998b). 'Managing Horizontal Government: The Politics of Coordination'. *Public Administration*, 76: 295–311.

——(1999). *Institutional Theory in Political Science*. London: Pinter.

Peterson, J. (1995*a*). 'Decision Making in the European Union: Towards a Framework for Analysis'. *Journal qf European Public Policy*, 2/1: 69–93.

——(1995*b*). 'Policy Networks and European Union Policy Making: A Reply to Kassim'. *West European Politics*, 18/2: 389–407.

——(1999). 'The Santer Era: The European Commission in Normative, Historical and Theoretical Perspective'. *Journal of European Public Policy*, 6/1: 46–65.

——and Bomberg, E. (1999). *Decision Making in the European Union*. Basingstoke: Macmillan.

Pierson, P. (1996). 'The Path to European Integration: A Historical Institutionalist Analysis'. *Comparative Political Studies*, 29/2: 123–63.

Pinder, J. (1995). *European Community: The Building of a Union*. Oxford: Oxford University Press.

Plaschke, H. (1994). 'National Economic Cultures and Economic Integration', in S. Zetterholm (ed.), *National Cultures and European Integration: Exploratory Essays on Cultural Diversity and Common Policies*. Providence RI: Berg, 113–43.

Pollack, M. A. (1994). 'Creeping Competence: The Expanding Agenda of the European Community'. *Journal of Public Policy*, 14/2: 95–146.

——(1996). 'The New Institutionalism and EC Governance: The Promise and Limits of Institutional Analysis'. *Governance*, 9: 429–58.

——(1997). 'Delegation, Agency, and Agenda Setting in the European Community'. *International Organization*, 51/1: 99–134.

Pressman, J. L., and Wildavsky, A. (1973). *Implementation*. Berkeley and Los Angeles: University of California Press.

Pretty, J. (1998). *The Living Land*. London: Earthscan Books.

Puchala, D. J. (1972). 'Of Blind Men, Elephants and International Integration'. *Journal of Common Market Studies*, 10: 267–84.

——(1975). 'Domestic Politics and Regional Harmonization in the European Communities'. *World Politics*, 27: 496–520.

——(1999). 'Institutionalism, Intergovernmentalism and European Integration', *Journal of Common Market Studies*, 37/2: 317–31.

Rawson, G. E. (1981). 'Organizational Goals and their Impact on the Policy Implementation Process', in D. J. Palumbo and M. A. Harder (eds.), *Implementing Public Policy*. Lexington, MS: D. C. Heath, 29–41.

Rhodes, R. A. W. (1986). *European Policy Making, Implementation and Sub-Central Governments*. Maastricht: European Institute of Public Administration.

——(1992). 'The Europeanisation of Sub-Central Government: The Case of the UK'. *Staatswissenschaften und Staatspraxis*, 2: 80–91.

——(1997). *Understanding Governance: Policy Networks, Governance, Reflexivity and Accountability*. Buckingham: Open University Press.

Richardson, J. J. (1996*a*). 'Policy-Making in the EU: Interests, Ideas and Garbage Cans of Primeral Soup', in J. J. Richardson (ed.), *European Union Power and Policy-Making*. London: Routledge, 3–23.

——(1996*b*). 'Actor-Based Models of National and EU Policy Making', in H. Kassim and A. Menon (eds.), *The European Union and National Industrial Policy*. London: Routledge, 26–51.

——(1996*c*). 'Eroding EU Policies: Implementation Gaps, Cheating and Re-Steering', in J. J. Richardson (ed.), *European Union Power and Policy-Making*. London: Routledge, 278–95.

Risse-Kappen, T. (1996). 'Exploring the Nature of the Beast: International Relations Theory and Comparative Policy Analysis meet the European Union'. *Journal of Common Market Studies,* 34: 53–77.

Rometsch, D., and Wessels, W. (1994). 'The Commission and the Council of Ministers', in G. Edwards and D. Spence (eds.), *The European Commission.* Harlow: Longman, 202–24.

Rometsch, D., and Wessels, W. (1997). 'The Commission and the Council of the Union', in G. Edwards and D. Spence (eds.), *The European Commission.* London: Catermill International, 202–24.

Rosamond, B. (1999). 'Discourses of Globalization and the Social Construction of European Identities'. *Journal of European Public Policy*, 6/4: 652–68.

——(2000). *Theories of European Integration.* Basingstoke: Macmillan.

Ross, G. (1993). 'Sidling into Industrial Policy: Inside the European Commission'. *French Politics and Society,* 11/1: 20–43.

——(1995). *Jacques Delors and European Integration.* Cambridge: Polity Press.

Sabatier, P. A. (1986). ' "Top-Down" and "Bottom-Up" Approaches to Implementation Research: A Critical Analysis and Suggested Synthesis'. *Journal of Public Policy*, 6/1: 21–48.

——(1988). 'An Advocacy Coalition Framework of Policy Change and the Role of Policy-Oriented Learning Therein'. *Policy Sciences*, 21: 129–68.

——(1991). 'Towards Better Theories of the Policy Process'. *Political Science and Politics*, 24/2: 147–56.

——(1998). 'The Advocacy Coalition Framework: Revisions and Relevance for Europe'. *Journal of European Public Policy*, 5/1: 98–130.

——and Pelkey, N. (1987). 'Incorporating Multiple Actors and Guidance Instruments into Models of Regulatory Policy Making: An Advocacy Coalition Framework'. *Administration and Society*, 19/2: 236–63.

Sainteny, G. (1995). 'French Communism: The Challenge of Environmentalism and the Ecologism'. *West European Politics*, 18/4: 110–29.

Sandholtz, W., and Stone Sweet, A. (1998) (eds.). *European Integration and Supranational Governance.* Oxford: Oxford University Press.

Santer, J. (1991). 'Some Reflections on The Principle of Subsidiarity'. Paper presented at the Jacques Delors Colloquium on Subsidiarity, organized by the European Institute of Public Administration, Maastricht, 21–2 Mar. 1991. Reproduced in *Subsidiarity: The Challenge of Change.* Maastricht: EIPA, 19–30.

Sasse, C., Poullet. E., Coombes, D., and Deprez, G. (1977). *Decision Making in the European Community.* New York: Praeger.

Scharpf, F. W. (1997). 'Introduction: The Problem Solving Capacity of Multi-Level Governance', *Journal of European Public Policy*, 4/4: 520–38.

Schein, E. H. (1996). 'Culture: The Missing Concept in Organization Studies'. *Administrative Science Quarterly*, 41/2: 229–40.

Schmidt, S. (1998). 'Commission Activism: Subsuming Telecommunications and Electricity under European Competition Law'. *Journal of European Public Policy*, 5/1:169–84.

Segura, A. R. (1996). 'Reflexiones Sobre el Reglamento Agroambiental Europea y el Programa Nacional Espanol'. *Quercus*, 125: 46–8.

Shepsle, K. A.(1989). 'Studying Institutions: Lessons from the Rational Choice Approach', *Journal of Theoretical Politics*, 1: 131–47.

Siedentopf, H., and Ziller, J. (1988) (eds.). *Making European Policies Work*, ii. *National Reports*. London: Sage.

Smith, J. (1999). *Europe's Elected Parliament*. Sheffield: Sheffield Academic Press.

Smith, M. J. (1990). *The Politics of Agricultural Support in Britain: the Development of the Agricultural Policy Community*. Aldershot: Dartmouth.

Smith, M. P. (1996). 'Integration in Small Steps: The European Commission and Member State aid to Industry'. *West European Politics*, 19/3: 563–82.

Smyrl, M. E. (1998). 'When (and How) Do the Commission's Preferences Matter?' *Journal of Common Market Studies*, 36/1: 79–99.

Spaargaren, G., and Mol, A. P. J. (1992). 'Sociology, Environment and Modernity: Ecological Modernization as a Theory of Social Change'. *Society and Natural Resources*, 55: 323–44.

Spence, D. (1994). 'Structure, Functions and Procedures in the Commission', in G. Edwards and D. Spence (eds.), *The European Commission*. Harlow: Longman, 97–116.

Stapleton, R. G. (1935). *The Land*. London: Faber & Faber.

Stern, A. (1994). *Lobbying in Europe after Maastricht: How to Keep Abreast and Wield Influence in the European Union*. Brussels: Club de Bruxelles.

Street, A. G. (1937). *Farming England*. London: B. T. Batsford Ltd.

Swidler, A. (1986). 'Culture in Action—Symbols and Strategies'. *American Sociological Review*, 51: 273–86.

Swinbank, A. (1993). 'CAP Reform, 1992'. *Journal of Common Market Studies*, 31: 359–72.

——(1999). 'CAP Reform and the WTO: Compatibility and Developments'. *European Review of Agricultural Economics*, 26/3: 1–19.

Swyngedouw, E. (2000). 'Elite Power, Global Forces and the Political Economy of "Glocal" Development', in G. Clark, M. Feldman, and M. Gertler (eds.), *A Handbook of Economic Geography*. Oxford: Oxford University Press, 541–559.

Taylor, P. J., and Flint, C. (2000). *Political Geography: World-Economy, Nation State and Locality*. Harlow: Pearson Education.

Thelen, K., and Steinmo, S. (1992). 'Historical Institutionalism in Comparative Politics', in S. Steinmo, K. Thelen, and F. Longstreth (eds.), *Structuring Politics: Historical Institutionalism in Comparative Analysis*. Cambridge: Cambridge University Press, 1–32.

Tinbergen, J. (1966). *Economic Policy: Principles and Design*. Amsterdam: North-Holland.

Touzard, J.-M. (1995). 'Regulation sectorelle, dynamique régionale et transformation d'un système productif localisé: Exemple de la viticulture Languedocienne', in G. Allaire and R. Boyer (eds.), *La Grande Transformation de l'agriculture*. Paris: Economica, 293–322.

Tracy, M. (1994). 'The Spirit of Stresa'. *European Review of Agricultural Economics*, 21: 357–374.

Tsebelis, G. (1994). 'The Power of the European Parliament as a Conditional Agenda Setter'. *American Political Science Review*, 88: 128–42.

——(1996). 'More on the European Parliament as a Conditional Agenda Setter: A Response to Moser'. *American Political Science Review*, 90: 839–44.

Tsinisizelis, M. (1990). 'Neo-Corporatism and the Common Agricultural Policy: The Case of Adjustment of the CAP'. Paper presented to the Joint Sessions of the European Consortium for Political Research, Bochum, 1–6 Apr.

Vail, D., Hasund, K., and Drake L. (1994). *The Greening of Agricultural Policy in Industrial Societies: Swedish Reforms in Comparative Perspective.* Ithaca, NY: Cornell University Press.

Van Meter, D. S., and Van Horn, C. E. (1975). 'The Policy Implementation Process: A Conceptual Framework'. *Administration and Society*, 6/4: 445–88.

van Schendelen, M. P. (1996) 'The Council Decides: Does the Council Decide?' *Journal of Common Market Studies*, 34/4: 531–48.

van Tattenhove, J. P. M., and Liefferink, J. D. (1992). 'Environmental Policy in the Netherlands and the European Community, a Conceptual Approach', in F. von Benda-Beckman and M. van der Velde (eds.), *Law as a Resource in Agrarian Struggles*. Wageningen: Netherlands Agricultural University, 267–93.

Verlaque, C. (1987). *Le Languedoc-Roussillon*. Paris: Presses Universitaires de France.

Viladomiu, L., and Rosell, J. (1996). 'Preliminary Report about the Income Compensation Scheme in Mancha Occidental and Campo de Montiel (Castilla la Mancha, Spain)'. Unpublished paper, Department of Applied Economics, Autonomous University of Barcelona.

Wallace, H. (1984). 'Implementation across National Boundaries', in D. Lewis and H. Wallace (eds.), *Policies Into Practice: National and International Case Studies in Implementation*. London: Heinemann, 129–43.

——(1999). 'Politics and Policy in the European Union: The Challenge of Governance,' in H. Wallace and W. Wallace, *Policy Making in the European Union*. 3rd edn. Oxford: Oxford University Press, 3–36.

——and Wallace, W. (1999). *Policy Making in the European Union*. 3rd edn. Oxford: Oxford University Press.

Weale, A. (1993). 'Ecological Modernization and the Integration of European Environmental Policy', in J. D. Liefferink, P. D. Lowe, and A. P. J. Mol (eds.), *European Integration and Environmental Policy*. London: Belhaven Press, 196–216.

Weick, K. (1985). *Der Prozess des Organisierens*. Frankfurt am Main: Suhrkamp.

Weingast, B. (1996). 'Institutional Theory', in R.E Goodin and H. D. Klingemann (eds.), *A New Handbook of Political Science*. Oxford: Oxford University Press.

Wendon, B. (1998). 'The Commission as Image-Venue Entrepreneur in EU Social Policy'. *Journal of European Public Policy*, 5/2: 339–53.

Wessels, W. (1991). 'The EC Council: The Community's Decision-Making Centre', in R. O. Keohane and S. Hoffmann (eds.), *The New European Community: Decision Making and Institutional Change*. Boulder, CO: Westview Press,133–55.

Westlake, M. (1994). *The Parliament and the Commission: Partners and Rivals in the European Policy Making Process*. Sevenoaks: Butterworth.

——(1995). *The Council of the European Union*. London: Catermill.

Whitby, M. C. (1996) (ed.). *The European Experience of Agri-Environment Policies.* Wallingford: CAB International.

——and Lowe, P. D. (1994). *Incentives for Countryside Management*. Wallingford: CAB International.

Wilks, S. (1990). 'The Embodiment of Industrial Culture in Bureaucracy and Management', in S. R. Clegg and G. S. Redding (eds.), *Capitalism in Contrasting Cultures.* Berlin: De Gruyter, 131–52.

——and Wright, M. (1987). *Comparative Government–Industry Relations*. Oxford: Clarendon Press.

Wilson, G. A., Petersen J.-E., and Holl, A. (1999). 'EU Member State Responses to Agri-Environment Regulation 2078/92/EEC—towards a Conceptual Framework?' *Geoforum*, 30: 185–202.

Wincott, D. (1995). 'Institutional Interaction and European Integration: Towards an Everyday Critique of Liberal Intergovernmentalism'. *Journal of Common Market Studies*, 33/4: 597–609.

Winter, S. (1985). 'Implementation Barriers'. *Politica*, 17/4: 467–87.

——(1986). 'How Policy Making Affects Implementation: The Decentralization of the Danish Disablement Pension Administration'. *Scandinavian Political Studies*, 9/4: 361–85.

——(1990). 'Integrating Implementation Research', in D. J. Palumbo and D. J. Calista (eds.), *Implementation and the Policy Process: Opening Up the Black Box*. Westport, CT: Greenwood Press, 19–38.

Wright, V. (1996). 'The National Co-ordination of European Policy-Making: Negotiating the Quagmire', in J. J. Richardson (ed.), *European Union Power and Policy Making*. London: Routledge, 148–69.

INDEX